ROUTLEDGE LIBRARY EDITIONS:
TIBET

Volume 3

BUDDHISTS AND GLACIERS OF WESTERN TIBET

BUDDHISTS AND GLACIERS OF WESTERN TIBET

GIOTTO DAINELLI

Routledge
Taylor & Francis Group

LONDON AND NEW YORK

First published in 1933 by Kegan Paul, Trench, Trubner & Co., Ltd.

This edition first published in 2019
by Routledge
2 Park Square, Milton Park, Abingdon, Oxon OX14 4RN

and by Routledge
711 Third Avenue, New York, NY 10017

Routledge is an imprint of the Taylor & Francis Group, an informa business

© 1933 Kegan Paul, Trench, Trubner & Co., Ltd.

British Library Cataloguing in Publication Data
A catalogue record for this book is available from the British Library

ISBN: 978-1-138-32747-4 (Set)
ISBN: 978-0-429-44145-5 (Set) (ebk)
ISBN: 978-1-138-33451-9 (Volume 3) (hbk)
ISBN: 978-1-138-33461-8 (Volume 3) (pbk)
ISBN: 978-0-429-44526-2 (Volume 3) (ebk)

Publisher's Note
The publisher has gone to great lengths to ensure the quality of this reprint but points out that some imperfections in the original copies may be apparent.

Disclaimer
The publisher has made every effort to trace copyright holders and would welcome correspondence from those they have been unable to trace.

BUDDHISTS
AND GLACIERS OF
WESTERN TIBET

By

GIOTTO DAINELLI

WITH 32 PLATES AND MAP

LONDON
KEGAN PAUL, TRENCH, TRUBNER & CO., LTD.
BROADWAY HOUSE, 68–74 CARTER LANE, E.C.4
1933

Translated from the Italian by
ANGUS DAVIDSON

Printed in Great Britain by Butler & Tanner Ltd., Frome and London

PUBLISHER'S NOTE

IN the original Italian version of this book the author expresses his views upon the very vexed question of the transliteration of Tibetan and Turki words. He finds the existing system, or lack of system, so confusing and misleading that he has elaborated a transcription of his own. "I proceeded to a minute inquiry," he says, "assembling the most important local 'authorities' in every village and every valley, and evolved an Italian transcription which should come as near as possible to the native pronunciation most generally in use. Thus I was able to make some interesting corrections of errors which I will explain more in detail. The most typical is perhaps the one relative to the name of the village at which we arrived during our difficult and agitating descent from the Zoji-la. Everyone has always called it, and continues to call it, by the name of Pandras, as did also the Italian expedition previous to mine. Since there is another and larger village a little way down the valley, which is called Dras, many travellers have supposed that the name Pandras obviously has some reference to the nearest large village; some of them have even tried to prove that the syllable 'pan' is derived from a root of some Indian language or other, meaning 'below'. Thus 'Below-Dras'. But the trouble is that it is a question of a village which is not below, but above Dras—apart from the unreasonableness of discovering a root of Indian origin in a region where the language is Tibetan. The truth is much simpler: it is not Pandras, but Prandas. 'Das' in Tibetan means 'little plateau', like the one at the foot of the village on top of some rocks; and 'pran', also in Tibetan, is the name of a particular grass which grows there in great quantities."

Unfortunately, though naturally, his transcription was made for Italian readers and this book will be read by many who are not acquainted with Italian. Such a transcription would be entirely useless to them. The publishers, therefore, have given the generally accepted transcriptions of Tibetan and Turki names as recognized by the Royal Geographical Society and the Survey of India. Where it has been impossible to trace place-names mentioned by the author, an Anglicized version of Professor Dainelli's Italian transcription has been given.

CONTENTS

vii

CONTENTS

LIST OF ILLUSTRATIONS

ix

MY BASE CAMP ON THE SIACHEN

[front

PREFACE

THIS is a faithful diary, written on the spot, but not meticulous to the point of recording pedantically the things I did and the things that happened to me day by day, of my recent expedition to Western Tibet.

It was a journey I had thought over and longed to make for many years, and which I organized and arranged in advance right from Italy to its distant goal—the heart of the Karakoram —with such rapidity of movement that I may be permitted to say that, from the point of view of speed, it could not be surpassed. But this, more than anything else, was the natural result of past experience.

My past experience had been this—the great expedition organized, in 1913-14, by Filippo de Filippi, the greatest, certainly, that those regions had known, and the most widely productive as regards scientific results of any that have been conducted by Italians to any part of the world. To have shared in it—considering, especially, the speed of movement necessary to the geographer-naturalist and allowed us by the leader of the expedition—may well constitute a reason for being profoundly happy and satisfied at having lived. In that marvellous country where the majesty of mountains assumes its grandest forms, among people who are instinctive artists even in the humblest manifestations of their life, I had felt an unspeakable joy, both of an eye and a mind which were never wearied with looking and learning. I had retained a subtle feeling of nostalgia for the country, for the people, for the unconfined freedom of caravan life, for the attraction of the unknown and unforeseen, for the need of making prompt and effective decisions in difficult circumstances, for the satisfaction afforded by responsibility and by the feeling of being in command of a little handful of natives who trust themselves entirely to our superiority of intellect and will and who follow us faithfully towards the unknown—an unknown which, living as they do in perpetual contact with nature, exercises so power-ful an attraction upon them.

With nostalgia went desire, with desire long-continued day-dreams and plans, in which it would be hard to say whether the stronger influence was the instinct of curiosity (without which no one can be an explorer), or the passion of the student who yearns to fill a gap in human knowledge by snatching some small new thing from the manifold face of the Earth.

Such, in substance, was the preparation for this new journey of mine, a preparation which I may describe as being principally spiritual and intellectual, as well as long and continuous, for an enterprise treasured as a prize, as a rest after toil, as a goal beyond which one might stop and look back over life and collect the threads of experience for the weaving, perhaps, of one's last task.

My expedition was entirely the result of my own personal initiative: I did not allow, because I did not want, either advice, help, or subscriptions from Societies or Committees. There was thus no need for me to expound my treasured plans to anyone, nor to give anyone an account of expenses incurred or results obtained. But being undertaken on my own per-sonal initiative, my expedition had to be small in numbers, an element which was in any case essential in order that it might travel light and overcome difficulties which I foresaw would be considerable. Therefore I had neither caravan-leaders nor interpreters: with my own previous long experience I was able to take direct command of the men—who were always extremely faithful. I had chosen few companions, few and trustworthy —Desio, my old pupil, a skilled mountaineer and explorer, who would have had the task of helping me in my scientific researches, since I foresaw how much I should be absorbed in general administration, in the leadership of the caravan, and in the solution of the complicated problems of commissariat; Miss Elly Kalau, an experienced climber and ski-er, who comes of a family of travellers and naturalists and has been for many years a faithful and intelligent collaborator in my various activities (she showed herself worthy of the choice by the excellent way in which she carried out all the tasks entrusted to her, i.e. the conduct of a correspondence in many languages, the charge of what may be called the domestic management of the camp, the forming of a botanical collection which is the richest that has ever been brought back from the high mountains of the Karakoram, and the addition to my collection of a marvellous series of photographs, among which are all those in this volume); and thirdly, Hashmatullah Khan, who had been my friend from the time of the De Filippi Expedition, when he was Governor of the District; no one could have been more skilful than he in arranging for the purchase of provisions at different points on the journey for the caravan of native porters, in accordance with orders received from me. Desio, however, was prevented from coming with me by his duties in Italy, so that my personal labours were increased. But with Desio, Miss Kalau, and Hashmatullah I should again feel ready for any undertaking.

And so, while our rocks and fossils and plants and anthropological measurements and observations of every kind will add some new contribution to the knowledge of my beloved Western Tibet and my beloved Ladakhis, this diary will serve to revive in my mind from time to time the memory of a wonderful journey, of an enterprise which was perhaps not altogether commonplace. I hope that the reader too may catch a glimpse of the grand and majestic beauty of the country and of the fine and essentially artistic intelligence of its inhabitants, and will understand why it is that my nostalgia is not allayed, but is perhaps, on the contrary, augmented.

Chapter I

IN THE FOOTSTEPS OF PREVIOUS ITALIAN TRAVELLERS

BETWEEN the desert plain of the Punjab, fertilized only by such irrigation as is allowed by the volume of water of the great "Five Rivers" which cross it and give it its name, and the vast stretches of sandy desert, burnt and arid, which fall away towards Central Asia, rises a gigantic bastion of mountains, the greatest on Earth. They are not always real mountains, however: the vast extent of this mighty mass thrown up from the Earth's surface consists rather of plateaux than of mountains—an immense altar, rising almost everywhere to more than 16,000 feet, wide and open, as though stretching towards heaven, from the Pamirs to Tibet, the real roof of the world. But the plateau rises at its outer edges, as though to emphasize the contrast with the wide lowlands which lie at its feet. It rises, along its northern edge, in the range of Kunlun; even higher, along its southern edge, in the range of the Himalaya, so that the latter, for a great part of its extent, forms not so much a real chain of mountains, as merely the highest point of the southern flank, deeply broken with valleys, of the immense Tibetan plateaux. About half-way along the southern edge of the Tibetan plateaux opens out the wide mirror of the sacred Lake Manasarowar, where storms are not unknown, and round which long processions of faithful Buddhists, intoning the short but eternal prayer of their faith, accomplish their pilgrimages. From here the Brahmaputra towards the East, the Indus towards the West, run close and parallel to the outer edge of the great zone of plateaux—at first calm and slow-moving through elevated, wide, rolling plains, then steadily more and more swollen and impetuous as their course plunges more deeply into the mass of mountains, cutting valleys of rough, wild grandeur. It is only here that the Himalaya no longer forms the outer edge of the plateaux, but becomes a majestic chain of mountains, embracing in their wide semi-circle the whole of India, with its seething humanity and boiling passions. Where, towards the West, the chain of mountains is bounded by the deep channel of the Indus, beyond this river another gigantic range lifts its crests and peaks, rough-hewn from rock and ice: this is the Karakoram, which, as it were, forms a link between the Tibetan plateaux and those of the Pamirs. It is the upper valley of the Indus, with all its tributaries, shut in between the opposing flanks of the Himalaya and the Karakoram, which constitutes Western Tibet. Farther to the East open out suddenly the immense stretches of Great Tibet, naked and desolate, uninhabited for whole months of travelling, until one reaches the region where villages and little towns are assembled round Lhasa, the sacred, forbidden city.

Western Tibet, as far as the point where it joins Great Tibet with its capital city of Lhasa, was, for the second time, my field of action.

It was not a new field for the activities of Italian explorers. In fact it may be said that during this last century they have chosen this part of Asia—second only to East Africa—as their favourite goal. It must also be added that among the considerable number of travellers, from every country—principally English, of course, but from almost every other part of Europe too, and even from America—it is the Italians who have left the most memorable record of their enterprises.

It was an Italian who may be said to have initiated a period of increased knowledge of this country; or, at the least, he may be said to have concluded that very much longer period during which the knowledge of it—from the writers of antiquity and of succeeding ages to the Chinese writers and the representations of the greatest cartographers of the time—was confined merely to a few scattered ideas, often vague and often, also, faulty. This was Father Ippolito Desideri of Pistoia, a Jesuit missionary, who, from Srinagar in Kashmir (which is also my point of departure) crossed the Himalaya (as I also intend to do) by the Zoji-la, followed up the whole course of the Indus into Western Tibet, then traversed the desolate stretches of the plateaux, finally reaching Lhasa,

2

the sacred city, which at that time, however, was not forbidden.

To Lhasa, then—this was two centuries ago—went, first
Jesuits, then Franciscans, as missionaries, attracted perhaps
by the ancient legend that there existed in Tibet a forgotten
and long-lost centre of Catholicism—a legend which was
probably due to analogies in certain external forms of worship.
These missionaries did not really succeed in forming any
proselytes (any more than the Protestant missions of to-day
who attempt to carry on their work in the Buddhist districts
of the Himalaya), chiefly because the Buddhist religion in
Tibet is closely bound up with a whole monastic hierarchy
and with a whole form of social structure, both of which have
roots in the general economy of the country which are too
strong to be easily torn up. The missionaries were nevertheless kindly welcomed, and also given a hearing in the discussions of dogma which they held with the wisest of the
lamas. Many of them, Jesuits or Franciscans, were Italians;
but, in order to get to Lhasa, they went generally by the
shortest and most direct way from the plain of India, which
goes much more to the east and skirts Nepal.

Desideri did not do this: he went to Srinagar in Kashmir,
crossed the Himalaya by the Zoji-la, like almost all later
travellers who were going direct to Western Tibet, and went
right across the latter towards his distant goal, leaving a faithful
description of it—of his whole journey, of the country traversed,
of the people he met, of the customs of their material life and
the forms of their cultural life—a description which even
to-day may be read and consulted with advantage.

Travelling was very different two centuries ago. To-day,
with my 4½ tons of very varied equipment, I have come all
the way from my study in Florence, as though in a dream,
in only 18 days—all the way to this marvellous Kashmir,
with its enchanting lakes blossoming with water-lilies, its
long roads flanked with gigantic poplars, its canals shaded by
the thick leaves of plane-trees. Anyone who feels strongly
the attraction of his own parish might find even this a
journey to be well considered before being undertaken. But
to the young Desideri, two centuries ago, the arrival in
Kashmir from Italy must have been a further spur to the

passion which urged him on to so much more distant a goal. Let us for curiosity's sake follow him: on September 27th, 1712, he left Rome for Genoa, where he only succeeded in embarking two months later; but the weather was so contrary that he did not arrive at Lisbon till the middle of the succeeding March. He changed ship and left again on April 7th; he circled right round the Continent of Africa, and at the end of September, just a year after leaving Rome, arrived at Goa, on the Indian coast. He re-embarked; disembarked again; by short stages he passed through Surat, Delhi and Lahore; he arrived finally on November 13th, 1714, in Kashmir —26 months, instead of the 18 days which I have taken. Another half-year at Srinagar, waiting for the propitious season;—then, at last, he started out for the unknown country beyond the Himalaya, for long months of travelling over the limitless desolation of the high plateaux of Tibet, cold and bare, whipped by squalls of wind.

That was travelling indeed—travelling which demanded passion, will, perseverance, hardness against every discomfort and quick adaptability to every novelty of country or people. How much easier does it seem for us! It is true that the greater speed of life nowadays causes us to consider time differently, and that the stage of progress at which we have arrived makes us, if not actually more exacting, certainly more foreseeing, more scrupulous, even meticulous, in the preparation and predisposition of equipment, and in all the rest of the organization of an enterprise of exploration. It is also true that our routes almost always diverge from the caravan-routes which have now been known for a long time, and that our endless curiosity, often accompanied by the stronger, more exacting curiosity which is the desire to know, takes us out of the accustomed paths in search always of something new, through valleys, over glaciers, passes and peaks, where our modern courage can display itself and compete with that ancient courage which may sometimes, perhaps, seem to us more modest, though actually, considering the times, and considering the means available to our predecessors, it was by no means so.

Even though the Italian Father Desideri marks the end of a long period which has its beginnings in distant antiquity, and marks also the beginning of modern progress in the knowledge of Western Tibet, his work had no immediate successors. A gap of a hundred years brings us to the first half of the last century, when the conquest of Western Tibet by the Maharajah of Jammu and Kashmir seems to have facilitated and almost invited European visitors to the district —nearly all English, at that time. It was the desire for sport which urged them there, but never far from the usual caravan-routes, and the desire to see new countries, mixed with a certain spirit of adventure. In a very few cases they were moved also by the desire to explore new ways of opening up the country to commercial penetration.

The middle part of the last century was a stirring and active time as regards journeys of exploration. It cannot be said that travellers were always scientifically equipped; however, they had an infinite curiosity to observe and to learn, and showed very often so acute a power of observation that the accounts of their journeys are still a source of accurate remarks and facts which we may consult with advantage in the light of the more exact knowledge which has since come to us. They represented a type of traveller which has since almost entirely disappeared: to-day travellers are either genuine naturalists and geographers, or they are people who apparently travel with the sole object of pursuing some kind of game, or, simply, of moving their legs and carrying about a restless spirit, passing, almost without noticing them, through landscapes which are nearly always marvellously beautiful and full of interest, and among peoples utterly different from our own. The accounts of their journeys are very often of little more value than waste paper.

Among the former class of travellers Western Tibet can count one Italian—the Marchese Roero di Cortanze, of an old noble family of Piedmont, who had become a planter on the outer slopes of the Himalaya, the range of which he crossed more than once between 1850 and 1860, exploring the larger of the valleys that descend from the Karakoram and pushing on as far as the first plateaux of Tibet. Later he re-told the story of his peregrinations in a simple, plain form, but with such a wealth of accurate observation that, with all the experience that I have of the country, I do not hesitate to

5

assert that Roero was a much more acute and sagacious observer than other travellers of the same period who are generally considered more important.

Between the period to which Roero belongs, and the modern period of the new type of exploration—more intent on pure exploration and more strictly scientific in method and object —there was another intermediary period during which little was done to advance the further knowledge of Western Tibet. Routes were marked by preceding travellers: new travellers could follow them with greater ease, and, being no more fully equipped than their predecessors, travelled mainly for their own pleasure, without contributing much—often not even little—to the experience of their successors. In this period there was also an Italian, the Duca Grazioli Lante, who travelled just half a century ago and afterwards related in simple form, without pretence, but also without novelty, his own journeyings in the Himalaya along the tracks already trodden by preceding travellers.

Finally there began the last period, which still continues, the period of climbing and exploration on a large scale. The chief caravan-routes along the bottom of the valleys were by now well known: an assault had to be made upon the hidden recesses of the mountains, the gigantic glaciers, the peaks of fabulous height. It was now necessary to have not only a passion for new things, but also the sacred fire of the mountaineer, and to organize caravans in special ways for special purposes, to equip them for long sojourns in uninhabited places, on ice and snow, and to have men who were sound and experienced in the technique of climbing and accustomed to the difficulties which have to be overcome in a region which consists essentially of high mountains. It was for this reason that Italian mountaineers, the robust Alpine guides from the Val d'Aosta, began to flock to Western Tibet: I believe that Courmayeur alone sent about fifteen—foremost of all was the master of all of them, Giuseppe Petigax—to whom it may be said that the conquests in exploration and climbing achieved by European caravans during the last period in the high ranges of Western Tibet are largely owing. And not only caravans of Italian climbers and explorers, but also those of other nations.

6

With foreigners, such as the Workmans, there have been not only Italian guides, but also an Italian naturalist and topographer, Count Cesare Calciati, on two successive expeditions —in 1908, to the Great Hispar Glacier, in 1911 to the glaciers of the upper Hushè and Kundos valleys, south of the Baltoro Glacier. The latter—which at its head is dominated by the giant of the whole range, K², and which perhaps for that reason has been chosen as goal by a greater number of climbing and exploring expeditions—had already seen an Italian caravan, which ascended its long tongue of ice as far as its upper basins and there made a victorious attempt upon the mountain ridges that surround its mighty valley of fantastic beauty. The greatest climber-explorer of modern Italy certainly could not resist the fascination of that great glacier and of the gigantic peaks which shut it in at the sides and surround it at the head, and just as he had been victorious in Alaska and at the Pole, just as he was to be afterwards at Ruwenzori, so he was also victorious in the heart of the Karakoram.

It was in 1909 that His Royal Highness the Duke of the Abruzzi—shining symbol and precursor of present-day Italy— brought his enthusiasm and his experience of organization and exploration to the Baltoro Glacier. He was accompanied by the Comandante Negrotto Cambiaso, Filippo de Filippi, Vittorio Sella, greatest among photographers of high mountains, and, at the head of a small handful of Alpine guides, Giuseppe Petigax. And even though K², attempted by various ways of approach, proved unassailable with its mighty walls of ice, still they attained, on the snowy shoulders of Bride Peak, to the altitude of 23,460 feet which no man had ever before reached, and which for long years remained, thanks to an Italian, the record mountain altitude reached by men by their own efforts.

This was essentially a climbing expedition. However, it did not neglect what may be considered as a duty towards science which must be paid by all who are drawn to visit and to gain knowledge of little known or new regions. So also Mario Piacenza, who in 1913 made the ascent of the double peak of Nun Kun (23,448 and 23,277 feet), brought back his contribution to science, through the researches of his two companions, Calciati and Borelli.

When, in the summer of the same year, Piacenza returned to Srinagar on his way home, there was just arriving also at Srinagar the greatest expedition Italy has sent to Western Tibet, that organized by Filippo de Filippi.

This expedition was different in character: it was not a climbing, but a purely scientific expedition, and its programme was to collect new contributions towards the knowledge of certain physical properties of the Earth, and also towards the knowledge of the whole region. Apart from its leader, the Comandante Alessio, Dr. Abetti, the Marchese Ginori, Lieutenant Antilli, Dainelli and Giuseppe Petigax constituted the first group: to which, the year following, were added Olinto Marinelli and Dr. Alessandri, besides two English topographers. No other expedition had ever been organized on so large a scale, for so long a period—a year and a half—or with so wide and varied a programme of methodical research, and the 16 thick volumes which represent the result of so great a sum of activity will be sufficient proof that the De Filippi Expedition was one of the most widely fruitful there has ever been, including not only the region in which it was working; it is a source of pride to all who had the honour of taking part in it.

Finally, last year, another Italian expedition, led by His Royal Highness the Duke of Spoleto, pitched its camp again, as is well known, on the Baltoro Glacier, and a detachment of it crossed the chain of the Karakoram and explored part of the Shaksgam Valley, which forms a deep cleft at the northern foot of the line of the highest peaks. The memory of this expedition is still fresh.

In virtue of these expeditions, especially of the one led by De Filippi, it may be claimed that Italy takes one of the first places in the scientific exploration of Western Tibet. This, though it may be a cause of pride to one who has contributed to such a result, must nevertheless make him tremble at the thought that he must live up to tradition in the new enterprise on which he has determined.

I left Italy, as an ordinary private individual entirely on my own free initiative; I am therefore under no obligation to anyone to divulge my programme. I can only say that, from the point of view of organization, the programme is a difficult

8

one, and that I may come across serious obstacles in conditions of country, rivers and glaciers. But it will be a joy to me to end my own career as naturalist and traveller by leading a caravan that entrusts itself to the will of its commander, through ways which, certainly, will not always be easy.

Srinagar (*Kashmir*), *April* 27*th*, 1930.

CHAPTER II

IN KASHMIR

The other morning, at the end of our motor-drive, we went along a long straight road, flanked by a double row of poplars with gigantic regular trunks, which, apparently, is the majestic avenue to the summer residence of the Maharajah of Jammu and Kashmir. At moments I felt I was dreaming. The last months in Florence, from October onwards, had been an intense, maddening struggle to get each task completed, to keep every promise, and to leave nothing behind me unfinished. This had been, in a way, a preparation for my departure; but it had been a preparation which, absorbing every activity and all my time, had made me almost forget that in a few months, in a few weeks, and, finally, in a few days, I was to leave on a long journey, for an undertaking perhaps by no means easy. Only about three weeks ago I was still frantically correcting proofs in Florence. Then there were hurried good-byes to a few friends, a quick journey to the port of embarkation, a speedy crossing from Italy to India: the dream began, and lasted for eleven days of blessed leisure on board ship, of complete relaxation of the nerves after so many months of intense work, in the absolute calm of the sea and the first warmth of the Red Sea and the Indian Ocean, which was yet mitigated by the movement of air produced by the swift motion of the ship. Then, disembarkation at Bombay, rapid completion of baggage—rapid, because of the precise orders already sent on from Italy. Finally, the journey across India already inflamed by the first heat of its long summer, and then the journey by car which took me from the sunburnt plain of the Punjab up the whole valley of the Jhelum, in behind the first spurs of the Himalaya, still snowy on all the peaks, to Srinagar, which claims to be the Venice of the Indian Orient. The dream still continued.

Then, scarcely had I arrived here in Srinagar when the

work of the final completion of the baggage began, the last and perhaps the most delicate part of my preparation for the life we were shortly to lead. Since then I have been utterly and finally absorbed in the full reality of my undertaking, which will lead me into unknown country and which will certainly call forth every quality of resistance, of perseverance, and also of adaptability and endurance in conditions of unavoidable hardship and in difficulties which the country will almost certainly raise in opposition to my intended programme and itinerary. Since then—inspired by the marvellous view of the mountains which surround this enchanted valley and by the memory of another journey of mine, long ago, which also had its point of departure here—since then I realize to the full that a new life is beginning and a joy for which I have longed for many years, ever since the experience I once had of long wanderings through the valleys and mountains and plateaux which, to the north of the Himalaya, extend almost to the summit of the world, and, beyond, to the scorched and dried-up deserts of Central Asia.

The general public—for whom life nowadays is, from a certain point of view, very easy, in cities where the slightest necessity, the smallest desire, can be easily satisfied—in order to understand what the organization of a journey like mine really means, must remember that in a few days I shall leave Srinagar, where there are motor-cars and offices and banks and shops, and that for six months on end I shall have to proceed, at best, by caravan-routes passing only through little villages of the most meagre resources; they must also reflect that, of those six months, four will be passed in entirely uninhabited regions, almost all the time on glaciers, often at a height of over 16,000 feet—that is, in regions where we have to trust entirely to our own foresight, even though we are prepared to give up many things and adapt ourselves to others which we ourselves, when living in cities, would not care to put up with. The greater the foresight, the less the renunciation, the easier and lighter the task to be accomplished and the manner of life to be lived. So one must, if possible, forget nothing. I am not speaking so much of actual provisions, which should be plentiful, good, and above all, varied, for monotony of diet, in regions where loss of appetite may at any moment overcome the heartiest of eaters, can easily become a cause of failure owing to the various consequences, physical and moral, which go with it. Nor yet am I speaking of camping outfit or mountaineering equipment, which even the uninitiated can order beforehand by himself, with the guidance of a good catalogue. I mean, above all, the minute details, from stationery to boot-grease, from a small supply of nails and tacks to things such as pins and needles! Patiently, month after month, one must note down from time to time in a pocket-book everything that casually occurs to one as necessary or useful, then complete the lists, perfect them, simplify them if possible: for an insignificant object that has been noted down may suggest others, or may allow of certain eliminations. This is really the essential kind of preparation: when the lists can be said to be complete—for it is possible to make them complete, provided one does not live cut off from everyday life, and particularly if one already has experience of the very special needs of caravan life—then it becomes almost a mechanical matter to put them into practical form.

But there are other things too, since we are not going simply for pleasure, or with the mere object of pursuing some particular kind of game: we are going with the higher purpose of contributing in some way to the progress of human wisdom and knowledge. Owing to the abnormalities of the conditions in which we shall find ourselves, that is, in countries where everything has an interest, where it would be a mistake to examine only this or that condition which physical or human nature presents, but where every sort of condition should be observed with a wide and complete—I might almost say philosophical—vision of man's knowledge of the Earth, we must also have a full equipment of instruments and means of bringing back as rich as possible a harvest of observations and collections, from geological specimens to anthropological measurements.

Such is the preparation which an undertaking like mine demands. I arrived only a few days ago, and if not a new life, at least a new work, has already begun. While loads are being prepared, the instruments of registration are already working in a small improvised observatory, which will be established along our route at every halt that is not merely for a few hours, as the ordinary stages are; an intelligent Balti, who has been with me before for months during my Himalayan wanderings and has rendered me valuable services, has been sent off to collect me some real Kashmiri natives—for here at Srinagar there is a considerably mixed population—whose measurements I wish to take in order to make a new contribution to our knowledge of these people of the high mountains of Asia. And the 'kansana', that is, the native cook—an important element in a caravan—has begun to receive instructions with regard to the composition of the cases of provisions; and Ramsana, the old merchant, whose chatter is inexhaustible but who is as quick in his work as with his tongue, is preparing light 'kilta' of interwoven osiers which are to be substituted for the heavy cases, and 'gilgit-boots', which come up above the knee like old-fashioned riding-boots and should make us feel the cold less acutely during our evenings on the glaciers.

And so our preparations may be said to be nearly finished. In a few days the caravan, the 'kafla', will take its way up the Sind Valley, towards the snowy gap in the Himalaya, towards the wonderful country of my Ladakhi friends, and then, at last, some distance into the unknown.

Srinagar (Kashmir), April 29th, 1930.

At last we have started! But it has been, and will be, a continual starting. We started from Florence, from Brindisi, from Bombay, from Rāwalpindi; now again from Srinagar; but I cannot say when, for us, it will be a question of arriving. Our wandering life has begun, from one place to another, never turning back on our tracks, carrying with us all our belongings, our movable houses, our victuals, everything, like primitive people for ever wandering.

We had come with extreme rapidity as far as Srinagar. It was not, however, possible to be so rapid during the last pause before the beginning of our Tibetan wanderings. Everything was ready before we left Florence, and everything travelled to Kashmir with the same speed as I did—this too, I believe, created a record as regards Himalayan expeditions—

13

but at Srinagar I had to organize the baggage into its final form (from the provisional form in which it was), and therefore acquire and arrange 'yaktan' and 'kilta', the cases and boxes of Kashmir make which are indispensable for anyone travelling in those regions. I had, too—this also was essential—to complete the numbers of my caravan and to organize transport, which was not at the time easy, across the Zoji-la, the pass through the Himalaya which would bring us right into Western Tibet.

There was one man whom I had known during my long wanderings in the Himalaya, who had been of the greatest assistance in my researches. He was, at that time, 'wazir wazarat'—that is, governor of the district—Afghan by origin, of reliable intelligence, having attained a considerable degree of culture on his own account, and eager to learn something on every subject. He had realized immediately, at that time, that his knowledge of the district would be of incomparable assistance to me in my inquiries and researches into its various peoples, who differ in religion, language, origin, race and traditions. And he perhaps understood that, in relation to his own work of governing, the administration of the district might derive some benefit from the experience and knowledge of this European who had come, unlike so many others, with an unlimited and insatiable curiosity to see and study everything. So Hashmatullah Khan and I became good friends, with a friendship which showed itself on his side in unlimited devotion and decisive promptness in making every possible arrangement to facilitate my work; perhaps this was because such confidence placed in him by a European must have appeared to him unusual, for Europeans who come to these parts generally show indifference rather than confidence.

Hashmatullah knew exactly what the plans were for my new journey to Tibet. I notified him of my arrival from Bombay. A telegram came from him asking when and where he could meet me. I replied, "At Srinagar, at once." And the day after our arrival, Hashmatullah also arrived and placed himself at my disposal. It was characteristic of the man that, when I asked him how I could recompense him for the immense help that he would undoubtedly give me by joining my expedition, he replied that to be allowed to travel with me would be in itself the greatest recompense he could wish. From that moment Hashmatullah Khan became officially part of my small staff, and was ready to carry out any orders that were given to him with untiring energy.

There was, however, one exceptional element in my projected caravan. This latter required also a *personnel* of lower grade. From the knowledge which I already had of the country and owing to the manner in which a great part of my journey was to be conducted, I had made one simple decision—as small a *personnel* as possible. I did not want a 'shikari', or caravan-leader, because *shikaris* easily become insolent and are unpopular, if only because of that, among the people of Tibet, and because I felt that I should get on quicker by myself both in finding and in managing the native porters. Besides, I should now have the most valuable help of Hashmatullah Khan. In the matter of servants, also, I wished to avoid, if possible, the Kashmiri element: they are not always adapted for long and difficult journeys, and are not beloved by the Ladakhis, among whom our time would be spent. But while we were working at the final preparation of the baggage, a little group of Ladakhis used to arrive faithfully every morning to watch us: they were not petulant nor did they get in our way and chatter like the Kashmiri, but were silent and almost supplicating as they gazed fixedly at me, joining their hands as though in prayer, without speaking a word. As I have long felt a sympathy towards these people, I approached them one day. There were three men from Nubra—the exact valley which was to be my base of operations—and an 'argon', that is, a half-breed, who was characterized by the little red fez which he wore instead of the typical woolly Ladakhi cap of his three companions. I discovered that the *argon*, Gulam Rasul, was a cook, a *kansana*, and had good 'chits', that is, references, from travellers with whom he had served. I engaged him without more ado. Of the others, one—the one who seemed to have the most supplicating eyes and hands of all of them, Tashi Serin—I engaged as my personal 'coolie', to carry the 'tiffin' and the photographic material. As my own servant or 'bearer' I had to take a Kashmiri; but this man, next day, gave me back

15

his advance of wages, declaring that there was too much snow on the Zoji-la. So I had to begin all over again.

But one day, as I was looking out of the little porch of my bungalow at the hotel, I saw among the natives who were crowding round with their usual impatience, a lean-faced, sharp-eyed man looking at me intently, but without offering me his services—which was odd in a Kashmiri. These two facts interested me, and I looked further at him and realized that his face was not new to me. A sudden flash—Kadir! It was Kadir Mir, head cook of the De Filippi Expedition. I called him: "Atcha, huzur!" and he showed me a little ticket on which he had got someone to write, in English, that he had been a willing and careful servant to his former master. I engaged him, and transferred Gulam Rasul to the post of bearer; he can take on the office of *kansana* again if by any chance our little company increases.

Tashi Serin is now very proud, but he has become livelier, nor does he now always have that humble and supplicating air. The day after I had engaged him he appeared before me with his head completely shaved instead of with long hair in the Tibetan manner. 'Tum nehin ladaki'—'you are no longer a Ladakhi,' I said to him in my very limited Hindustani. Then he took off a comical mountaineering cap which he was wearing instead of the usual cap of his countrymen, and showed me a long pigtail hanging down from the middle of his shaven head which looked like a billiard-ball. He laughed heartily, as though he had surprised his new master in a mistake.

Transport organization has been much more difficult. The Himalayan pass, the Zoji-la, is officially closed—which means that prices are ten times higher than usual, but also means that, even at these prices, the natives can refuse their services, or, alternatively, impose even higher prices. The British Commissioner for Ladakh (he is a kind of political agent of the Indian Empire, who is established during the summer at Leh, mainly in order to supervise and control the trade from Yarkand, and obviously to see that no arms are brought in) had informed me that conditions on the Zoji-la are exceptionally bad this year and that to organize the transport of a fairly heavy caravan like mine would be difficult: however, he would try to help me in every possible way. Though very grateful for his offer, I had no need to make use of it, and I make no attempt to conceal the fact that, when all is said and done, I am glad that it was so, since, whether one wished or not, and even though in crossing India we were not in the least conscious of the disturbances of which the European newspapers speak with such an excessive wealth of detail, there is yet no doubt that at this particular moment English officialdom does not meet with very great sympathy from the natives. So that the fact of not making use of its assistance may be preferable in the circumstances.

I succeeded in my object by entrusting all the transport to the responsibility of a Kashmiri agent recommended by Hashmatullah Khan. The heavy baggage left three days before us; a second and lighter caravan precedes us by one day, and only our personal baggage, including beds, a table and a kitchen, will go with us. It is arranged that the whole *kafla*, or caravan, shall reassemble at Dras, beyond the pass, and therefore quite safely beyond snow, avalanches and the most dangerous bits of the road.

All this, of course, is more easily said than done. The fact of having to do with Orientals always implies a certain exercise of patience on the part of Europeans who are accustomed to place considerable value upon time. But I cannot complain: one day of negotiation was sufficient for arranging the whole of the transport from Srinagar to Kargil—that is, along the only portion of our route which, at the present season, presents really serious difficulties.

So passed my nine days in Kashmir, in bargaining from morning to night. But this did not prevent me from finding the time to re-explore Srinagar, the so-called Venice of the East, and to admire again the country round the town. It is almost like a landscape of legend in the exuberance of its trees, the many-coloured variety of its flowers and the thick foliage of its orchards. At times, as one passed along avenues of gigantic poplars, or floated on tortuous canals overhung with huge, ancient plane-trees which raise their thick foliage to the sky or droop till they gently touch the water, or as one crossed open country where shaven meadows like lawns alternate with wide beds of white and purple-flowered iris, while all round a circle of high snowy mountains encloses, as though in a complete cup, this enchanted valley, one had to make an effort of imagination to convince oneself that one was under the sky of the tropics, only one day's distance from that flat, uniform, scorched, dried-up, almost suffocating Punjab which we crossed in the train.

One day I sailed again in a light 'shikara' on the calm waters of Lake Dal, the lake of Srinagar. It was too early in the season to see Lake Dal in all its magnificence, when it appears to be transformed into a vast meadow in which the water-lilies stretch out their great leaves and lift their rosy flowers which look as though made of wax. But all the same it is beautiful and romantic in its clear stillness which reflects the thick vegetation on its banks and the line of the neighbouring mountains. And its life is always interesting—the life of the men who fish in it, gather herbs in it, and cultivate the characteristic floating vegetable- and flower-gardens which they move about, according to convenience, from one part of it to another.

Another day, again in a *shikara*, I went down the river Jhelum as far as the dam just outside the town which keeps the river at a constant level: Srinagar passed in front of me, with its palaces, its Hindu temples with their lofty, delicate, shining domes, its ancient pagoda-shaped mosques, its picturesque houses adorned as though with lace and broken up with projecting balconies and open galleries, its wretched hovels which are perpetually threatened with imminent collapse, its roofs which appear—and, indeed, actually are—flowery meadows where peasants climb to scythe the grass and pick the flowers, its numerous bridges that constitute the principal landmarks of the whole city, its crowds which jostle on the frequent flights of stairs down to the river to wash clothes, to wash themselves, to grind rice in huge primitive mortars and to air garments of every colour, and its other crowds, on *shikaras*, barges and house-boats of every shape and size, of every grade of poverty and wealth and elegance, gliding up and down this great high road made by the river, accompanied by the rhythmic stroke of the short, webbed oars and the sharp or harsh voices of the rowers—all Srinagar passed before me like a fantasy of the East, amazing in outline, colour and sound.

Another day I returned to the enchanted gardens which the Moguls, lords of the land, have scattered along the banks of Lake Dal. I had already admired the Chashmashai Bagh with its play of fountains and its lawns bordered with flowers: it is certainly charming, but seems a mere trifle when, a little farther on, are the marvels of the Nishat Bagh and of the Shalimar Bagh. All the fountains sent forth crystalline jets of water and a crowd of natives moved over the wide lawns under the thick foliage of the plane-trees, among the flower-beds, over little bridges thrown across canals which spout water from a thousand jets, in kiosks which are jewels of stone and wood-carving like lace, planned and built with the innate sense of beauty which belongs to all these people of the East. One is reminded of our old Italian gardens, perfect in design and with perfectly kept lawns and hedges; but here there is a greater beauty of flowers, a greater luxuriance of trees, and, in addition, the thousand colours of the picturesque crowd of natives and the view of Pir Panjal with the long, softened line of its top all white with snow.

But to-morrow—to-morrow, at last, we start!

Srinagar (Kashmir), May 5th, 1930.

CHAPTER III

CROSSING THE ZOJI-LA

Our departure from civilization has been gradual, for we left Srinagar in a car, which took us as far as the opening of the Sind Valley, thus accomplishing in less than two hours a distance for which, in former times, a caravan took a stage and a half. When the car could go no farther, saddle-horses were waiting for us, and with them began our real wandering life. It began at the same quick rate at which we had already accomplished the journey between Italy and Srinagar, for we have already passed what would normally be the second stage, Kangan, and have arrived, as it were in one breath, at the next— Gund, that is, three stages in only one day.

This Sind Valley is very beautiful. As in all high mountain valleys, and in all the valleys of the Alps, the flat country seems to be insinuating itself along the bottom of the valley, which is still wide and not, as yet, steep. Here it is the flat country of Kashmir which insinuates itself, with its little regular terraces for rice-growing, its great walnut-trees overshadowing small groups of cultivators' houses, with their very characteristic thatched pointed roofs, their walls made of rough, sun-baked bricks, and their little barns which are exactly the same shape, on a small scale, as the houses, and look almost like children's toys. But the sides of the valley, right down from the high ridges already beetling with rock except where their shoulders are still covered with snow, are entirely clothed with thick woods of pine and Himalayan cedar.

Just as our progress has been rapid, so also is the change in the country. At Gund it was cultivated everywhere, with a sprinkling of typical Kashmiri houses. But the next day, as we went up the valley, the bottom became steadily narrower. The leaves of the trees were smaller and smaller, because later and later in their cycle of vegetation; the cultivated fields disappeared and conifer woods invaded the bottom as well as the sides of the valley, which became narrower and wilder but

more and more impressive. This impressiveness was due also
to the snow—not snow which had fallen straight from above
so as to clothe the earth with a uniform blanket, but snow
which had hurtled from the walls of the valley, through steep
clefts and gorges, and had accumulated at the bottom in great
shapeless half-cones of vast size and rather terrifying when
one thinks of the mighty rumbling and the blast of wind which
must have accompanied their headlong fall.

Often these furious avalanches stretched across the bottom
of the valley from one side to the other, and the river, the Sind,
disappeared beneath them, to reappear a little farther on from
beneath a great overhanging vault. Our path, from a little
beyond Gund, began to lie over this avalanche-snow, which is
irregular in surface and often in shapeless lumps, almost always
with a very steep slope down to a headlong leap over the river,
and often broken by deep crevasses between the two banks,
over which sometimes a thin snow bridge afforded the only
means of crossing both for men and horses. But one must
know these little, lean, humble, Himalayan horses in order to
realize that their surefootedness finds no difficulties of surface
or of passage; they measure the distance with their large eyes
and place their feet firmly and carefully.

The valley grew narrower and narrower, wilder and wilder,
and more and more snow-covered; but after a final ascent up a
steep slope which seemed almost to bar the way, just as its
summit was reached the steep sides of the valley vanished as
though by magic, and in their place opened out the wide basin
of Sonamarg, pleasant in shape, even though hemmed in by
mountain ridges of rugged dolomite, and by small glaciers
which glinted in the setting sun. There was nothing but snow
around us: one could almost imagine oneself in one of those
Alpine valleys which, near their head, become suddenly wider
and pleasanter as though to accentuate their contrast with the
wild mountains which stand above them, completely mantled,
in winter, in an even, untouched blanket of snow.

Even at Sonamarg we found the shelter of a bungalow.
But this one had none of the refined simplicity of certain Indian
bungalows: it had only the name in common. Its rooms were
small and miserable, but we put up our beds in them and they
soon convinced, even those who doubted, of the advantages

which four walls and a roof, however primitive, have over a tent, when there is nothing but snow all round and a penetrating wind is blowing. And so, while I worked, a good fire warmed me through and kept me company.

At Sonamarg we were already near the Zoji-la: only one stage, and we ought to attack the mountains. The lowest pass of the Himalaya, which descends here to almost 11,500 feet—in the midst of mountains, the humblest of which is higher than Mont Blanc—had left me with the impression that it was quite an ordinary pass. I had crossed it in the height of summer; the caravan-route wound easily upwards from the bottom of the Sind Valley, over its steep flank, following all its twists and turns, then suddenly became flat, coming out immediately above the Zoji-la. The latter must not be thought of as a narrow, clearly-defined saddle beyond which the slope, on the opposite side, again becomes steep; on the contrary, it is like a long level corridor, so level that, as one goes down the Tibetan slope, one has to go miles and miles before one has descended a hundred feet or so, or little more—so level, in fact, that the waters become stagnant over certain short distances, so uncertain is their course made by the particular conditions of the ground. But towards Kashmir, that is, towards the Sind Valley, there is the deep cleft, sudden, steep and wild—a real rocky glen—of the Baltal ravine.

When I crossed it before, in the height of summer, the Zoji-la seemed to me quite ordinary from the point of view of the tourist, even though of great interest owing to its particular conditions of soil and water, which had attracted the curiosity of many travellers but had not yet been explained. In winter, however, the Zoji-la is quite a different affair.

Almost all expeditions—like mine—have crossed it at the beginning of spring; and all have had to adopt the rule followed by the natives, that is, to start the ascent from the Sind Valley so early that the first streak of dawn has not appeared in the sky before they have reached the pass, with the whole caravan. This is a necessary precaution against avalanches, which, at the first warmth of the sun, may come tumbling down the horribly bare, precipitous sides to the bottom of the ravine by which, in winter, the ascent is made. If there chances to be a snowy period, one must wait in the Sind Valley until it is over and also until the sides of the ravine are cleared of the newly-fallen snow.

Approached even in this way, the crossing of the Zoji-la, with a relatively heavy caravan like mine, may give some cause for thought. To me it gave even greater cause. Scarcely three days before I had left Florence a Tibetan correspondent of mine had telegraphed to me to put off my departure for a month, because exceptionally heavy snows had made the Zoji-la impassable for a long time to come. To put off was impossible: it would have spoilt the whole of my projected summer plans. So I started, but the Zoji-la remained a doubtful point in the initial phase of my programme. A doubtful point which was not cleared up even in Kashmir; in fact, all sources of information were agreed: the snowfall had been exceptional all through the winter, and even during this first beginning of spring there was snow actually while we were at Srinagar; the pass was officially closed for an indefinite period; no caravan had yet ventured to cross it, apart from the usual postal couriers and a few isolated wayfarers.

But, while I was going up the lower part of the Sind Valley, where the hot sun had already brought out the buds and re-clothed the trees with tender green leaves, I met various caravans coming down, and caravans coming down the Sind Valley could only have come from Ladakh by the Zoji-la. They were caravans of Purighis—a quite separate people which I thought to have distinguished last time I was here, and whose existence and individuality were later confirmed by the measurements I brought back—caravans laden with 'namdah', the lovely felt rugs from Yarkand, which the clever embroiderers of Kashmir adorn with a design of interlaced plane-leaves and water-lilies, the characteristic, almost symbolic, plants of the country.

The passing of these caravans was a good sign, but, when we made inquiries of them, the reply was always the same: 'Resta bohot carab, huzur; bohot, bohot baraf,' that is: 'The road is very bad, sir: there is much, much snow.' Greater details, beyond the comprehension of my elementary Hindustani, were given to Hashmatullah Khan—avalanches, above all, avalanches.

We realized, on arriving at Sonamarg, how we should find

the Zoji-la: the vast avalanches in the defile of Gaganjir, and then the snow which uniformly covered the whole basin, had caused us to pass almost without transition from a warm, spring-like landscape to one of wintry rigidity.

At Sonamarg, as already at Gund, I took measurements of a certain number of Kashmiris—all the individuals in the little village, who were, indeed, few; then we took the road towards the uncertainties of the Zoji-la: we were the first, this year, to cross it in the direction of Tibet. The sky helped us, a sky of serene and luminous radiance, against which, at the first light of day (I have already gone back to my old habit of rising almost with the sun, even though I have arranged 'chota hazri', or breakfast, at a time which allows longer in bed to those who wish it), all the peaks of rock and snow stood out in clear relief.

That first morning we had an enchanting ride up the Sind Valley, between Sonamarg and Baltal. The bottom of the valley was still wide and slightly sloping, but the sides, still partly wooded, were extremely steep, and from them pines and cedars spread across the bottom, forming picturesque dark spots against the immaculate whiteness of the snow. The landscape was entirely wintry, and to me who always love mountains, especially when they are sleeping their solemn sleep under the white blanket which covers them, this seemed like one of my winter excursions in the Alps—except that I had no skis, but was comfortably carried along by my lean little horse. Snow bridges over the river, invading avalanches from the mouths of lateral ravines—everything was wonderful to look at; but I felt a considerable curiosity as to what was waiting for me in the future.

At Baltal the Sind Valley closes in quite suddenly and takes a decided bend to the right; on the left (as one goes up it) a narrow ravine opens, up which the view is soon interrupted by the tortuousness of its course. This is the ravine which comes down from the Zoji-la. In front of the entrance to it, on the flat bottom of the Sind Valley, is a little bungalow, with a hut beside it for travellers' servants. The hut, however, had been completely wrecked by a winter avalanche which had fallen upon it and the bungalow was almost completely buried in snow: nevertheless it was an excellent shelter.

There was a magnificent view of mountains from here, with the last buttresses of Kolahoi, actually one of the highest summits in Kashmir; it also afforded an instance of the power that the mountains can display, for from the mouth of the Zoji-la ravine descended an immense avalanche of unusual shape, long and narrow, which came right down into the Sind Valley and was enclosed at the sides by two fairly high terraces; its surface was all broken up into shapeless blocks piled up in disorder, and was everywhere uneven and irregular, even in its minor details; its course stopped suddenly in a kind of sheer wall several yards high. If it had not been for its brilliant, spotless whiteness, it would have looked more like a great flow of lava than an avalanche of snow. This was to be our path on the next night.

We got up at midnight. And in spite of delay, due to the snow and to the complete darkness (for the moon had already set) and to the distance at which the loads had had to be stacked, it was still completely dark when we started on our way up the avalanche, penetrating at once into the Zoji-la ravine. How different from summer! In summer the ravine is at first level as one goes up it from Baltal, then slightly inclined—so deeply has the torrent hollowed it out—and only at its head does it become all at once extremely steep, until one reaches the pass. But now it is entirely different. The avalanches of snow have filled it up to such an extent that the steep slope comes at the beginning, and after that is passed all fatigue and difficulty is at an end, and one proceeds up a nearly level slope.

There is, of course, no mountaineering difficulty, but it is a fatiguing climb; the horses followed us, jumping hither and thither, and I thought of the poor coolies who, in order to relieve the pack-animals, had to carry all my heavy, irksome baggage on their shoulders.

After $2\frac{1}{2}$ hours of rapid ascent we arrived at the summit, before dawn: a cold wind lashed our faces and quite numbed us. We made a brief halt in the shelter of the snow causeway of an old avalanche. We could still see the last of the birch-trees which come right up to the pass on the Kashmir side. It is they, in fact, which give it the name by which travellers generally call it. The Kashmiris have a different name for

it, but the Tibetan name has now been adopted. The inhabitants of the country beyond the pass, when they climb up to
it through their great valleys which are desolate and without
vegetation, must be surprised at seeing the sparse birch-wood
appearing from the Kashmir side at the top of the pass; they
called it, therefore, the pass (la) of the birches (Zoji).

Beyond the pass, down the long, slightly sloping corridor,
it is easy going. But in the meantime the sun came out, and
soon warmed us up and softened the snow, and progress
became tiring. The little bungalow of Machoi, which,
especially now, looked like an Alpine shelter, close to the
beautiful glacier which descends in cascade after cascade from
the jagged ridge and precipitous sides of Mount Kanipatr,
seemed to have been put there on purpose for us to take a
short rest and eat our picnic lunch. The pack-animals, in
the meantime, passed us and went on down the slope towards
Matayan. But, shortly after, one of the drivers came back to
tell me it was impossible to get on, owing to the snow being so
soft from the sun, which was now high. I insisted, on principle, that they must go on to the stopping-place decided upon,
but meanwhile, wishing to be just, I made inquiries of some
natives who, overcome by fatigue and exhaustion, were coming
up one by one from lower down, laden with bales of the beautiful
Yarkandi silk which is not woven in regular designs but in
flames of the most brilliant colours, with contrasts which, at
first sight, offend the European eye and taste, but always end
by pleasing it with the strange fusion of their tones and colours.
All were agreed: a man might still pass, though with difficulty;
a pack-horse, no. I went to find out, and found in fact that
the first group of my little caravan had stopped just below
Machoi, and that the animals were unloaded and struggling
hard to get out of the snow, into which they sank with all four
legs. I made a rapid decision: we must stop at Machoi, and
consequently modify the programme for next day. In the
meantime I had word that the main part of my baggage had
also crossed the Zoji-la and had stopped a little beyond the
pass.

I should like to point out to those who have had experience
in Himalayan travelling that, one month ago, at this time, I
was walking along the quay at Brindisi, inspecting the big pile

of baggage which was awaiting the steamer in which I was to sail. One month ago—and now, with all my *impedimenta*, I have already overcome the uncertainties of the Zoji-la and penetrated into Western Tibet.

I have arrived in Western Tibet, certainly; but the difficulties of approaching the base of operations for my summer campaign are not yet over. On the other hand, the natives whom we met during the day all made the same assertion—that the difficulty lay not so much in crossing the Zoji-la, as in the descent to Karbu and even as far as Kargil. If one thinks about this a moment it is quite easy to understand; high up, the snow made a complete and uniform covering for the ground and was thick and even, but as one comes down lower, arriving again in temperatures which are already spring-like, the covering becomes gradually broken up and the snow more and more treacherous under one's feet. We proved this during a few days of travelling.

Next day, as we descended the valley, we passed the wretched village of Matayan, which should have been our stopping-place of the day before. The whole valley was still in its full winter clothing; there were majestic mountains on every side; high, snowy peaks were visible at the top of every ravine, and the whole scene was a vision of glittering light. In the midst of such splendour Matayan seemed anxious to make its poor hovels look as humble as possible: they were wretched little houses, reduced, quite contrary to the custom of the country, to one floor only, and their flat, dark roofs scarcely showed above the wide shining surface of the snow. The whole population, men and women, children and babies, had come out on to the roofs to enjoy the sunshine and perhaps also—why not?—to watch the passing of this first caravan of strangers.

We made a brief halt for lunch and then again took the road, which still reserved for us one real 'mauvais pas'. In order to cross the river there was nothing but a bridge formed of treacherous avalanche snow: beyond, the surface was very steep, irregular, full of cracks which threatened the collapse of one crust after another. The poor horses, if they had had even a fraction of the fear, for themselves, which I had for their loads, would certainly have refused to go on. In a few

27

minutes one had a bad fall on its side, and another was dragged by the weight—perhaps unevenly distributed—of its load, off the tracks marked by the passage of those in front. One fell right over at what was perhaps the most delicate part, and its load started off on its own down the short snowy slope towards a point whence it seemed it must inevitably take a final leap into the swirling muddy waters of the river. How my heart sank at that moment, as I stood watching the passage of the caravan: that particular load included, among other things of mine, the big 'treasury' box! But the promptness and skill of the men saved the situation. After this 'mauvais pas' the rest seemed a mere walk, though always on melting snow, as far as the next village, Prandas.

There I installed myself in a native house. Each of us had his own big room, from the door of which, giving on to the roof of the floor below, one dominated the whole village, the valley and the beautiful snowy mountains.

Next day I went on down the valley. Right at the beginning there was another 'mauvais pas', very much worse than that of the day before—the slender, insecure edge of an avalanche, extremely steep, hanging above the river—but we all passed it safe and sound.

The valley, broad from Matayan to Prandas, narrows down again; the river runs tumultously through a narrow rocky gorge which shines as though varnished with a dark wine-colour, reminding one of the patina on a certain kind of lovely old Oriental pottery. But suddenly, after a bend, the landscape opens out again, assuming in all its lines the grandeur which is an essential characteristic of this majestic fold in the Earth's surface. We had come out into the basin in which lies Dras, a wide stretch of the valley from the bottom of which rise huge rocky humps, almost smothered by the accumulation of great alluvial deposits which are terraced at different levels. Little groups of houses, one or two little villages, are scattered here and there; one or two small clumps of trees—willows and poplars which are not wild, but cultivated—are the first signs of vegetable life in this part of Tibet which is naturally so bare and desolate; the fields still sleep under snow; here and there wander, in search of who knows what food, flocks of sheep and shaggy 'zo'—a cross between a cow and a yak, the type

28

PRANDAS, IN THE JHEMBUR VALLEY

[face p. 28

of buffalo which belongs to the high mountains of Tibet. A large bungalow welcomed us hospitably. During the day all the main part of the caravan joined up with us. The sky, clear till now, is becoming covered with mist and threatening clouds. But what does it matter now? We have crossed the Zoji-la.

Dras, May 11*th,* 1930.

CHAPTER IV

ACROSS PURIG

During that day at Dras, the sky, which had grown more and more heavily overcast since we had arrived, fulfilled its threats in a great downpour of water. It stopped raining, then began again, and the sun, so hot in the morning, ceased completely to show its face through the clouds.

Our departure next morning was fixed for a relatively early hour, six o'clock, for it was a long stage and not easy all the way, judging from information received. At half-past four I was up; but when, half asleep, I put my head out of the bungalow, I saw that it was snowing in large flakes, looking for all the world like the pictures of one's childhood. But better snow than rain, after all: and I got ready to start at the time arranged. I started, actually, at eight, because the small caravan of personal baggage did not come to life till then, and when it did finally come to life, it was very different from what it had been the day before. The horses of my 'kafla' were weary from their efforts of the preceding days, and about twenty of them had not even the strength to rise from the ground. After vain attempts on the part of the men, the Kashmiri agent who had undertaken the responsibility of my transport as far as Kargil had to go in search of fifty porters or so to take the place of the exhausted horses.

Directly we had left the rocky soil of the basin—where, near the path, engraved stone columns with inscriptions remind one of the time when this valley too was Buddhist—the snow on the ground diminished rapidly. It made a strange impression upon me to see fields again, and peasants at the plough, and more numerous hamlets, almost always huddled at the junction of the flat valley-bottom with the rocky side; a little group of willows near each group of houses now made an almost unvarying element in the landscape, and, lower down, of poplars also. Otherwise it was entirely naked; naked, but

30

ANCIENT BUDDHIST STELES AT DRAS

[face p. 30

impressive. It is perhaps here more than anywhere—that is, after leaving Dras—that one gets an exact idea of the grandeur of Himalayan scenery.

We went quickly down along the River Dras, to the point where it turns towards the left, in the neighbourhood of Dendel, and the valley becomes narrower and wilder. Just at the bend, there was the remains of an avalanche, broken by long crevasses and giving way beneath one's feet; we were only able to cross it along a thin ridge between one crevasse and another. There were several more avalanches farther on, as far as Karbu (our day's stage), and some were dangerous, at least for the horses. It was a long stage, but we made up for this by our speed. The wretched Tashgam oasis offered us a mediocre shelter in a little grove of poplars; then, after a little, we arrived at Karbu.

Owing to our speed of travelling we hardly noticed a certain monotony in the landscape from Dendel onwards: the valley is not wide, the sides are steep, rocky, sprinkled with snow low down but entirely covered higher up. Anyone new to the country might be surprised at the nakedness of the mountains, but ·I am surprised rather at the relative amount of juniper-bushes scattered here and there on their sides. But not even at Karbu had we come down low enough for a plantation of trees to break the bareness of the landscape near the village itself. The little bungalow is farther down, near the river, and near a tiny plantation of willows and poplars; but the village is above, high up, on a great moraine terrace, and from below one cannot even see it.

Beyond Karbu the Dras Valley becomes deeper and deeper, that is to say, its two sides become steadily steeper, and often sheer precipices, and the road, when there is not space enough for it to continue along the river, is forced to mount high above it, in order to get past the precipices of rock. So it is a perpetual up and down: but this, owing to the continual twisting of the valley, afforded us, when high up, truly impressive views of the wild bareness of the valley-sides—a bareness undiminished by the usual dark sprinkling of juniper over the yellowish-maroon colour of the rocks—of the snowy peaks and ridges which always appear, incomparably beautiful, as background to the occasional lateral ravines, and of the milky

31

turbulent river below, as it follows the windings of the valley, closely shut in between its lofty granite banks.

Below Karbu, the road was almost all easy. The very fact of its going up and down over the steep sides of the valley means also that work has been put into its making and that it has been adapted to the nature of the ground, which is unusual on this wretched road, although it is the only connection between Turkistan and the great world of India. All trade between the two countries has, from time immemorial, passed along this main route, which is generally little more than a track left by the caravans, and which might be destroyed all at once or interrupted for a long time by even a mild display of violence on the part of the forces of nature. It is like this even below Karbu. There are no longer avalanches of snow, but an immense landslip, or rather an immense fallen mass of earth and rock and lumps of stone, has completely effaced the road along the river, for a distance of over two miles. To find a way past this we had to climb quite high up, cross the irregular surface of the landslip and then come down again beyond. Though it was easy for us, it was not so for the poor horses: at intervals they had to be relieved of their loads, which were then transported by the men, and then loaded up again directly the ground became less treacherous. The difficulties, or rather uncertainties, of the passage were not due merely to the possibility of a fall down the slope of the landslip into the river, but also to the stones and lumps of rocks which might become detached from the earth, which was so unstable that at moments it seemed actually to be moving: an enormous lump only just missed one of my horses.

We had scarcely passed this new 'mauvais pas'—rather a long "step", indeed—when, as though to make up for it, we saw down in the valley encased in its walls of rock, a sight which was entirely new and unexpected and quite refreshing in the heat of the midday sun: on the far bank of the river there was a little oasis. We had seen others on the way down from Matayan, but between Matayan and Dendel they were almost entirely covered in snow, and after that were uncovered but bare, both in their black-earthed fields and leafless trees. Kirkitchu, on the other hand, was quite green, both in its trees and fields, with a lovely bright green, fresh and shining and looking almost impossible; and in the midst of the green there were pink patches of apricot-trees in full bloom. A little later we had halted, for lunch, in a grove of apricot-trees, near the oasis of Chanagund, and the light of the sun seemed actually to be pink as it filtered down to us through the little thick clusters of flowers which clothed the branches.

Then we started off again. There were more little oases and more patches of thin green sprinkled with pink in the midst of the yellowish bareness of the rocks—until the Dras joins its milky waters with the turbulent yellow waters of a larger river, the Suru, with which it runs henceforth to join the Indus, now not far away.

We turned up the Suru. Soon, after going through a final defile, it opens out into the great basin of Kargil—our objective. At Kargil, however, a halt seemed to be necessary, and so I stopped yesterday in this little capital of Purig.

The Kargil basin is rather a singular one. It is not exactly formed by a widening of the valley, but by the confluence between the Suru, which comes down from the principal chain of the Himalaya, and its tributary the Vuacca, which, on the other hand, runs parallel with the Indus. There is no spur of mountains dividing the two rivers before they join, merely an immense mass of alluvial deposit, flattened, almost level, at its top, and in which the two water-courses are hollowed out to a moderate depth. And so, even though there is no real plain and no typical basin, the country nevertheless widens and opens out unexpectedly after the rocky defile through which the road of the previous days took us. At the foot of the sides which enclose this great triangle hollowed out in the spurs of the Himalaya, there is a line of oases, one after another, all filled with trees and blooming with green.

The importance of Kargil is due to the fact that in its immediate neighbourhood the caravan-route which comes over the Zoji Pass divides into two, one road going to Skardu, capital of Baltistan, the other to Leh, capital of Ladakh, and then over to the high Karakoram Pass and Chinese Turkistan. For this reason a tiny bazaar has come into being here at Kargil, to serve the numerous caravans which pass through.

The principal occupation of the whole day and the chief reason why I decided to stop was the necessity of rearranging all the cases of supplies. I had ordered a certain number of identical cases, each of which should contain everything required for a certain number of days—the number of days, of course, varying according to the number of travellers. I thought my orders had been understood, but, instead, each case turned out in practice to be different from the other, and the management of my little family of wanderers threatened to become exceptionally complicated. I emptied all the cases, and rearranged them according to my previous plan. It was an extremely long job: we worked the whole day, with the aid of Rasul and Tashi; Hashmatullah Khan helped me too, also the 'tessildar' of Kargil (who was actually a prefect), and a missionary who passed almost the whole day at our bungalow (so great was his joy at seeing European faces), and then the 'chokidar', the 'zaildar', the 'chuprassi', and I don't know how many other local authorities of second and even third rank. But now our domestic arrangements should go 'comme sur des roulettes'!

The normal stage from Kargil takes one as far as Mulba— the longest stage between Srinagar and Leh. It was too long to fit in with my plans, which included one or two further pieces of reorganization and a visit to the Kargil bazaar. It is certainly not a large bazaar—merely a narrow, inclined alley flanked by two rows of little shops for the exclusive use of natives. The modesty of the wares and the simplicity with which they are displayed and offered to clients may be imagined. The *clientèle*, however, is extremely varied, since it is made up of all the caravan-dwellers between India and Turkistan. Though Purighis, naturally, are in the majority, there were also Ladakhis and Baltis and Brokpas, also Kashmiris and Punjabis and Yarkandis to complete the variety of the little picture, which aroused the curiosity of Miss Kalau to an extraordinary extent, for she was new to this life, though not unprepared for it. Hashmatullah, of course, was perfectly at home.

It was midday when, preceded by the little caravan of personal baggage—for the heavy baggage had already started on its own account direct for Leh—I left the large and hospitable bungalow of Kargil which looks out over the swift and muddy Suru and the chain of green oases spread out along the opposite bank of the river. We crossed the wide, flattened

34

stretch of great alluvial terraces which forms the angle of confluence between the Suru and its tributary the Vuacca.

A winter avalanche had destroyed the bridge across the
Wakka near Pashkum; one can make a *détour* a few miles
longer and so avoid the risks of a ford. But we, who had so
many fords in prospect, and many of them, perhaps, difficult
and certainly alarming, did not allow ourselves to be too much
frightened by the Wakka, which united its waters with those
of the Suru in quite a modest-looking fashion, almost opposite
the bazaar. It was for this reason that we crossed the whole
of the wide level stretch of the Kargil terraces and descended
thence towards the Wakka, opposite the fine cultivated area of
Pashkum, whose delicate green gave a feeling of freshness in
the midst of the dry, burnt appearance of so many bare rocks.
The ford was almost a joke, even though the current was
strong and we had to cross obliquely in order to break its
force. We made a brief halt for lunch on the strand of the
river, then started off again.

Our road was indicated by the Wakka Valley, sometimes
along the river-bank, more often rising high up, and keeping
to the right bank. The landscape was a little dull in its
uniformity which was not even broken by the presence of
villages. The valley is not wide, nor yet is it a proper gorge.
It is enclosed on both sides by steep banks of rock—a rock
which has in it strange tones of green alternating here and
there with a bright wine-red—but they do not rise to very
imposing ridges or peaks. But within these banks, the bottom
of the valley appears to have been heaped up, to a height of
some hundreds of metres, with a conglomerate mass of large
rocks, through which both the river and the lateral torrents
have cut deep courses. These masses at the bottom are the
only element of real beauty in the landscape of the Vuacca
Valley—steep walls, perpendicular or even overhanging, now
solid from their topmost edge down to the river, now again
pierced with niches, caverns and holes under the rocks, and
broken by the furrows cut by lateral torrents into tremendous
pillars, great towers and even vaster masses which look like
ruins, so that it is easy to imagine them as castles and fortresses,
bastions and towers of defence which have been more or less
completely destroyed by time.

Before sunset we arrived at Lotsum, a poor Purighi village at the opening of the lateral valley of Kerit. I remembered how I had come there before, in the middle of winter. From the lower Bot Karbu Valley I had come over a high pass so deep in snow that I had had to engage about ten natives simply to trample the road for me and my few porters. Then I had come headlong down from the high ground into Kerit, at the bottom of a little valley which was a horribly narrow gorge, until finally I emerged here, dead tired, in the Vuacca Valley, and the wretched house which sheltered me seemed to me a palace fit for a prince.

It was not: nor was the one that yesterday evening received my party, which, though small, is large for resources such as Lotsum can provide.

Someone may perhaps ask how it is that a wretched house in a wretched village in a remote valley of Purig, in the midst of the Himalaya, is capable of suddenly giving hospitality to a party of travellers and their *personnel*—which is by no means small, considering that Kadir and Rasul have been paying, on their own account, two Ladakhis from Nubra as personal assistants ever since we left Srinagar: such things happen almost as an established procedure in these strange parts. But perhaps the moment has come to explain how a house is constructed in Western Tibet.

The valley-bottoms, in which the villages are almost invariably found, are characterized climatically by these conditions—long icy winters and long sun-baked summers. It would be difficult to design a house which should provide equally good shelter from intense cold and from violent heat. So the people of these parts evolved a type of house with two distinct divisions, one for winter and one for summer, each adapted for one or other of the two opposite climatic conditions of the year. That is why we are always able to find, in any native house, empty quarters at our disposal: at present, of course, it is the summer quarters that are available.

All over Purig and Baltistan the winter quarters have exactly the same characteristics. One enters, generally, a first enclosed space in which the sheep are kept; from it one goes into another which is the stall for the oxen; then there is a third, for the bullocks; and finally one arrives in another room

36

in which the family lives. It has no windows towards the
outside, only an opening in the middle of the ceiling for the
smoke to escape, and between it and the entrance door there
is the double or even triple protection of the beasts' stalls,
which not only keeps out the low outside temperature, but
even provides an animal warmth. In their one living-room
they cook, eat and sleep: the entire family life takes place
between those four smoky walls. Our rules of hygiene may
not be observed, but undoubtedly they achieve their aim of
wasting as little heat as possible and getting the greatest
possible protection against the icy cold of the air outside.

With late spring comes the first heat, and then the family
migrates to the floor above, to its summer quarters. Here
there are no stables, because no protection against cold is
needed; nor is there only one living-room, but more than one,
so as to have more air; there are windows, too, and doors
opening to the outside, and partition-walls of hurdle instead
of masonry, so that the air may circulate more freely. As one
goes down from Purig through Baltistan, just as the heat of
the summer is ore intense, so also the summer quarters
become more airy and better ventilated: in the Skardu basin
they are almost always made entirely of hurdles, and have most
of their rooms open in front.

But, with all this luxury of summer and winter quarters,
it must not be imagined that the houses are palaces. They
are mean huts, with walls put up anyhow, and made of small
stones or rough bricks summarily baked in the sun; the roofs
are flat, and in the summer quarters (which are generally
smaller in space than the ground floor) form large open terraces.
The terraces and roofs, which are easily accessible (either by
means of steps, or directly from the ground if the house, as
often happens, is built on a slope), form a setting for the whole
of family life—always in summer, and in winter also during
the hours in which the sun is at its height or has any warmth
in it, even if the whole countryside is covered with snow. At
these times roofs and terraces are full of people and even of
animals; both people and animals go from one roof or terrace
to another, as if the whole life of the village were concentrated
there and nowhere else. And it is unnecessary to say that,
the moment the information of our arrival spread, all the roofs

were covered with even more people than usual, and the travellers were saluted from above with a chorus of *salaams*. But yesterday evening at Lotsum it was the travellers and their varied suite of servants who populated the roofs and terraces of a Purighi house, and looked out from them over the valley, the village, and the comings and goings of all its inhabitants. We passed a fairly comfortable night—except for the smoke which came up through all the walls from the winter quarters below and thoroughly suffocated such of us as were not accustomed to Tibetan houses—as I, from long experience at other times, have learned to be.

Lotsum, May 16th, 1930.

CHAPTER V

INTO THE BUDDHIST COUNTRY

The Wakka Valley continues, even higher up, to have the same characteristics as before: it is relatively narrow, so that there is no room at the bottom for cultivation or villages— there is, in fact, only one more small oasis for as long as the valley maintains this character—and is monotonous both in form and colour, though always rather theatrical, with its lower walls of conglomerate broken up into gigantic towers and bastions and riddled with cups and cavities and grottoes.

The sky was overcast: since we crossed the Zoji-la and passed Dras, the weather has not been so favourable. Man is by nature discontented; I hardly remember the great advantage the perfect weather gave us during our crossing of the Himalaya, threatened as we were by avalanches, and complain because the sky is no longer clear.

Certainly it would be good to have the sunshine to show up the colours and forms of the landscape which to-day has started to be characteristically Tibetan. The Sind Valley, for us, was like an old childhood's acquaintance, like a typical Alpine valley. The Dras Valley and the lower Wakka Valley were not old acquaintances for all of us, and were perhaps too unchanging, too monotonous, their rocks too ferruginous and rusty-looking, too uninhabited, to give us much satisfaction—in spite of the real impression of grandeur they might well give—when we knew that there was waiting for us a landscape which is, if possible, even grander, even more theatrical, more varied in form and colour, and enlivened by a people full of geniality, of artistic sense, of cheerfulness and humour, who succeed in impressing these qualities of their own upon surroundings which by nature are desolate and bare of vegetation, a desert of rock and alluvion. But I yearned for the sunshine, to go with me and display to advantage the fantastic beauty to which I was returning after so

39

many years of longing, and to which one of my companions
was coming for the first time under my guidance and initiation.

Going up the Wakka Valley, one arrives at the junction of
another river, which marks the end of its long, monotonous,
uninhabited lower stretch.   From here onwards one must keep
one's eyes open and not be absorbed in thought; one must
be on the alert, like a sentry, so that nothing may escape one's
notice.   This is the doorway of Western Tibet proper, and
through it one goes—if I may use the expression—into its
vestibule; and in a vestibule strangers may come and go, but
the occupants of the house are already to be seen.   The
strangers are Purighis in particular; the occupants are Ladakhis.
From here onwards we shall begin to appreciate the Ladakhis;
then we shall quickly grow to love them, when we see how
they welcome and entertain us in this great house of theirs,
the bare vastness of which their natural genius adorns so
splendidly.

The valley widens out: its real sides recede from each
other, as do the two opposing walls of the conglomerate which
occupies the valley-bottom.   One seems to breathe more freely,
and as the view opens out one also appreciates better the
beauties which indeed existed before, but upon which it was
impossible to dwell owing to the narrowness of the valley.
There were two qualities in the landscape which accompanied
us from now till the end of to-day's journey—both apparent
on the opposite slope to that at the foot of which the path
runs.   On the first level, lower down, there are the usual
walls of conglomerate, broken up, with even more fantastic
results than before, into the castles and fortresses of an imaginative stage-designer, into great towers and massive bastions,
into graceful, slim steeples and spires.   Then, on a second
level, can be seen the real side of the valley—mountains of
such shape and boldness of outline as to resemble the Dolomites,
though not violently broken up, as they are, into almost detached
shafts; they constitute, rather, a continuous, compact wall,
jagged only at the summit of their dizzy ridge.   On the other
hand, on the side at the foot of which our path runs, the mountainous landscape has a strange softness: the sides and summits
are extremely gentle, almost smooth, and rounded, but here
and there a rocky point sticks up, small but extremely rugged,

40

as if it were trying to imitate the rough grandeur of the opposite side.

In the midst of this landscape, the whole wild beauty of which we were able to admire since it had become more open, we saw, down at the bottom of the valley, on the first and lowest level of the ground, some unusual objects. They looked like the large, rough bases of pillars with something smaller stuck on the top, and were white, pink, orange or blue in colour. They were isolated, or in small irregular groups, or three of different colours in a short alignment. Or, on some little piece of rising ground, were small stone figures of men from which projected branches and boughs adorned with fluttering banners. The former are "chorten", the latter "lato", which faithful Buddhists raise in memory of their honoured dead, or to placate and invoke spirits. We were, in fact, just entering into the Buddhist world of Tibet, and *chorten* and *lato* enliven the bare grandeur of the natural landscape—even from the first moment.

But if one looks into the lateral valley which here joins that of the Wakka, one sees something even more strange and wonderful. The wall of conglomerate penetrates into this valley with its fantastic shapes: at its foot is a little cluster of large, pink *chorten*: but the wall itself, of a uniform, pale rust-colour, is interrupted by a square white patch, framed in colour, and pierced as though by so many symmetrical, dark eyes. It is the façade of a "gompa", or monastery, with its little windows, and it goes back into a natural cavity in the conglomerate. It is a fantastic sight, suspended half-way up the precipice of rock, and created by the genius of this imaginative race.

There is nothing interesting inside it, especially if one has before one the prospect of the wonders of all the *gompa* of Ladakh; for this reason I did not turn the caravan aside to the little *gompa* of Shargol, but pressed on farther up the long valley of the Wakka. But soon afterwards something even more fantastic appeared in front of us: from the bottom of the right-hand wall of the valley—the one at whose foot the path runs—in the midst of smooth, gentle, rounded slopes, a point of rock stood up towards the sky, erect, pointed and sharp as the tooth of a feline animal. Right on the top, surrounded by a little ring of ruined walls, were perched the remains of an ancient castle, a little *gompa*, and then another, facing on to the abyss which surrounded them on every side. These are the two *gompa* of Mulba. The tiny bungalow at the foot of the rocks, on the river-bank, is completely dominated by them.

Mulba, the first Buddhist village on our route, gave a worthy reception to me, the old friend of the Ladakhis. Two "mon"—the *mon* are musicians, who hand on their art from father to son—gave an impetuous, rhythmic roll on their drums and played modulations in a simple, very quick time on their long silver trumpets; the few lamas from the two *gompa* had come down to join them, and added the dull beat of their characteristic big drums and the hollow sound of their long copper trombones, adorned with flowery silver ornamentations; the whole of the small population of the village lined the way for me to pass, welcoming me with the usual "ju!", spoken more drawlingly, the more profound the respect they wish to express.

A visit to the two *gompa* made an incomparably fantastic impression upon us, even though they are rather poor in comparison with many which we shall be admiring during the next few days. But their situation is truly fantastic, on the very top of the precipitous point of rock which dominates the whole of the valley and looks as if it were trying to reach heaven. This point of rock has also a documentary value in the history of the district, for an inscription in the rock near its foot actually repeats an order given by an ancient local king.

It is cold, the sky has become more and more overcast during the day. I have not left off the habit I have adopted so far, and while I write I am comforted by a good fire crackling on the hearth.

Mulba, May 16th, 1930.

Anyone who comes for the first time into Ladakh must think he is entering a land of dreams. Even I feel this, though almost every detail of this wonderful journey had remained impressed on my memory.

42

ROCK-CARVING OF BUDDHA AT MULBA

[face p. 42

We had not yet lost sight of the great rock with the *gompa* of Mulba perched on its extreme summit, like two sentries guarding the valley, when we saw a smaller rock, of which the whole of one face has a figure of Chamba, the Buddha of the Tibetans, carved in relief upon it, in gigantic dimensions. But even when one has passed Chamba, and the two airy monasteries have disappeared behind a side-curtain of hills, one feels nevertheless that one has arrived in another world. One feels this even from the houses.

I have already initiated my readers into the secrets of the houses of Western Tibet. Those of the Purighis and the Baltis have, it is true, the choice of quarters which is more or less imposed upon them by the climate, but they also have, almost always, an appearance of wretchedness—walls put up anyhow, without any sense of the straight, walls in which river-pebbles and rough sun-baked bricks display their poverty without attempting to hide it, walls replaced by even more primitive hurdles, sometimes and sometimes not covered with mud; haphazard roofs, from every side of which protrude branches and boughs which form a support to the final covering of earth; no choice of aspect or of exterior structure which might lead one to credit the inhabitants with even the beginnings of an artistic sense or, at the least, of natural taste. Certainly they are convenient for the needs of their occupants, and also for passing travellers, as they are easily adaptable, but nevertheless, for the majority of travellers, they are nothing more than wretched huts.

One enters the land of dreams, and even the houses seem to invite one to dream. The structure of the interior is the same—winter quarters well protected from the cold, summer quarters splendidly ventilated, often also quarters for the seasons between; however, there is more space even in this universal method of internal arrangement. But their outside appearance is different and cannot escape the notice even of the least serious traveller—well-built walls, with a perfect sense of the straight, but built in such a way that the house tends to become slightly narrower towards the top and thus assumes a quite special elegance, whereas its dimensions would perhaps make it look squat and massive; the framework is often invisible, because covered with a thick layer of white

43

plaster; there are very small windows in the walls at different levels, with elegant projecting wooden jambs; and on the top floor almost always a large projecting balcony, sheltered by a pretty little pent-house, or a big open terrace which breaks the compact massiveness of the building; and both the windows and the balcony or terrace are placed so as to give the house a general symmetry—a symmetry which, even to one who detests it on principle, gives character and grace to these first typically Tibetan habitations.

Then, as if this were not enough, a certain amount of colour, apart from the white of the plaster, begins to appear. Some houses have their top edges painted red in a band which goes all round, all of them have the edges of the roof surmounted with tufts of hay and boughs, so nicely arranged that they look like an intentional ornament, and at a corner of the roof a small branch is placed upright with little flags hanging or fluttering from it. Then there are *lato* and *chorten* scattered along beside the path through the fields, half hidden in a grotto, or erected along the edge of a ridge or the top of a rise; one also begins to see "mani", long, low, wide walls, upon which the faithful place stones with the eternal prayer of the Buddhists carved upon them—"om mani padme hum".

In this way the country, which in itself becomes more and more impressive, though always bare, becomes also more and more embellished—one might almost say populated—by the houses, the *lato*, the *chorten* and the *mani*—very gradually, because we are still right in the zone of transition. But the inhabitants themselves also contribute towards animating the landscape.

As I came down from the Zoji Pass and crossed Purig, the inhabitants all crowded round as I passed, not so much from curiosity as in sign of respect; but it was a dumb, silent, surly respect, as though imposed upon them. But from Mulba onwards the people came to meet me smiling, cheerful, festive, bringing their women with them, and their musicians and lamas if there were any in the village. Just as the others had been surly and lacking in spontaneity, at least in appearance, so these people are ingenuously and naturally festive and joyful. If one glances by chance at a Purighi or a Balti, he seems anxious to assume an expression which is

even more dark and depressed and reserved than usual. If
one looks at a Ladakhi, on the other hand, he breaks at once
into a bright open smile, with his eyes, his mouth and the whole
of his face; he repeats his greeting and looks back at one as
if one were an old friend. But, in the case of the Ladakhis,
I am indeed an old friend.

Yesterday, after leaving Mulba, we passed through fields,
and I observed the difference between country life here and
in Purig. In Purig there was very little activity in the fields,
in appearance at least—solitary men at the plough, and if by
chance there was a woman, she would hide behind a low wall
or squat down on the ground till we had passed. Here the
whole family seems to be in the fields: the woman leads the
oxen while the man carefully guides the plough behind them;
others sow; two or three girls break the clods turned up by
the plough, with a rapid, rhythmic movement of their whole
body and of the hoe, moving quickly along the upturned
furrow; and the children follow the adults, amusing themselves
happily with some trifle, as children will do all the world over
if they have not already grown "blasés" about toys. The
whole country-side appears filled with life and animation by
these people, who stop their work as we pass to greet us with
smiles, and then take it up again with the cheerfulness which
they bring to the whole of life.

From the Wakka Valley we went up a small lateral valley
which comes down from the right, in the middle of that pleasant
country of mountains, little knolls, and gently rounded hillocks
which forms such a strong contrast with the precipitous, lofty
mountains facing it, though in it, here and there, a few teeth
of solid, compact rock, of roughly pointed shape, rise sheer
into the air. We went up the valley as far as a pass which
is almost 13,000 feet high. This pass, too, is pleasant and
gently rounded like all the neighbouring landscape; but near
it there rises, from the line of rounded summits, a rocky point
higher than the others, lofty, erect, naked, precipitous.
"Namika"—the prop of heaven—the inhabitants appropriately
call it, and the neighbouring pass is called Namika-la.

From here there is a rapid descent into the valley of Bot
Karbu or of Chiktan. A few miles lower down from where
one comes out into the bottom of the valley, there is still to

be seen at Chiktan, in almost perfect preservation outside, the old castle of the feudal period which lasted in the district till almost a century ago. Boldly poised on a great, sheer peak of rock, and in the perfect Tibetan style, alert and at the same time powerful, it looks like a castle of legend. It was impossible to include a visit to it in my present programme: we had to hurry on up the valley. Pairs of crows, black and glossy, were wheeling low down, alighting here and there on the ground and then taking flight again; high up, vultures were circling majestically, almost touching the peaks as though they wished to settle there, and then going off again with their wide, sure flight. We met caravans, but only small ones— few with porters, the majority with horses, and donkeys also. We came across them on the road, and also during the halt which they usually take half-way on their day's stage: the loads would be heaped up in good order, generally in a semicircle, the animals scattered in that search for a blade of grass which must be a kind of torture for them, or—if the search is hopeless —standing together in long lines in front of primitive, makeshift mangers marked by two rows of stones, into which the men throw a handful or two of straw, gathered God knows where. The men themselves, close to the loads which, if necessary, protect them from a suddenly-rising wind, light a little fire to make tea and crouch round it, repairing their clothes and pack-saddles until the tea is ready.

The other day, before we arrived at Mulba, a man in one of these little groups rose to his feet—as indeed they always do, as a mark of respect; he was a Ladakhi, and immediately, without hesitation, he came forward to meet me with the most frank and friendly signs of greeting. Coming to the edge of the path, his hands joined in the attitude of prayer and his face wreathed in smiles, he began, after the usual Tibetan greeting, to speak to me, striving to mix a few words of Hindustani with his own language and even calling me by name, 'Danelli sahib'. But his speech was short, for I too recognized him. He was one of the twenty coolies from Timosgam who had followed me faithfully in my summer exploring expedition from the Depsang to the Lingzi-Tang plateaux and to the great glaciers of the upper Shyok and up the Rimo Glacier. They were wonderful people, who

46

would have thrown themselves into the fire for me, knowing
that the sacrifice would be appreciated and rewarded . . . with
a tin of jam! And Sonam Kontchok, most faithful of all?
At Yarkand. And Namghial, that robust old man, who had
been head of my little company? Dead. And Ghiazo, un-
rivalled as a hunter and collector of fossils? He had not seen
him since that time. And I, who was labouring under the
illusion that I should find them all and take them all into my
service again, my faithful followers of a time which is now so
distant!

Since our first meeting I have found my former porter
every day, halted by the wayside near the fire making tea; and
in the evening, at the end of the day's journey, I go and see
him when he also has arrived and is preparing the evening
meal with his companions.

The Chiktan Valley also is beautiful. It too is characterized, in its bottom and its low sides, by those rocks which
make for a gentle landscape punctuated with sharp, erect
points of rock; but behind them, on one side—the left—there
is that other kind of rock which we have already admired
along the Wakka, and which here too rises up into steep
ridges and peaks of marvellous beauty. On the other side—
the right—there are rocks of yet another kind, less fine to look
at, but, from their compactness and power of resistance, resulting in shapes and effects of high relief which are a complete
contrast with the smooth, rounded surfaces that form the sides
of the valley nearer the bottom. At the edge of the latter
are the villages. There is one—Tankse—which is especially
picturesque: its fine houses and green fields, which look as if
they had been combed, stretch right across the mouth of a
short but wide lateral valley. At the end of the village rises
one of the typical points of rock, but more than usually sharp
and toothlike: on the top of it are the ruins of an ancient castle,
while all down the less steep side are the remains of peasants'
houses which were protected by the solid walls of the residence
of their lord—traces of the feudal period, of which Chiktan is
the most notable monument. Further on is Mundik, which
is also picturesque, but in a different way. Its houses extend
along, and are supported against, a wall of conglomerate which
follows the bottom of this as of the Wakka Valley, and seems

even to penetrate into it. But here everything is picturesque, and I do not see how there could well be a greater harmony between natural landscape and the manifestations of humanity. Men, here, seem to have wished to be inspired by the landscape and to harmonize with it: certainly they have done nothing to disturb its lines or its beauty. Many of our own people might well learn from them.

In front of us, meanwhile, a fantastically theatrical view was growing steadily clearer. All that could be seen was, or seemed to be, unbelievable, to be the fruit of a genial imagination which conceived and saw everything as being daringly beautiful and noble. Often, if one shut one's eyes and gave one's imagination play, one felt oneself to be in contact with old popular legends or with the enterprises and adventures of knights of supernatural powers. But opening our eyes honestly, we had to convince ourselves that we were confronting actual reality. We had no other word to express our wonder except—utterly fantastic, completely and utterly fantastic.

The side of the valley at the foot of which our path lay was marked, ahead of us, by an immense rock, one of those which break the smooth uniformity of the pleasant rounded landscape. An immense rock with irregularly broken sides, ferruginous and rusty-looking in colour. The whole of its summit was crowned with the ruins of an ancient castle, sharply outlined against the sky. Another smaller rock leaned close up against it, like a younger brother, but the walls of this one were straight, perpendicular, almost polished, as though some genius of nature had cut it out clean, in this way, with huge strokes. Its summit, of moderate size, was as though levelled, and upon it was a forest, a veritable forest of tumbledown walls, from which a thin tentacle of smaller walls reinforced with little towers wound its way down, apparently taking advantage of the slightest roughness in the rock, to a neighbouring ravine. The ancient castle on its larger summit, the ancient village on the rock below it; and the fortified descent to the stream for the necessary water-supply. It is a world which seems so very far away, but which was preserved intact here until a century ago. Then came the Dogra conquest which laid low and destroyed everything, like

a scourge. The genial nature of the people created the picturesque new villages, the handsome houses, the *chorten*, the long
mani, the *lato*, and established its own happy, laughing serenity
beside the rather surly, fearsome ruins of old local feudalism.
We were still intent upon the view of the great rocks crowned
with ruins when, suddenly, the inhabitants of Bot Karbu
brought us back to the realities of actual life with the dis-
tracting music of their *mon*, the strange discords of their
lamas' orchestra, the offerings and the 'ju' of the women,
and the fluttering of all the flags hoisted on the tops of the
houses. Here at Bot Karbu I gave my companions their
first experience of Ladakhi dances—both of men and women
—on the small space in front of the bungalow.

Our march to-day continued, without stopping, up the
Chiktan Valley. The natural landscape was, as usual, always
impressive, but even more naked and deserted. The bold
and jagged mountains on the left side come closer to the
central line of the valley, and between them open ravines
which look like wild dark holes; the opposite side, on the
other hand, is smooth and pleasant. In this part the one
and only village, Hiniskut, takes advantage of one of the usual
pointed rocks. There are the ruins of an ancient castle on
the top, and the houses are still built down the sides: the scourge
of conquest has not destroyed everything here.

The horses limped up the slope; every now and then they
stopped, panting. Then we arrived at a pass, the Fotu-la,
over 13,000 feet high. On the other side a valley descended;
it also was smooth in the lower part of its sides, but, like the
others, was shut in by two rows of high, steep mountains.
Far away in the background was a snowy ridge: this was
beyond the Indus, it was already the Karakoram, no longer
the Himalaya. We made a brief halt to enjoy this new sight,
in the lee of a large *lato*, for there was a cold wind blowing.
There were masses of clouds moving across the sky. Then
on, down the new valley; quickly down, following its smooth
windings. As I went down I had a foretaste of the wonder
which would soon be re-born in me, even though not unexpected. At every turn of the valley I imagined that the
great surprise would catch me unawares, and I held back my
horse to be near my companions and to read in their faces

that which words would not be capable of saying. But here was the decisive turn: I recognized it, marked by two great *chorten*. We reached them: passed them: and suddenly, in all its magnificence, Lamayuru appeared.

Lamayuru, May 18th, 1930.

CHAPTER VI

FROM ONE *GOMPA* TO ANOTHER

The two *chorten* at the last turn in the valley before Lama-yuru are but the first of a long series which, alternating with *mani*, follow the path as it curves gently down across the side of the valley. At the end there is a veritable forest of *chorten* and *mani* of every size and shape, all up the slope, leaning against each other and mingling with the few houses of the village. Behind the village rise high cliffs of yellowish clay, pierced with caves and broken vertically, like narrow chimneys, into towers and more or less detached shafts, and the even line of their summit is topped by a mass of buildings, the temples and chapels of the *gompa* of Lamayuru. It is a picturesque and impressive sight; and the first effect of its unexpected appearance does not alter or wear off. As we approached the village, the details, becoming more clearly visible, increased the grandeur and intensity of the first impression. In the meantime the little streets between one *chorten* and another, and from house to house, and the upper terraces of the houses, had become peopled and animated with, I believe, the entire population of Lamayuru. At the entrance to the village there was a dense crowd of people, in the midst of which a brilliant, many-coloured patch—violet, green, red—indicated the presence of women in their best clothes, ready with hospitable offerings—flowers and meal and 'chang', the Tibetan beer. As we approached nearer we heard a roll of drums and a flourish from the trumpets of the *mon*, from the lower part of the village; this was immediately answered by the music of the lamas, drawn up on the highest terrace of the monastery. When finally we arrived at the little bungalow, where our personal baggage waited in heaps, deposited shortly before by the caravan which follows all our movements (the heavy baggage goes direct and separately to Leh), the whole population crowded round on the small space in front, and men and

51

women performed alternately, in my honour, their characteristic dances with little steps against the beat of the music,
moving at first slowly and with an almost complete immobility
of the whole body, then gradually quicker and quicker till they
end with extremely fast movements accompanied by contortions
of the body, the arms, and even the hands.

Late the same afternoon we went up to the *gompa*: the path
clambers up the slope of the valley-side among long *mani* and
chorten like a pilgrimage to prepare one for a forthcoming
initiation. Arrived at the summit, we were on the platform
up above the strange clay cliffs with their tower-like forms,
from one to another of which some bridge is thrown boldly across
to link up the inhabited area of the *gompa*, or to make a passage-
way from one to another of its many buildings. The lamas
were all ready to be our guides and to do us honour, majestically
clothed in their flame- or wine-coloured robes. I was again
conscious of the delicacy and refinement of Tibetan art, as
shown in the wall-paintings, in the little statues representing
the thousand Buddhist divinities and venerated lamas, in the
ceremonial objects, in the ornamental patterns bordering their
buildings, windows and balconies, in the spontaneous but
skilful distribution of the temples, cells, courtyards and porticoes, among which are *mani* which can be turned by hand,
little *chorten* set into the walls or larger ones erected in the
middle of the little streets of the monastery, tall posts which
carry long pennons with prayers printed on them, banners
fluttering from every roof, little gables from which project
branches of burnt juniper which serve to scent the air—everything goes to make up a complete picture, harmonious in its
picturesque variety. It would be worth while coming all the
way from Europe just to see and admire the *gompa* of Lamayuru:
for us, on the other hand, Lamayuru merely marks the beginning of a long pilgrimage which will lead us day after day from
one *gompa* to another.

Early next morning we started off again down the Lamayuru
Valley, straight towards the Indus. The rising sun, with its
strong contrasts of light and shade, threw into new relief the
chorten and chapels and temples of the *gompa*, perched on top
of the clay cliffs. A little below the village the clay seems to
have invaded the whole valley-bottom up to a considerable

ARRIVAL AT LAMAYURU

[face p. 52

height on the sides: above that it is again broken up by
torrents. It is a smooth, yellow clay, which the water has
twisted strangely into the shape of domes, of hillocks, of vast
nipples, each of them incised with almost regular furrows
which radiate outwards from the smoothly rounded summit
in all directions. If one goes up the valley one is prepared by the sight of this strangely formed landscape for
the view which unfolds directly one has turned a particular
corner—great towering cliffs broken into vertical chimneys, at
their feet the village and the forest of *chorten*, and the *gompa*
on top.

Up to this point, however, the valley is composed, on the
whole, of gentle, smooth forms, and slopes gently at the
bottom. But suddenly the sides close in and rise up sheer,
showing the bare compactness of rocks in which all the colours
of a rich palette seem to have been mixed; the valley becomes
a gorge and the torrent, delving down into it, almost disappears
in its depths. The path, too, plunges down into the bottom
of the narrow gorge. One has to look straight up above one's
head in order to see a thin slice of sky, and it was a sky in
which the masses of morning cloud of the last few days had
now formed into a solid curtain of leaden grey. The valley-
bottom widens a little, but it still remains, none the less, a
deep, rocky gorge; the path is like a tortuous balcony, cut into
the rock and hanging above the river. Finally it opens out
into the larger valley of the Indus.

The landscape is then no longer shut in nor the view
restricted, but there is not the impression of grandeur which
might perhaps be expected from the great river which, from
near the sacred Lake Manasarowar in Central Tibet, forms the
dividing line between the Himalaya and the Karakoram, two
of the greatest ranges in the world. Certainly the Indus is
not large at this point, for in its upper course there are scarcely
any glaciers to feed it: above the Zanskar, as we shall see in a
few days, it appears sometimes, in the middle of summer, to
be quite a smallish river and is of no great importance to a
traveller who understands the difficulties and dangers of fords.
But I think it is also the grandeur of the whole landscape
which serves to lessen the impressiveness of the Indus as it
first appears at the bottom of its terraced valley. When the

lines of the whole landscape are on such a magnificent scale as
they are in this region of Tibet, any single detail, however
imposing, seems to grow smaller and less important, sometimes
almost to disappear. I had this same impression on another
occasion, when I came out suddenly upon the Indus from the
Suru Valley, on the way to Skardu in Baltistan, but it is an
impression which gradually ceases to have effect as one becomes
accustomed to comparing the relative sizes of all the various
elements in a landscape of such vast scale.

There is a suspension-bridge over the Indus, which, on
the other side of the river, leads into the enclosure of a Dogra
fort, built by the conquerors at this key situation on the great
caravan-route. There are some admirable designs carved on
old granite blocks with the *patina* of time upon their surface,
among them one of an archer on horseback pursuing a gazelle,
which shows, in the few, rough strokes of its outline, a complete mastery of the representation of movement. It was
probably the work of some young shepherd, of a fairly remote
period, done to relieve his enforced idleness while guarding his
flocks at pasture.

We went on up the great valley and the great river, by its
right bank.

Since Khirkitchu and Chanagund in the Dras Valley we
had seen no green fields; from Kargil to Lamayuru the fields
were either newly ploughed or in process of being ploughed,
but the reddish or grey earth did not change or break the
general nakedness of the landscape. But now there appeared
in front of us, at the bottom of the valley, a great patch of
green—Khalatse. One large field of this cunningly-terraced
area is devoted to crops; the trees—willows and poplars and a few
apricots—are already clothed with little leaves; along the banks
of the small canals are low tufts of a darker green, in the midst
of which grows a purplish iris which looks like a flower in
miniature. There were *mon*, women, lamas; on our arrival
we were offered flowers, *satu* (flour made from parched barley),
chang; there were sounds of drums and trumpets, cymbals and
trombones, and greetings from the people we met along the
road and from others who had gone up on to the roofs; indeed
our journey is almost a triumphal progress.

To go on and on, always, without stopping or resting—it

seems as though Fate had ordained this for me, sometimes—quite often, in fact—against my own desire. But, so far, mine is but a journey of approach, of advance towards a very distant goal. We must hurry on all the time, never stopping.

When we arrived, on our way up the Indus, at Balucar—a little point of rock with ruins which have a certain importance in the history of the country, and fossils which are even more important from the point of view of the geology of the Western Himalaya—we left the valley and started to climb up its right side. This was a deviation from the ordinary route which I was anxious to make both for old sake's sake and also for the carrying out of my future plans.

There is, in a small lateral valley, a village called Timosgam which I once visited during my long wanderings in Western Tibet, and the memory which I had of it impelled me to return there. But there was also another reason. It was from Timosgam that the porters came who had formed the light caravan that followed me so faithfully in forced marches over the Rimo glacier and the plateaux of Lingzi-Tang, by ways which were often unknown before, experiencing severe fatigues and sometimes strict rationing of provisions. The men had remained completely loyal all the time. I wanted to see them again and hoped to be able to take them with me once more. The men of Timosgam, in fact, have acquired a much better reputation for endurance than those who live nearer and in closer contact with the high mountains and glaciers; those of the Nubra Valley, who live almost face to face with the vast glacier, had been indicated to me as the least ready to venture into unknown country. Perhaps, knowing more, they are for that reason more inclined to be afraid.

It was for these different reasons that I was going to Timosgam. There was a steep ascent; then we crossed a kind of level plateau opening out between the channel in which the Indus flows and the high granite mountain-side; then all at once we came from above upon the Timosgam Valley, with its green fields, pink flowering apricot-trees, and little scattered groups of houses festooned with flags with prayers printed upon them. A small ridge of rock rises above the lowest group: on its top there are the ruins of an ancient castle, and the old walls enclose it in a circle, with an extra wall going off down the side to the neighbouring torrent, for drawing water. The great towers of defence on the neighbouring hill-tops are also in ruins, but on the highest summit, in the midst of the ruins, there is a little *gompa* which, with its walls of flaming red, looks as though it were on fire, and a little below it is another of dazzling white.

We went rapidly down a steep slope to the bottom of the valley. The triumphal progress continued, with the usual welcome and the usual offerings and music. I am occupying the best house in the village, the same one in which, sixteen years ago, I had a little room on the terrace at the end, near a little chapel in which a lama intoned evening prayers, accompanying himself with the regular beat of the big drum. I found none of my old porters. However, a whole crowd came asking to be taken on. Negotiations—extremely laborious— began yesterday evening. They continued this morning, and were finally concluded: 40 porters, to be with me for the whole of my summer campaign, are to join me at Leh in a week. I shall, of course, need a great many more supplementary ones; but these 40 will be the regulars, always with us and equipped for high altitudes, and they will operate, in particular, above my base-camp—a base-camp which, if the difficulties are not too great, will already be well amidst the glaciers.

Timosgam has already given us an insight into Ladakhi life. On our arrival we were offered tea, with ' chupattis'— thin round flat pieces of dough, a substitute for bread—in the big family kitchen. There was a regular exhibition of brass teapots, kettles for making *chang*, and enormous copper pots, on the shelves all round the room; in the middle was a smoking stove, and in one corner, strips of soft Chinese carpet on which to sit cross-legged, in the manner of the country. The wife, with her great glittering 'perak', which hangs from the forehead right down the back to the waist, bristling with turquoises and little gold and silver reliquaries, moved about between us and the stove.

We also went up to the *gompa*. The one which is all red outside contains a gigantic statue, at least five times life-size, of Chamba, the Buddha; the other contains I don't know what divinities, but, particularly, some charming 'tanca', votive pictures which hang from the walls and columns of the temple.

This morning, having finished the laborious negotiations with the men of the village, I started again on my ever-lasting march, going up a little valley which comes out into the valley of Timosgam. Beyond a little pass the village of Himis Shupa welcomed me triumphally. 'Shupa' means juniper: about twenty juniper-trees, gnarled and gigantic —a great rarity for the whole of this region—give the village its name. Some slight percolation of water, in the level, wide bottom of the valley, produces an unusual carpet of natural grass, very short but thick, on ground which is all covered with very small mounds, like certain high, turfy plateaux in our Alpine valleys: this also is rare.

Into the saddle again: a third climb and a third descent. But after the descent, instead of going straight on in the same direction, as we did since leaving Timosgam—that is, going over a series of low passes which succeed each other at regular intervals and mark the so-called "high road" to Leh, we turned to the right, following a small valley which descends straight to the Indus. A handsome yellow lama was waiting for me on horseback, with a Ladakhi: he bowed to us, and then took the head of the company.

One explanation may be necessary. Lamas, i.e. Buddhist monks (who have their heads entirely shaved, in contrast with the laymen, who wear a long pigtail, obviously a belated adop-tion of the Chinese fashion), wear a monastic habit entirely of bright red, rather inclined to wine-colour, round which they drape majestically a long piece of cloth of the same colour: the band which girds them at the waist is also red, as is the odd-shaped cap, circular, with wide flaps turned up except above the forehead. There is no doubt that the lamas form a supremely picturesque element in the Tibetan landscape. It seems that at one time the mode of life of these innumerable servants of the Buddhist religion (and perhaps, later on, I shall explain also how their great numbers are intimately con-nected with the general economy of the country)—it seems that at one time their mode of life was not so pure as it should have been. Customs were degenerating. Then there arose among them a reformer, seeking to restore the purity of their life—his name was Tsongkapa—who imposed stricter and severer rules on his followers. The latter, to distinguish themselves from other lamas, adopted yellow as the colour of their girdles and caps, and so were called 'Yellow Lamas'. To-day there is no great difference between the Yellows and the Reds. They live side by side, but not in any propagandist rivalry, nor with any great difference of life. Perhaps in the past it was so, and it is perhaps owing to this that quite often, where there is a 'red' temple, there is a 'yellow' one near by: hence the two at Mulba, and at Timosgam.

Here, then, was a yellow lama, very elegant in the flaming draperies in which he was clothed, on a little prancing horse with a beautiful Chinese embroidered horse-cloth. He was administrator of the *gompa* of Rigzon. As usual in my triumphal progress, I had been met by the established authority at the boundary of the territory under his direct jurisdiction. At the boundary of the territory of each village the 'lambardar' —a sort of mayor—would come to meet me, and would not leave me till I left the village; at the boundary of the territory of each group of villages constituting a regional and administrative unity, its chief, or 'zaildar', would also come to meet me and not leave me again. Each formed a faithful guard of honour—not to mention what was done for me also by the representatives of the State. To-day I have arrived in the territory, not of a village, but of a *gompa*; and that is why to-day I had a picturesque flame-red lama as my guard of honour.

Rigzon-Gompa, May 20th, 1930.

CHAPTER VII

AMONGST THE TIBETANS

The little valley down which we went had one unique quality: it was extremely narrow and its sides were bare, but all along its tortuous bottom there was a thin continuous line of bright green willows. This also was a rarity, like the ancient junipers and the soft grass of Himis Shupa. But even though a rarity, this thin string of willows winding its way down the valley and, as it were, caressed by the murmur of the little stream, could not efface our memory of the picturesque beauty of the fields of the Timosgam Valley, laid out in terrace below terrace and all green with the first sprouting of the crops, sprinkled with flowering apricot-trees and close groups of houses, each of which, with its jutting balconies—the 'rabsal'—and tiny windows, the big terraces at the ends, and the fluttering of banners and pennons, formed a complete picture in its grove of willows and poplars. Here there was the thin twisting line of little trees and then, on both sides, a desert of rock. Soon the latter became universal, as the valley was joined by a much smaller valley opening on one side; it became entirely rock, with little narrow windings, so that it looked all the time as though it were completely blocked. Miss Kalau wondered what in the world could be the objective of my programme, and where we could be going. But there is no use in being impatient, in this country where every day brings a surprise. A few more turns—the Yellow Lama still pranced along in front of us, now appearing, now disappearing in the windings of the narrow gorge—and then, suddenly, Rigzon, amazing, incredibly theatrical, like all these Tibetan *gompa*.

Rigzon is not, like most of the others, on a height: it spreads out in a sort of amphitheatre against the side of a little spur of rock which forms another narrow turn of the gorge. Thus it actually appears to block the valley. From the bottom to the top, one above the other, are the little houses of the lamas—of the usual Tibetan type, with a terrace at the end, but small, as though in miniature—and the temple buildings: the roof of each house and each building forms, as it were, a step to support the houses and buildings above it. The monks' dwellings have tiny windows, but the halls for the worship of Buddha and of the most holy and venerated lamas have large balconies and porches. These balconies and porches are made of wood, and a most exquisite grace is achieved with the simple means available to Tibetan architecture. The edge of every roof is adorned with a deep border of wine-colour, which makes an excellent frame for the whiteness of the walls. I believe I have discovered the origin of this ornamental *motif*, which is repeated in every *gompa*, in every temple, and in all the houses of the wealthier inhabitants.

They have a custom all over Western Tibet of piling up the hay they have mown—which actually is very little—or straw, or the fodder required for daily use, all round the roof, in such a manner that its weight comes only on the outside walls and not on the ceiling of the rooms underneath. The Baltis—a poor people, who have lost all æsthetic sense, owing, probably, to their loss of the Buddhist religion—pile up their straw and fodder in utter disorder. But as one goes farther east, and above all, as one comes into the zone of transition between Musulmans and Buddhists which we passed through between Lotsum and Lamayuru, one notices that the piles at the edge of the roofs are more tidily and more regularly made: straw and fodder are better arranged, better put together, so that they do not jut out beyond the walls of the house but keep an even thickness all round. In this way they become an ornamental element in the houses of the Tibetan peasants. The step from this to real conscious ornamentation is not difficult, and it is for this reason that every *gompa*, every temple, every house belonging to rich inhabitants has its walls surmounted by a wide border of branches and twigs arranged in perfect order and covered in its turn with a layer of earth; this border, in which the branches and twigs are arranged transversely to the walls, is painted red or maroon, and often, on this plain-coloured background, there is a series of white circles for further ornament. In this way, I think, may un-

THE LAMÁS OF RIGZON

[face p. 60

doubtedly be explained the chief ornamental *motif* that recurs in Tibetan architecture.

We had a great welcome at Rigzon. We are accommodated at the guest-house, a little separate house at a certain distance from the *gompa*. But we went up to the *gompa* soon after we arrived. Our guide took us straight into a large temple, where we were offered tea. The tea was completely Tibetan: we sat on the floor on soft Chinese rugs, each with a little lacquered table in front of him, and on the table a cup and a dish of Ladakhi sweetmeats, which are by no means all to be despised. It cannot be said that the tea, which is boiled with salt and butter, is exactly delicious: one has to shut one's eyes and drink it slowly in little sips, for otherwise the lama, ready with the big copper teapot ornamented with fine silver decorations, immediately hastens to fill up one's cup again. But one can easily make the small sacrifice of drinking Ladakhi tea when one is in such interesting surroundings. Great statues of Buddhist divinities, of copper gilt, and great *chorten* of silver bristling with turquoises and precious stones are placed along the long wall in front of us; an infinite number of little shining brass goblets have wicks lighted inside them in honour of the divinity, and these tremble in the breeze which comes in through the wide-open doors and windows; long fringes of *tanca* hang from the ceiling, and large frescoes of Chinese workmanship, illustrating the life of Sanghiès, the greater Buddha, cover the walls. A lama holds, almost religiously, the sacrificial teapot, assisted by yet another lama, who slowly burns thin sticks of perfumed benzoin in our honour.

Then we visited the *gompa*—which is the most recent in foundation and in the most perfect order, because its lamas are notoriously the best, the purest, the most cultured, the most profoundly faithful to their religion, of any in the whole of Ladakh. Certainly, when the door of the largest temple was opened for us and we went into a place frescoed with paintings and adorned with *tanca*, in which the long rows of little lamps lighted in honour of the divinities did not break a twilight full of mystery and meditation, when we saw the lamas inside, in two long rows on the ground, repeating their eternal prayer, intoning it on one note accompanied by the muffled beat of a drum, without the slightest movement of surprise or curiosity at the sudden entrance of strangers or any change in the fixed expression of their eyes and of their faces which looked as though modelled in bronze—certainly, at that moment, one could not be unconscious of the deep feeling of mysticism which seemed to emanate from the walls, from the light, from the very air, perfumed with benzoin, and from these calm, indifferent, inspired, ascetic men. At a pause in the prayers, the Superior of the lamas, an old man with eyes so clear and transparent that they seemed to be looking beyond this life, turned to me, stretching out two trembling hands from beneath the great yellow cloak which enveloped him, to give me his greeting and tell me that he hoped I should take back from Rigzon a remembrance for all time. We went out again and the door closed, and the lamas again started to intone their prayers and the drum to repeat its muffled beat.

The remembrance that the Superior of Rigzon wished me to take back with me for good was a present: it was the great copper teapot ornamented with fine silver decorations, which the lama had held almost religiously, ready to fill up our cups, when, in the temple dedicated to the glory of Sanghiès, we had felt almost that we were taking part in a ritual.

Rigzon-Gompa, May 20th, 1930.

Yesterday morning, before starting, I went up from the guest-house of Rigzon to the monastery to thank the Superior and leave him an offering for the *gompa*. I found him, with his lamas, already at prayer in the temple filled with mystic twilight. This is the entire life of these "pure" lamas of Rigzon.

We have come right up the little valley which we descended the day before yesterday, back past the thin, twisting line of willows, in the midst of which little birds flew about and chirped; on the rocks at the sides, on the other hand, pairs of partridges chased each other, not in the least frightened at our large party riding by. The lama-administrator of Rigzon went in front of us to the end of the territory of his own *gompa*.

At the top of the little valley we took again the "high road" which starts at Balucar on the Indus and, passing through

Timosgam and Himis Shupa, goes direct to Leh, crossing alternately hills and short belts of plateau and valley-bottoms; this was the old, original road avoiding the bottom of the Indus Valley, which the more modern caravan-route follows. The same thing has happened here which also happened, in different times, in the Alps, where the old roads avoided the bottoms of valleys, preferring to cut across their sides.

So we took the "high road" again, that is, the old road to Leh. In those days they had preferred this route, in spite of its continual ups and downs over the hills between the numerous little valleys, not only to avoid the bottom of the larger valley which is more exposed to floods and alluvial deposits, but also because up above, between one hill and the next, there is one village after another, in the bottom of each valley, like the continuous beads of a necklace. Beads of green and emerald, fields and little groves of trees, are scattered at almost regular intervals in the midst of the rocky desert of these last southern spurs of the Karakoram. It is a rocky desert, however, which is not without attractions in spite of its bare desolation. It is always and at all times impressive. It is also varied; every type of rock has its own special shapes, and the high road runs at exactly the junction of the different kinds of rock, so that the landscape on each side is always different. On one side, where this characteristic belt of plateaux extends as far as the Indus, the rock is generally softer, often clayey, and therefore smooth in shape, even if in the middle of it there is the ruggedness of a more compact and harder stratum. On the other side it is granite, and the slopes are suddenly steeper, rougher, at times even overhanging. The surface of the granite is as though rudely carved into the shape of huge rounded nipples or blunted turrets, which sometimes form a gigantic chaos of shapeless, twisted, piled-up blocks, like an immense ruin. The colour also varies. I really cannot understand how it is that certain travellers have asserted that the Karakoram is colourless. From the pink of the granite, which passes to light yellow and orange, there are, in the prevalent type of rock on the other side of the old road, broad brushstrokes, as it were, of every colour and tone: red predominates—dark wine-red—but here is a bright yellow, here a pale green which from a distance looks like a meadow of young grass,

63

here a dark green, a violet, a maroon. There is no question
of lack of colour in the ground: it is a riot of colour. This was
one of the usual ready-made remarks which are repeated from
one traveller to another, like the one to the effect that it never
thunders in the Karakoram. Obviously it rarely thunders,
because storm-clouds generally break into rain before crossing
the chain of the Himalaya. But I remember that once in the
Eastern Karakoram, for two weeks at a time, I had a violent
hailstorm every day, accompanied by tremendous claps of
thunder. And even in the last few days, during which the
sky has been overcast all the time, rumbles of thunder have
accompanied the frequent snowstorms up on the mountain-
tops, from which we had a certain amount of sleet, carried by
the wind.

We climbed some rising ground, crossed the head of
another little valley, climbed a second hill, and from there
descended into a second valley. But this one, which was
larger than the others, we did not cross: instead, we went up
it. A lama, extremely elegant in his flaming draperies and
high yellow cap, awaited us on horseback a little beyond the
second hill. He had not at all the look of a monk, in spite
of his habit—which indeed often, as is well known, "does not
make the monk"—but as he sat erect and perched up on a
high saddle adorned with a beautiful Chinese horse-cloth,
with his sunburnt face, his enormously long pointed moustaches
like those of an old-time Austrian officer, and his rather proud
but frankly smiling eyes, he looked much more like a disguised
medieval 'bravo'.

Under his guidance, therefore, we turned to go up the
new valley, which is the valley of Likir. Just beyond the
bend, in fact, where the two sides come close together and the
snow comes right down from the uniform covering on the
ridges, getting thinner towards the bottom of the valley, there
appeared, on a small shelf of rock, a large building at the end,
surrounded by a forest of smaller buildings—the *gompa* of
Likir. It was still a long way off; in contrast to Rigzon which
appears only when one has already arrived, we had this in
front of us during a whole hour's march, and so great was our
desire to see this new wonder that we felt we should never
reach it. Likir-*gompa* is perhaps the most ancient of all the

monasteries of Ladakh. It was founded by a powerful and pious king, a 'gyalpo', and for this reason had a period of wealth and splendour. Then, since all things on earth are changeable, including the favours of the great and those of the populace, Likir-*gompa* declined, and the signs of its decline are naturally all the more visible as time passes. But, both as an institution and as a constitution, it is a typical Tibetan monastery, which one cannot but admire even though, on coming nearer, one sees that the walls have several cracks and that some of the roofs have fallen in, and that inside also everything gives the impression of age and desertion.

The upper part of the Likir Valley is cut deeply into the solid granite; then, suddenly, the two sides appear to branch off, getting farther and farther from each other, and the bottom rapidly widens, opening out in the direction of the Indus. At the point where the valley changes its character in this way, there rises from the bottom a not very large shelf of rock, on the top of which is the *gompa*, which also spreads a certain way down the sides with its many little houses, the lamas' dwellings. So that, from any point in the lower valley, which is like a great wedge driven into the mountains, one cannot prevent one's eye lighting finally on the *gompa*: the latter has the upper valley as background—very rocky, but quite often snow-covered even in the height of summer.

The principal temple buildings crown the summit of the hill, arranged like a flight of steps but without really appearing to be detached from each other; in front, on the side of the *gompa* open to the view, they have little porticoes and wide terraces which break the compact solidity of the whole construction. The lamas' little houses continue, very close to each other, in steps down the hillside, and beyond them a little irregular forest of *chorten* and *mani* ends by dividing into two long rows following the two paths which come up the valley towards the *gompa*, at the foot of each of its lofty sides.

Even from close by, Likir looks picturesque and imposing, hanging above and dominating the valley as it does. A grove of tall poplars surrounds the base of the hill on one side; on the other, a gigantic juniper, supposed to have been planted by the 'gyalpo' who founded the monastery, makes an unexpectedly dark spot among the whiteness of the houses and the *chorten*. We

entered amid the usual festive, noisy welcomes—the music of
the lamas, drawn up above beside one of the temples, that of the
mon, at the entrance to the sacred enclosure, the women grouped
at the place where we had to dismount, and the whole population
of the neighbouring village lined up on each side of the path.

It is true that the walls were full of cracks, that the plaster
was peeling off, that the masonry of the buildings was no longer
white, that the high flights of stairs in the usual labyrinth of ups
and downs which forms the inside of a Tibetan monastery were
beginning to crumble, but there was still a wonderful wealth of
tanca and of statues and all the other religious furnishings in the
twilit temples and in the Superior's little private room, which is
a treasure in itself. This Superior is a 'kushok', one who has
been reincarnated, a sort of superman.

I left Likir with a certain regret. I had remembered, from
my previous visit, a little chapel—really a little cell—quite dark
and dusty, against whose farthest wall was a whole crowd of
little statues of Tsongkapa, the lama-reformer. They were of
clay, brass, wood, bronze, some silvered or gilded, others
adorned with jewels and turquoises, almost all of admirable
workmanship, especially in the way in which they rendered the
attitude of repose in the face and the whole figure, showing
the spiritual calm to which the great and pious lama had
attained. This time I again saw the little cell, darker, dustier,
more deserted than ever, and it seemed to me that, when the
door was opened, the calm, smiling face of the reformer
Tsongkapa was lit up in all these little statues for the benefit
of an unbeliever who was very ready to venerate them for the
supreme plastic beauty of their modelling.

We came quickly down from Likir—down the side of the
hill, and down the valley, till we came again to the belt of
plateaux, the "high road" to Leh. These plateaux are simply
the upper surface of an immense alluvial deposit which at
another period choked up the great Indus Valley and the lateral
valleys of its tributaries. Then the Indus re-carved a deep bed
for itself, digging a deep channel through the alluvion; it is on
our right here, but has disappeared from sight. The alluvion
still fills the lateral valleys, giving them a strange appearance,
because the relative height of their sides, which are very rugged,
is diminished, and the bottom is unexpectedly wide and flat.

RUINS OF THE ANCIENT CASTLE OF BASGO

[face p. 66

The surface traversed by the "high road" to Leh is also flat, flat and uniform, sandy and pebbly, and looks almost like a desert—an illusion which is increased at moments when a gust of wind blows up the sand violently. Nor is it entirely an illusion: for, even though mountainous, the absolute nakedness and absolute aridity of its whole surface makes it a desert. A few ancient *mani*, of a different type and completely neglected —the "high road" is also the "old road", it must be remembered—marked the traces of our path. We met very few people, a few isolated peasants, for caravans have now for some time followed the road along the Indus. However, we also were getting nearer the Indus: one could not see it, but one could imagine it in the wide, impressive channel which, in front of us, makes a deep hollow among the mountains. It began to seem as if the monotony of our way over the flat surface of the plateau would never end, but suddenly the plateau was interrupted by a steep slope; we went quickly down this into a small valley between sides of greenish clay which look as though they must melt in the first heavy shower, and came out at Basgo, a picturesque village at the point where a lateral valley opens into that of the Indus. The fields at the bottom of the valley were all green, but the opposite side, which is not very high, but is steep and has a rough, jagged ridge at its top, looked as if its dark red rocks were all on fire. The majestic ruins of an old feudal castle seemed to look with contempt at the houses of the 'zemindars', the peasants, clustered at its feet. On the two most prominent summits of the fiery ridge two *gompa* raise their whiteness to the sky.

This morning, before starting, we went up to the two *gompa* of Basgo; the *mon* greeted us with their impetuous music as we came out of the thick grove of poplars in the middle of which we had camped in a little hut. I do not know whether the *mon* of Basgo who plays the trumpet knows the real artistic value of his instrument: it is of silver, traced with flowers and dragons and peacocks, and bristling with lapis lazuli and turquoises. But I know that he will not part with it, because it is the instrument which his father played, and his grandfather and his great-grandfather and goodness knows how many generations of his ancestors, in all the village festivities. For these *mon* (whom someone, in the warmth of his imagination, has

67

declared to be the descendants and representatives of the primitive population of the country) are a sort of caste to which the practice of the musical art is reserved; and, in spite of the wide conception of life which these Tibetans have, and the lack, among them, of any and every form of exclusiveness, or, rather, of snobbishness, they are rated—the *mon*—at a lower social level, simply because they are musical performers. This suggests the influence of Indian beliefs and customs. They are attached to the exercise of their art, just as my *mon* at Basgo proved himself to be proudly attached to his trumpet.

However, as one climbs up to the two *gompa*, one immediately forgets both *mon* and trumpets adorned with silver and turquoises; one forgets everything.

No pen can possibly describe the amazing theatrical phantasmagoria of forms and colours which suddenly appears and fills one with astonishment the moment one reaches the ridge on which the two *gompa* are perched. It is a scene of strangely distorted rocks of a curious red with wide strokes of green, which no imagination of painter or stage-designer could devise —and, if he did imagine it and realize it, it would seem unreal. But here, in this country, it is a reality. The tremendous ruins of the old castle, portions of the old surrounding walls, ascending and descending according to the ups and downs of the fiery rocks, great towers of defence scattered here and there on outlying points of the rocky heights, complete an improbable landscape which might well have been the inspiration of certain old imaginative prints.

One of the two *gompa*, the upper one, contains the gigantic statue—very much more gigantic than the one at Timosgam— of Chamba, the Buddha: it is made of gilded copper. The other, of more modest appearance, is perhaps still more interesting. Small in size, square, with four rough symmetrical columns of wood, a sort of square altar in the middle, and a low doorway with broad wooden door-posts finely carved in repeated bands of ornamental design in which the *motif* of the swastika recurs more frequently than any other, this little temple shows clearly its extreme antiquity. It is one of those little chapels, all alike, which Buddhism, when it penetrated this region perhaps a thousand years ago, scattered along the valley-bottoms, along the principal roads. All these chapels are alike and built

68

on the same model. The best preserved are at Alchi, near the bank of the Indus not far from Basgo; then comes the one at Basgo itself, inside the enclosure of the ancient ruined castle. I know of one other, near Chiktan in the valley of Bot Karbu —a particularly interesting one because the inhabitants, who have been converted to Islam, continue nevertheless to frequent it, and on occasions both men and women circle round it, moving in the little rhythmic steps of the Tibetan dances and wearing long, slender wreaths of flowers. They do not pray there to Allah, their new God; they no longer pray there, as they once did, to the divinities of the multiple Olympus of the Tibetan Buddhists: they go there to pray to "the Spirit", as they themselves told me—that is, to something above and outside all corporeal and terrestrial things. All the other chapels of the same age are in complete ruin, but the traveller who has eyes—and something else as well—may recognize them by the square walls which rise solitary here and there in the flat bottoms of the valleys between Mulba and Leh.

Piang-Gompa, May 22*nd,* 1930.

CHAPTER VIII

ARRIVAL AT LEH, THE CAPITAL

We left Basgo later than we had intended, but the road was easy, almost all the time on the flat. Flat, and nearly on the level of the Indus: sand and pebbles, desert again. However, this desert, over which the two roads to Leh, the old and the new, now run together, was populated with *chorten* and *mani*. There is a forest of them on the way out of Basgo, but after that there are a few only, the largest in the whole district: these were built, not gradually, by the piety of the inhabitants, but created by the faith and power of a king, a 'gyalpo'. There are *mani* hundreds and hundreds of yards in length, high, wide, regular, covered with innumerable stones with the usual inscription of the eternal Buddhist prayer, arranged in perfect order on the two upper slopes of roof, and at the end of each *mani*, a gigantic *chorten*, the lower part built in huge steps, the upper part consisting of an enormous globe, which is so large that it could quite easily give shelter to the whole of my party, servants included.

We go carefully round, like Buddhists, to the left of *chorten* and *mani*: if by any chance our attention is distracted, the horses themselves take care, on their own account, not to let us break this important rule of the Tibetan religion, so strong is the habit with them.

Caravans were now more frequent; villages were rarely seen, but one felt that life was nearer and more active. In front of us the great valley of the Indus widened out more and more, assuming proportions of the greatest magnificence: this is the heart of Ladakh, in which Leh, the capital, is situated, near the mouth of a lateral valley. Here the whole history of the country has been mainly centred, its most powerful dynasty, its most stormy vicissitudes; here Tibetan art has perhaps displayed its noblest forms, whether bold or delicate; here modern commerce has its centre of distribution, between India and

70

Turkistan, between the territory of Baltistan and the Great
Tibet of Lhasa. I had now almost arrived at an important stage
in my long march, the stage which would mark the end of the
long journey of approach; from Leh, in fact, the attack begins.

We went through the great rank oasis of Nimu. Neither
lamas nor musicians, nor men and women *en fête*, distracted us,
and we went quickly on. There was a short ascent over
another—the last—tract of desolate, bare plateau, pebbly and
sandy. Beyond, it slopes gently down towards the great
Ladakh basin, through which the Indus, broken up into small
branches, slow and calm, follows its shining course.

We went gently downwards, but not yet directly towards
our goal. I turned aside at the opening of a lateral valley,
because I did not wish to miss another of the largest *gompa*
in Ladakh. The experience that we had at Likir was repeated
again. We turned into the new valley and immediately saw,
on a little hill rising from the valley-bottom, just where the
narrow, rocky upper gorge opens into a wide funnel at the
end, the imposing mass of buildings of another monastery.
This was the *gompa* of Piang. And a lama, handsome, plump,
ruddy, smiling, extremely elegant and also—which was unusual
—very well cared for in his whole person, was waiting for us
on the path, and now placed himself at the head of the party.

I already had an indelible memory of Piang, for it was
there that I had been present at one of those Buddhist religious
ceremonies which are commonly called 'devil-dances'—a name
which is one of the usual ingenuous mistakes of superficial
travellers, unable to see or even suppose the existence of any
symbolism (and a profound symbolism at that) and judging
merely from the perfectly formal exterior of the ceremony.
It is true that the lamas dance with surprising agility, dressed
in rich and gorgeous costumes of old Chinese silk, their faces
covered with great masks, often of monstrous appearance; but
all this has nothing to do with devils, and actually the object
of these symbolic dances is to represent, in the combination of
their various elements, the supreme triumph of the Spirit of
Good, whose image, also purely symbolical, is kept from year
to year in the largest temple of the *gompa*.

It was at Piang that I had been present at this greatest of
Tibetan-Buddhist ceremonies, which lasted for two entire days,

from dawn to sunset, without a moment's pause; it was there I had begun really to understand the cast of mind, the soul, the spirit of my Ladakhi friends, and also that essential characteristic of theirs which pervades every phase of their life— their lively, gay humour.

On that occasion it had been a time of great solemnities at Piang. All the ornaments, all the richest and finest furnishings had been brought out; all the lamas were present, some of them having come in from the villages to which they disperse in order to spread their culture among the inhabitants (and in Ladakh it seems that 95 per cent. of the men are literate). A gay and many-coloured crowd of the faithful made a picturesque circle round the great open space in which the ceremony was taking place; the two orchestras of lamas, playing at full strength, and the incense-burners adorned with gold and silver arabesques, sent forth all their sounds and all their perfumes to the glory of the Spirit.

Now I saw Piang again at a time of quiet and repose. But, as always happened during this triumphal voyage of mine, the men and women of the neighbouring village had assembled with offerings of *chang* (the beer of the country) and *satu* (meal made from scorched barley)—symbols of Ladakhi hospitality; the *mon* drummed and trilled; the lama musicians, their heads covered with gigantic ceremonial hats, made a strange sort of crown on top of the highest roof of the *gompa*, outlined clearly and each one separately against the sky, and sent down to me from there the strange, dissonant, yet solemn notes of their greeting.

Piang has, in common with all the Tibetan *gompa*, an elevated, picturesque, commanding situation. It has, however, like all the other monasteries, a very special character of its own, for these people, so happily and richly endowed with an innate artistic sense, do not design and construct to pattern, as is the tendency of the latest Western civilization. Here, thank God, everything is still spontaneous, genuine, original, and represents the geniality which is common to the whole people and also a characteristic of almost all of them individually. So Piang, too, is different from other monasteries. There is not a number of temple buildings, as elsewhere, but one only, a large, massive, lofty, separate building, which crowns the smallish moraine hill which almost blocks the valley. Lower down, along the slope, are the little houses of the lamas ; then the enclosing walls and, outside, the usual forest of *chorten* and *mani*. Elsewhere, *gompa* take their character from the complete effect of their various buildings, harmoniously brought together and arranged so as to form a unique whole ; here, on the other hand, the smaller houses seem almost to disappear in contrast with the massive pile which dominates them from above.

I am writing in a little room in the guest-house, near the *gompa*; the outside wall of the room is not a real wall, but consists simply of a curtain that the lamas have put up as a shelter—not much of a shelter either—from the cold of the night. I think again of the time when the curtain was not there, when I looked and watched through this great opening and tried to understand the deep, hidden meaning of the fantastic scene of dancing which went on in the wide space below.

Piang-Gompa, May 22nd, 1930.

Yesterday was the last stage of our long journey of approach, the last, and a short and speedy one.

We went down from Piang as far as the opening of the valley into the larger valley of the Indus, and nothing but the last spur of a buttress of rock separated us from the great basin of Ladakh. The way over it is not long. But, just at its extremity, this spur breaks off into an isolated rock, which hangs right over the Indus, and from which the eye can wander far and wide over the whole of the basin and the high snowy mountains which enclose it all round. Upon this rock, whose marvellous situation naturally did not escape the genial eye of the Ladakhis, there is a *gompa*, Spituk. At its foot, along the river-bank, is the village. My coming had, as usual, been announced beforehand at Spituk, and the usual honours were not lacking: here, too, the lamas stood in a row on the highest roof of the monastery, wearing those strange, high hats, flame-coloured with a great yellow crest, which remind one, if one is inclined to be disrespectful, of the traditional firemen's helmets of light opera.

Spituk is no longer what it was at the time when I visited

it after I first came to Leh. At that time the *kushok* Bacula was alive. What is a *kushok*, you may ask ? He is the Superior of a group of monasteries, but he is also something more; he is one who has been reincarnated. Every *gompa* has its lama-Superior, but this merely represents a rank in the hierarchy of lamas. A *kushok* not only has an even more elevated rank, but he is chosen for this rank because of the quality he possesses of long experience in many former lives.

When I was at Spituk before, the *kushok* was a descendant of the ancient royal family of Zanskar. From his broad, slightly Mongol face and calm, clear eyes there seemed to shine a mystic piety like that of the Superior of Rigzon; but he had besides this an unsuspected quality, the gesture of a great lord who is conscious of dignity inherited in the blood. *Kushok* Bacula must have been a man of exquisite taste—judging, at least, from the sober, rich elegance of his private room, in which was a wealth of silks and of lacquer, of silver and brass objects, in perfect harmony, rendered, as it were, more intimate and complete by the subdued light.

He has been dead ten years, my friend Bacula. We had lunch in his private room which was now almost without ornament; there were merely two statuettes of Sanghiès and Tsong-kapa, and a few little *tanca*; round about were the chests containing his clothes, his silks, his treasures, and, hung on the walls, his beautiful hats lacquered with bright yellow and arabesqued with gold, which he used when he travelled from one monastery to another, riding on a richly caparisoned mule among lamas on horseback, carrying his great frilly umbrella, his great tea-cup, and his book of prayers.

Spituk seemed rather deserted, waiting for its new *kushok*. He has already, of course, been chosen, or rather discovered, according to the traditional customs and rules, for which purpose, upon the death of the previous *kushok*, a council of lamas of the greatest wisdom and dignity is held: these, guided by superhuman inspiration, conclude that the dead man is reincarnate in a baby which has certain distinctive signs and whose family lives in a certain village. They go to the village and search for the baby who corresponds with the indications foretold by divine inspiration. This is the new *kushok*: they take him and bring him up for his future exalted spiritual

LEH AND THE ANCIENT PALACE OF THE LADAKHI KINGS

[face p. 74

functions. It is an upbringing which may be said to be inten-
sive and also forced. It includes a first period mainly of educa-
tional and religious preparation, and a second, which may also
last many years, of complete seclusion, solitude, and meditation.
If the young superman is not made completely stupid by it, he
certainly turns out morally perfected. I know cases of both
results. Meanwhile the *gompa* of Spituk is without its baby
kushok, who is at Lhasa, the sacred city, being prepared for a
segregation of goodness knows how many years. And meanwhile the private room of my old friend Bacula has time to get
more and more full of dust and to look more and more abandoned.

There is a wonderful view from the top of the Spituk rock
and from the terraces of the *gompa*. This whole tract of the
Indus Valley, where it opens out into a basin which, strictly
speaking, is Ladakh, is spread out before one in shapes and
dimensions which it would be impossible to imagine when one
comes out to the Indus on the way down from Lamayuru.
This country seems to do everything by contrasts. Beyond the
vast, open Ladakh basin, towards the upper course of the river,
is a portion of the Indus Valley which, in contrast, is grand and
wild in the narrowness of its great rocky gorge. Over there,
in the distance, the Ladakh basin seems to close in: just there
begins the rugged country of the Rong. But here, on the
other hand, it is all so wide and open that it is a rest to the eye.
Part of the beauty of this Ladakh basin is due to its two sides
being quite different. The southern side, to the left of the
river, which looks dark and gloomy from a distance—though,
from closer, it is of every tone of green and red and grey—
shows clearly its formation of straight layers, parallel with the
course of the Indus and with the side of the valley actually
formed by them; the valleys cut out of this side—which are
never large, for the ridge of mountains which closes them in
at their heads can be seen rising not far off, culminating in
lovely snowy peaks and even a few small glaciers—have narrow
openings, owing to their having been forced to cut their way
across the line of these strata. But outside each opening an
immense cone spreads out, composed of a vast mass of alluvial
deposit; and all these cones, joining laterally one with the
other, form an immense, regular inclined plane of dark-coloured
shingle, descending gently and evenly from the foot of the

75

mountainous valley-side to the Indus, which is as though pushed back by them against the foot of the opposite side, the northern. This latter side is entirely different. It forms part of a chain of mountains which stretches for hundreds of miles and separates the Indus from its chief tributary, the Shyok—a chain formed entirely of granite; its short buttresses jut out towards the bottom of the great basin, getting thinner and thinner and finally breaking into isolated points; and as they get thinner, so they branch off from each other, in such a way that they form great funnel-shaped divisions between the lateral valleys which they enclose. The projecting cones which, as far as the left side of the valley is concerned, are entirely external to the lateral valleys and form such a typical feature in the landscape of the Ladakh basin, appear, on the other hand—on the right side—to be inside the lateral valleys and enclosed within the thin buttresses of granite.

In the midst of the broad basin is a belt of really flat country through which flows the Indus, slowly and divided into branches from which its waters are drawn to irrigate and fertilize the fields by means of hundreds and hundreds of canals which divide the Ladakh plain in every direction, like shining ribbons. In this plain there are fertile cultivated areas sprinkled with the houses of the farmers: these are the finest houses in all Ladakh—that is, ordinary farmers' houses. There are few, if any, real villages in the plain. The villages are all at the mouths of the lateral valleys—that is, on the left side, just where the valleys open into the basin, and on the right, where they widen out from the narrow defiles above into the broad funnels at their ends.

The landscape is so vast that almost all sign of the presence and the activities of man is lacking in the view from this marvellous point of vantage, the rocky pinnacle of Spituk— one of the pinnacles broken off from the thin buttress of the granite ridge. The only village we can see from up here is the one just below the *gompa*, with its houses, its fields traversed by canals, its *chorten* and its long *mani*. There is nothing else in the plain beyond; near the opposite side, beyond the river, one can just see the village of Stok, where the ancient royal family of Ladakh has recently come to live in a majestic palace in the perfect Tibetan style; and on this side of the Indus, only Leh, the capital, situated at the point where the wide mouth of the valley begins to open, merging into the even wider plain exactly below the rock of Spituk. Though far away and recognizable only by the massive palace of its ancient kings—a tiny cube, as seen from here—Leh attracts, almost torments me with longing: my eyes seek it out, my desire hastens to the moment when I shall again enter the great avenue of its bazaar, dominated by the splendid mass of the ancient palace of its kings. . . . But it was still so far away that my companions remained almost indifferent when I pointed it out to them again and again from the various terraces we passed under the guidance of the lamas of Spituk.

Too far away, indeed, to appreciate its real beauty, made up, not only of the stately mass of its ancient palace, but of many other elements as well; it would be hard to explain exactly why one considers each separate element beautiful, but certainly the whole effect is one of exquisite picturesqueness and harmony.

Leh, May 24th, 1930.

CHAPTER IX

MY DUTIES AT LEH

Leh is not so distant but that it can be reached in a short time, by riding quickly, from Spituk. It is an easy road over the even, gently rising surface of the wide funnel at the end of the valley, sandy, but strewn with blocks of granite which have fallen from the neighbouring side. The road is easy and straight, and marked by two parallel rows of stones which seem to go on for ever. Our little horses went forward with a steady, smooth pace until we urged them too strongly and they broke into an awkward, jerky trot. Half-way, a cavalcade which had come from Leh to meet us paid us their respects and then turned to join in behind us; then came another, and another, and then solitary riders who had tarried behind. We watched them come on at a good pace; then getting off the road they dismounted quickly and saluted us, bowing to the ground and raising their right hand to their foreheads; then they joined the others. And all the horses, as if in competition, quickened their rapid, smooth little steps, making more triumphal this unforgettable entry of mine into Leh. The unexpectedness of this and the quick pace at which we were going to a certain extent prevented those of us who did not already know it from observing the great tree-lined. avenue of the bazaar and the royal palace dominating it from the top of the short, steep ridge of rock, against which lean the closely-packed houses of the ancient capital of Ladakh.

We passed quickly on, as though in a dream, hardly noticing the respectful 'jul' which the inhabitants addressed to us, repeatedly beating their foreheads with their closed fists. Some of them, more faithful to old customs, stuck a small part of their tongues out of their mouths: this also is a sign of respectful devotion. We turned from the great avenue of the bazaar into a small street and then into a

78

second, until we came out into the lovely poplar-grove which surrounds the bungalow.

We took possession quickly and without delay—a room for each, a common room for meals, and a dark-room. The verandah and the little space in front were filled with the heavy part of the baggage, which had travelled separately since Kargil, and arrived here punctually, a little in advance. I was so well satisfied with the man—a Purighi—who has led the *kafla* here, entirely on his own responsibility, that I have kept him on for as long as we stay here, as night-watchman over all the baggage which is outside. In the evening he spreads a blanket on the verandah and sleeps the sleep of the just, for in this country one can keep guard just as well sleeping.

At moments the desire comes upon me to lie down, here in front of the house, and take my ease, revelling in the beauty which breathes from every rock and every plant in the landscape, and in the solemn calm which relaxes every nerve. In front of the house the tall poplars are just beginning to put forth their little leaves, and form a sort of transparent courtyard with their white trunks and slender branches. Just over there is a small pond for irrigating the fields: it is not really much to look at, but when it is quite full and shines like a small clear mirror, and when the boys of the village—I should say, of the capital—are plunging about in it, I feel it is a little mountain lake, picturesque as nature intended it, rather than a thing made by man to supply the wants of nature, which is so prodigal of beauty and so niggardly with wealth. Beyond the little mirror of shining water, a bank of rock, rough and steep-though not high, shows endwise on its top the imposing mass of the ancient palace of the Ladakhi kings, and, higher up, three little temples like cubes, looking as though they were striving to reach the heaven of the numberless Buddhist divinities, and also to protect the faithful, clustered at the foot of the short ridge of rock. The houses of the latter fly flags from the corners of their roofs, flags inscribed with all the prayers of a faith that is rich in prayers, that says them, repeats them, sings them in every shape and form, and makes the wind repeat them as it flutters the little banners, and the water as it moves the little *mani* everlastingly. Past

79

this bank of rock with its palace and its temples, with no transition of middle distance, I can see, far off, through the transparent curtain of the poplars, the chain of mountains which encloses the wide valley of the Indus towards the south: the lower part of their sides is nearly black, but their peaks are white with snow and are outlined clearly and sharply against the amazingly bright blue of a sky upon which the clouds brought by the monsoon are like cotton-wool.

But I am allowed only to feel this desire to stretch myself quietly on the verandah and revel in the beauty and interest of the horizon. A look, now and then, to refresh myself, and to breathe a big mouthful of healthy air—and then back again to work.

It began yesterday, directly after we arrived, and continued to-day without a pause—as it will still continue during the few days that I have planned to stop at Leh. Every piece of baggage must be gone over, so that anything which may be superfluous can be left here; I have also to organize transport as far as the Nubra Valley, and to work it out, at any rate roughly, for the region beyond the last village; I have to make up the number of the permanent porters and equip them for high altitudes; also to make the necessary arrangements for provisioning them, and therefore to organize a second caravan to carry, not our belongings, but provisions for the first, and also for themselves. These are calculations which, if one thinks of them, are enough to make one lose one's head, but I have to give them a great deal of thought, and, imperatively, to keep my head. My Ladakhi friends are all at my service, and Hashmatullah Khan is amazingly energetic in translating all my decisions into facts. There is no doubt whatever that no other expedition-leader could obtain here what I am able to obtain so speedily. If difficulties exist, they are overcome. There are people here who seem as if they had served me all their lives and wished never to do anything else—two people, in particular, and they are the two most important men in Ladakh. I do not even remember the name of one of them: I call him simply 'Kalon', which is his rightful title as descendant of the family which provided the ancient Ladakhi kings with ministers—*Kalon*. The other is Kalzan, the richest merchant here, who has a warehouse at

Lhasa and a large business in all the districts round. The two of them represent the highest and most legitimate aristocracy of the country. In fact, they do not dress like the other Ladakhis who are all tillers of their own soil, but wear a voluminous blue robe done up all down the front and a little Chinese cap. They appear silently, at any moment, at the bungalow, and silently deposit either a large jar of *chang*, or a dish of little Ladakhi cakes, or a vessel full of rice, or a parcel of Chinese tea; but they come mainly to listen to orders or expressed desires, and go away again silently to execute the one and fulfil the other.

To-day, however, has also been a day of visits, visits made and received from all the recognized authorities, among whom, owing to the wealth and dignity they have attained, may be included two or three big merchants, foremost of all Kalzan. I have already seen and acquired a few charming things which have travelled for months and months over the plateaux from Lhasa.

Many visits, and many invitations—tea-parties combined with 'tamáshas'—that is, local dances—and dinners. I have made two conditions with regard to the latter—that they must be completely Ladakhi and must not last more than an hour, for, if I did not make this latter stipulation beforehand, what would happen would be that, following the local custom on occasions of special dinners, the entire night would be spent in banqueting. And I must sleep at night, because at five, without fail, my working day begins.

Leh, May 24th, 1930.

My work at Leh has continued steadily and will continue up till the last moment, that is, till to-morrow morning, when I have arranged to start.

The elimination of part of the baggage has been relatively easy. But what a number of useless things we shall still be taking! My companions were very much astonished when I told them that I could not allow them more than one personal load—that is, 65 pounds—each. I did not tell them that when I was with Olinto Marinelli, and we did some good exploration work on the plateaux and glaciers, we had only one load between us—a small case, in which almost all our own belongings had to give place to instruments, maps, and collections of specimens. But this lightness is the first essential for travelling quickly in uninhabited districts, just as an easy adaptability is the first requisite of an explorer. Otherwise one may, indeed, imagine that one is an explorer, but one can never really become one unless one is able to renounce everything that constitutes the ordinary habits and customs of the everyday life of so-called civilized people.

Actually I am letting my companions travel like princes compared with the way in which I myself have travelled before, both here and in other parts of the world. As for myself— apart from keeping up external appearances, which, as leader, I am bound to do—I have gone back to my old habits of primitive simplicity. In this case, middle courses are no virtue: they are a defect which absolutely prevents one from becoming a true explorer.

But the limitation of baggage has been a mere trifle. The serious thing is the organization of the *kafla* for the glaciers. I will give an idea of this. The loads to be carried on the glaciers will be, roughly, 90 in number, and for three months. This is too much, considering the difficulties of a journey in an uninhabited region and over difficult ground. In two months, part of the baggage will have become useless and the number of provision-cases will also be reduced: it is a question of doing the third month with only 40 loads, and also of arranging to be met by a second caravan which will come by another route and relieve my own caravan until the end of the journey.

These are the fundamentals on which I have to construct my plans. I give them, for the practical instruction of future explorers. I shall leave for the glaciers with 90 loads, but not from here: from here I start with quite different baggage. I have engaged 40 permanent porters and have equipped them down to the last detail for high altitudes: these are the porters who will accompany me during the whole journey of exploration, and who will be sufficient for the third month too. I am engaging 30 others, whom I call the 'supplementary permanent' porters; they will work with me only during the first two months. Thus I hope to assure transport as far as my base-camp, which I shall establish on a large glacier. As for the difference between the number of loads and the number of porters, I hope to rectify this by making the 'supplementary permanents' go backwards and forwards with such loads as do not represent immediate necessities—food-chests and boxes of photographic material, which gradually get used up.

In this way I have achieved an economy of about 20 men. The sage, always ready to pronounce judgment, will declare that in enterprises such as mine one should not make economies. Let the sage first become an explorer, and then give judgment. Men have to be victualled: each one consumes, every day, 2 pounds of meal—'ata' made of corn, and *satu* of scorched barley—and 4¼ ounces of tea and salt and butter. My men, under the strict limits imposed upon a caravan during three months of exploration, will therefore consume about 6½ tons of victuals. This is all ordered, and is steadily accumulating on my account at the last village before 'my' glacier.

Six and a half tons of victuals! It may not be difficult to acquire them when one has at one's disposal the means, the moral means, that I have—to acquire them actually in a few days, and in a country which is extremely poor in local resources. The difficulty comes when this enormous mass of meal and salt, butter and tea—I have added tobacco and shall also, from time to time, add the luxury of a few goats—has to be transported by men, who carry not more than 65 pounds each and have also, themselves, to be fed. A whole battalion would not be enough to carry it, and then one would need a whole division to carry the provisions necessary to the battalion, and so on: the whole of humanity would soon, by a fantastic *crescendo*, be needed, and the last huge band of people would have no one left to provision them! And then? This is the explorer's secret: to provision the 70 men, who carry the 6½ tons necessary to themselves, with the aid of a minimum number of extra porters, who in turn must be self-supporting. It is a secret which follows no particular theory; one has to make use of every circumstance, to be prompt in decision, and to arrive, with the greatest economy of means, at a result which theoretically, according to calculations on paper, seems to be impossible.

Another decision has now been made—that of the route

to be followed in order to approach the glacier. A high chain of mountains, as I think I have already said, shuts off the valley of the Indus to the north, towards that other majestic valley of the Shyok. I have to cross this chain. There are three passes of almost equal altitude: they are all about 18,000 feet. The normal summer road is by the Khardung-la, just behind Leh; but this is completely closed at present by snow and avalanches. The way over the Chang-la, though still snow-covered, is open, but it is longer by some days' march, and more expensive by some thousands of rupees. Between the two is the Diggher-la road, which is not yet being used by caravans, but only by travellers on foot. It is decided, therefore, that we cross by the Diggher-la. But since mine is a heavy caravan—there will be not less than 120 loads starting from here—I have divided it in two: the heavy baggage has already left, so as to lessen the difficulties of finding local means of transport. It is already on the road, part of it to the Diggher-la, and part of it also to the Chang-la; and may all the Buddhas of my Ladakhi friends kindly protect it against the dangers of too much snow both in the passes and in the sky!

There is another difficulty, and owing to an entirely accidental happening: a maharajah has died in India, and three days of official mourning have been declared in Kashmir. My funds had been placed to my credit at the office of the 'tessil' in Leh, but the office is closed . . . owing to mourning, and for the moment I am without a rupee. It is rather annoying and inconvenient. But I have been given credit everywhere: there is not a merchant at Leh who has not given it me, and to an unlimited extent. But to-morrow morning, at the very last moment before starting, I shall have to draw upon the office (which will no longer be in mourning) for all I need, and shall have to go round paying all my debts—a business I would much rather have avoided.

However, it's an ill wind . . . and even the official mourning has had its advantages. It has made it possible to avoid, or rather, to suspend, some of the many invitations received, which would have taken up too much time in the midst of my exacting work.

I have not been able to give to Leh itself more than a very little of the time it deserves. However, yesterday morn-

THE SHYOK VALLEY, FROM THE MOUTH OF THE DIGGHER VALLEY

[face p. 84

ing I went up to the royal palace, and then to the three little temples higher up, on the edge of the ridge of rock which dominates the whole city. This is not a euphemism: Leh can justly be called a city, not only on account of its historic past and its traditions, but because it has been the capital of a vast and relatively powerful kingdom. It is a city also by its structure, for the area of its dwellings, even though not large, is compact and has a network of little streets composed entirely of houses, without any gaps for fields, vegetable-plots, or gardens. It is a city also in virtue of its importance and its commercial function as the centre of convergence and re-distribution of a considerable volume of trade, which has its points of departure in India, Chinese Turkistan and the Great Tibet of Lhasa.

I have never seen Leh at the time when the trade-caravans converge there from these three directions and leave in the same three directions again. But I can almost say that I have lived for months along the caravan-route of the Karakoram, and have seen the long processions of horses and camels, of yak and donkeys, crossing the highest chain of mountains in the world, with pack-saddles loaded with every kind of merchandise. One caravan behind the other, small and big, poor and rich, and all coming to Leh. I can well imagine the movement of animals and men which, in late summer, must enliven the quiet life of the capital of Ladakh, when not only those who have descended from the high Karakoram Pass, but also caravans coming from India and Kashmir, and others which have crossed the vast desolate plateaux of Tibet, all arrive here to exchange their merchandise. A sign of it is to be seen in the numerous *serai* in Leh, almost all at its outer edge on the side of our bungalow, towards the cultivated open country. There is one of which—to look at it now, closed and empty—one hardly realizes the purpose, or why the State should have built it; but there are also many others belonging to private individuals, for whom they are a kind of industry, since they let them as stabling for the animals and shelters for the men of the caravans passing through. There are also a number of them scattered about in neighbouring villages, so as to avoid overcrowding in Leh, where, in any case, there is a scarcity of fuel and fodder.

Leh, therefore, is an important centre of commercial exchange, which has not yet abandoned the ways and methods and customs followed for centuries and centuries by these peoples of the middle of Central Asia. Probably many more centuries will pass without these ways and customs and methods being abandoned.

Arriving by the Bazaar gate, one has no idea of what Leh is really like. The bazaar is a long, wide avenue bordered with poplars, with wretched little shops at the sides, and leads straight towards the base of the majestic, lordly palace of the ancient Ladakhi kings. One goes out of the bazaar, straight to the bungalow, almost without seeing anything of the city. Actually the inhabited area extends in the opposite direction, hidden by the long row of little shops. One must go up on to the rock in order to see its full extent and compactness; it stretches out, with its border of *chorten* and *mani*, into the middle of the flat country, and as far as the base of the rock from which the steep ridge rises. It is here that the best houses are, for the chief men of the city prefer this quarter, even if less convenient, owing to its being nearer the royal palace, which rises right above it—an immense mass, the lower part of the walls thick and solid, but relieved higher up by terraces and *rabsal* and by the gradual narrowing of the structure from the bottom to the top, according to the rules of Tibetan architecture.

The whole city is concentrated here round its ancient royal palace, which is the first thing one sees on arriving in Leh, and which dominates and protects the dwelling-houses lying at its feet as though in an attitude of devoted subjection.

It is a subjection which is nowadays only apparent and traditional. The descendant of the ancient kings still bears the royal title of *gyalpo*, but he no longer occupies the royal palace of his fathers, except when he comes from his estate at Stok to spend a few hours or a few days in the capital, and he has nothing royal about him to distinguish him from any other Ladakhi of good position. On the contrary, he seems all the more humble, when one thinks of the magnificence of his ancestors up till a century ago. He came a few days ago to pay me his respects, bringing me a little tray of dried cakes: he waited, humbly and alone, for more than an hour on our

verandah, because I had not the time to entertain him with
my more or less monosyllabic Hindustani conversation; then
he went away without even a servant following him, very,
very modest and humble, poor man, while from above the
majestic mass of the palace sang the glory and power and
magnificence of his fathers.

If I have been rather generous of my time with Stakchen
Ralpa, *kushok* of Himis, the most important lama of the whole
region, I have done it from diplomacy. I have known Stakchen Ralpa for some time: I do not know if it is his natural
character or a consequence of the long 15-years' segregation
for the perfection of his moral nature, but the fact remains
that his intelligence is not too bright. Large and robust,
with a big, round, full face, his eyes half closed behind coloured
spectacles, followed always by servants and by other lamas,
his dependents, he certainly has, externally, an appearance of
the power which is bound up with his quality of *kushok* of
the most important group of *gompa* in Ladakh. He walks
slowly, sits calmly down, closes his already half-closed eyes so
that his silence appears to be meditation, and one may easily
be mistaken into believing that he really has a sense of his
own spiritual and temporal majesty. But scarcely has he become familiar with his surroundings—particularly if there are
no strangers present—than he begins little by little to open
his eyes, turning his large head from side to side, looking at
everything; then he begins to ask questions. But—unfortunately—his curiosity is precisely and exactly the same over the
range-finder deposited in a corner of the room as over a piece
of blotting-paper on my desk, or the long row of cigarette-
boxes on the mantelpiece. I knew him well, Stakchen Ralpa,
and found him still the same, still irritating with the absolute
vacuity of that big round head, a vacuity which he tries, perhaps unconsciously, to hide by closing or half closing his eyes
behind the large coloured lenses. However, I had to entertain him and explain to him what the range-finder was, and
what the blotting-paper was—purely from diplomacy. The
future will tell whether my diplomacy bears fruit: for the
moment it is nothing but a seed sown with the object of
renewing an old alliance!

One would hardly think that Stakchen Ralpa was a Ladakhi,

and, if I remember rightly, he is not. The Ladakhis are a race of superior intelligence, quick, lively, and of an infinite spiritual serenity, happy, gay, eternally smiling. I shall have more to say of them later. A typical Ladakhi is my friend Kalzan, the biggest merchant in Leh, whose racial characteristics, even if restrained by his sense of personal dignity and deference towards me, often burst forth instinctively in the broad smile which lights up his large, slightly Mongol face, and in his gestures, attitudes, and even his speech: then all at once he restrains himself and recovers his composure, his dignity, and his attitude of reverent respect, joining his hands quickly in front of his chest, as though to ask pardon.

Kalzan's fine house is quite close, and I have often found the time to slip away there to ask him a favour, to give him a new job, and also to look at the charming objects brought from Lhasa which he, good merchant that he is, is always ready to yield to anyone who asks him for them: the most beautiful, in fact, have already passed from their old owner to a new one. But I have not had time to extend my search very far: I have been entirely taken up with calculations and plans of campaign, and discussions with the men who offer themselves as porters—'supplementary permanent' porters.

There are discussions and negotiations, and the business seems to be arranged; then everything comes to nothing again because of some new demand to which I will not agree. Nothing is settled; and then they come back one by one and I enrol them separately on exactly the same conditions as I had offered them all together.

Meanwhile the days that we had arranged to stay at Leh have already gone, and to-morrow we start, or rather start again. We begin, first, our wandering life from village to village, and then the solitary life amid the solemn loneliness of the mountains and glaciers. However, we shall have our caravan to remind us all the time of the festive gaiety of the Ladakhis. We have had this gaiety before our eyes here from morning till night, in the many-coloured bustle of people in front of the bungalow: also in the entertainments to which we have been invited, though these have been curtailed by the official State mourning.

The first invitation was for the day after our arrival—a

tea-party and 'tamasha', that is, native dances in the open, with both men and women. All the notables of the capital were invited and a crowd of the inhabitants came as spectators, squatting on the ground all round the wide space to which the palace of the ancient kings formed an admirable back-cloth. The *mon* rolled their drums and beat out rhythms in two, three and four different *tempi*—always varying even though to a less experienced ear they may appear to be always the same; and the dancers, alternately men and women, carried out their evolutions in a long file which broke up in the open space, each one gyrating by himself, twisting his whole body, making abrupt movements with the arms and even with the hands and finger-joints, moving with small steps against the beat, at first very slowly, then quicker and quicker until they seemed all movement.

But this—thanks to the State decree and . . . by the grace of God—was the one and only *tamasha*, for otherwise our departure would have had to be postponed. But official mourning did not necessitate the suspension of dinner-invitations—from Haji Mohammed Siddik, an important *argon* (i.e. half-breed and Musulman) merchant, and from Kalzan and the 'Kalon'. Here, however, we were in purely Ladakhi sur-roundings—wide, low rooms with ceilings decorated with the same exquisite ornamental paintings which cover walls and cornices and door-posts in the monastery temples; large carpets from Lhasa or China on the floors; little lacquered tables, one for each guest, and upon them one of those charming tea-cups with a saucer and cover of finely-chiselled silver. We sat on the floor with legs crossed, in the Oriental manner, behind each little table. Dinner began, and lasted one hour, but only because I had made this stipulation; otherwise it might have gone on all night. To me, as before, each dinner seemed excellent; but my companions also could not fail to appreciate a certain kind of tasty vermicelli which comes at the beginning of every formal Ladakhi dinner, and also a sort of dumpling with crisp, crackling pastry, filled with a hash of meat which might well be envied by our own domestic cooks. Dinner goes on for a long time, one course after another without any pause; the tea-cups are always full, though one only drinks a sip of tea, also the cups of *chang*, the intoxicating beer. But at this point, to avoid consequences which would imperil our own personal dignity, we rise, stretch our legs after their unaccustomed position, give a last look round at our extraordinarily picturesque surroundings, thank our host, and go off towards the bungalow. The servants and household of the host accompany us to light the way on this moonless night. And with this evening's dinner I hope that my duties at Leh are finally over.

Leh, May 28th, 1930.

CHAPTER X

CROSSING THE DIGGHER-LA (17,890 FEET)
TOWARDS THE SHYOK VALLEY

My day began, at Leh the other morning, at 5 o'clock as usual, owing to the many things I had to do: as usual, my companions were left to sleep peacefully till breakfast-time. Actually, I think the sleep which I allowed them and which they, perhaps, desired, cannot have been very peaceful. In the tree-bordered space round the bungalow there was a great coming and going of porters, who were all ready according to their orders. I was horrified when I saw them arrive in a long file: they had so many fur cloaks and other clothes, so many bags of personal belongings, so many pots and ladles, that it seemed to me that, with all this junk, their loads were already complete. The mountaineering equipment which I had provided for them had still to be added: how they were then to carry on their shoulders the normal load of 65 pounds as arranged for each, seemed an almost hopeless problem. But from long experience and knowledge I was sure of my men.

The first start of a caravan is always a long business. Each man looks for a load which, in appearance at any rate, gives hopes of being lighter than the others. Then, if a load is composed of several pieces, he will try to remove one surreptitiously and put it delicately on to the neighbouring load. One has to keep one's eyes open—there were two of us to do this—and at the same time be ready, to a certain extent, to be sympathetic—to be both severe and just, to make demands and to yield. One heaves a sigh of relief when, one behind the other, the 70 porters, bent beneath the weight of their loads, have left the bungalow enclosure on the first stage of the journey. Only two are left, who have been told to sit and wait on the verandah for special orders.

Soon afterwards they discovered what sort of special orders

these were to be. The official mourning being ended, I was at last able to collect my thousands of rupees, all in silver. The two boxes which constituted my treasury were still waiting in my room, and the two poor coolies had to load them on to their shoulders—not less than 110 pounds each, perhaps more. But I sent with them two spare men to relieve them every now and then of this really excessive weight. Then I had to pay off all the debts I had made here and there during the previous days, to make final arrangements for the special service of couriers I have organized between Leh and my various future camps, and to pay my respects to the authorities and say affectionate farewells to friends. Finally we started, at half-past eleven!

I might have said that my day's work was already over, but, instead, the day which was just beginning for my companions was beginning anew for me. And I had good reason to expect that it would be fatiguing.

Down to the Indus Valley we went, skirting the long *mani*—some of the largest in Ladakh. *Mani* are always more frequent along roads in the neighbourhood of villages; these, at the gate of the capital, certainly ought to be among the largest. Scarcely had we reached the wide Indus Valley than, in a short time, having gone up along its granite side for only a few hundred yards, we turned off into a small lateral valley, the valley of Sabu, which leads to the pass of Diggher-la. This was the beginning of new country for me, and I opened my eyes wider than usual.

The things I looked at were all the time both new and interesting. The first fields and poplar-groves of Sabu appeared in exactly the same relative situation as those of Leh, Piang, and Likir, that is, at the point where a lateral valley, narrow and rocky higher up, opens all at once into a great funnel-shaped end: here, too, on a small pinnacle near by, were the immense ruins of an ancient castle. But what seemed to me unusual was the distance to which the fields, though getting steadily poorer in willows and poplars, extended up the small valley—that is, of course, along the bottom— for they extended for some miles; and the other fact, that they alternated with wide belts which are not cultivated but have a natural covering of short, fine grass. It would no doubt

92

be possible to verify quite exceptional conditions of humidity in the soil, which might also be proved by certain trees—old and gnarled, but I do not know of what kind, since they were leafless and I only saw them from a distance—which are scattered at rare intervals in the cultivated area. It must by no means be imagined that they even form little groves: I think I only saw five specimens; but five trees in a country that has none at all are an obvious rarity. Sabu also exemplifies man's fight against nature, a fight all the more desperate here, where nature appears to provide certain favourable conditions in the humidity of the valley-bottom. But some impetuous torrents from the sides have caused vast falls of rock and swept away in a moment what has cost men long decades of patient toil: fields are overwhelmed, houses destroyed. How many ruins there are, how many houses razed to the ground, in the long oasis of Sabu!

Eventually one comes out of the oasis and continues to mount up the valley. The path now becomes more monotonous: we were between two gigantic banks of moraine which wound tortuously according to the windings of the valley: there was no view in any direction and the solitude was complete—nothing but formless shingle mixed with fine clayey earth upon which our poor horses found it more and more difficult to get along. Curiously enough, one had almost a feeling of fatigue too. It was already almost dark, partly because the sky had now become entirely covered with storm-clouds, when we arrived at the point where the two banks of moraine seemed to flatten out and disappear: this was the locality called Larsa Sabu, which is a usual camping-place. Two men who have carried up fuel for us; a few yak, shaggy buffaloes from the high altitudes, which I had brought up, as they might be useful to us next day; a small pile of baggage, left behind by the first caravan so that they might be lighter in crossing the pass; a leaden sky; biting air; snow all round; and our breathing rendered short and irregular. Larsa Sabu is 14,400 feet up. The porters did not arrive, exhausted, till ten: and last of all, my treasury boxes, when I was already fearing that they must have stopped half-way.

It was a sleepless night for almost everyone, sleepless and short, for at 4 o'clock yesterday morning we were already up.

The temporary population of Larsa Sabu had been increased meanwhile by a few men who had come up from the village, in the hopes that I would enrol them as porters. A few, in fact, were enrolled, and at once served to relieve my caravan on a march that was known to be exhausting. It was owing to this lightening of the loads that we started late: only when all the porters were on the path up the bottom of the valley was I myself able to leave. It was 7 o'clock: one coolie, his load on his shoulders, still delayed, and I approached him to hurry him up. He was one of the new ones engaged that morning, a big, tall, strong young man, and an older man was holding his hand tightly and speaking to him rather excitedly. Scarcely had I approached when the man turned to me and began to speak to me instead, still excitedly. Then, realizing that I did not understand, he simplified his speech into a few words, and touching my legs lightly kept on repeating, evidently much moved: "am baba, huzur; am baba, huzur," "I am his father, my lord." It was perhaps the first time that he had been separated from this big son of his, and he had come so far with him to see him off upon an unknown enterprise about which, probably, the whole of Ladakh is wondering. He wished to recommend him to the "lord" who was in command of the enterprise and controlled the destiny of the men concerned in it. Yes, my worthy *zemindar* of Sabu, I know you have feelings just like ours; go back contented to your village and your fields: in my evening visits to my people I shall always look out for this big boy of yours. He seemed to understand: he touched my legs again lightly, struck his forehead several times and shook his son's hand without saying another word; then the young man started on his way, and the old man remained all alone at Larsa Sabu, watching him as he went.

The yak, which the evening before had waited for us scattered over the slopes of the moraines, were collected next morning in a group near the dismantled camp, with our saddles on: I had had them brought up so far in order to spare us some of our fatigue. But the result was not what we hoped for: they sank into the snow, owing to their heavy weight, right up to their bellies, and remained there firmly stuck. We had to dismount quickly, before they began the violent, awkward movements necessary to free them from their un-comfortable position. After this short experiment we preferred to walk.

Progress at first was easy, almost pleasant, up the slightly inclined valley-bottom, and the rising sun seemed to caress us with the warmth of its rays, the force of which was weakened by thinly diffused cloud. But all at once, without transition, conditions changed completely. The valley still followed its widely curving course, with the same gentle slope at the bottom, but the pass, the Diggher-la, is not at its head: it is a gap—and only a very slight gap—in the thin ridge at the top of one side of the valley. The side is extremely steep and con-sists of long, very slippery slopes of snow with nothing but a few small, perfectly straight furrows in it, the marks of rocks which have tumbled down from above; here and there is a belt where the rock just shows through. We climbed up over the snow by cutting across and twisting backwards and forwards, but when on the rock tried to climb straight up in order to save time and distance. But the effort became rapidly more severe; one's breath became short and gasping, one's step slower and more laboured, and we had to stop every little while. Poor Hashmatullah, accustomed to the sun-scorched plains of his native Punjab, pressed forward with indomitable energy, in spite of his age of nearly seventy. Every now and then I felt it necessary to have a look at the porters, and was compelled to admire them. They came straight up, whether over rocks or snow, without a groan or a sign of impatience or weariness; they stopped frequently and in moments of very great stress uttered, as they always do, a peculiar whistling sound; but whenever the windings of the path brought me near them, they were always ready with a smile full of their usual frank, open gaiety. They are really admirable in every kind of circumstance, my Ladakhis!

Meanwhile the mist had become cloud and the sky was overcast. A fresh wind had arisen and sleet began to fall. Evidently the Diggher-la was in a difficult mood.

We took a deep breath when, towards 1 o'clock, we arrived at the top, at the slight gap in the ridge of mountains—17,900 feet high. The prayer-banners of a *lato* flapped violently on a rock near by. We took a short rest, out of the wind, which lashed us violently on the top of the pass. The porters appeared with their loads, one by one, put them down, and then produced, from the enormous, endless pocket formed by the overlapping of one fold over another of their huge cloaks, banners which they attached to the *lato*, murmuring a humble prayer. This is the practice of their faith, when a difficult trial has been overcome.

The descent was like an easy walk on our own native mountains, rather steep but on good snow right to the bottom of the valley, and very gradual thenceforward. And just because it was so gradual, one felt it would never end. Then the snow became soft, progress more tiring; in certain expanses one sank in right up to the thigh and one's feet were soaked in the icy water which covered the ground below. At last, at 6 in the evening, we were at the lower snow-line, at Larsa Diggher—15,100 feet. The caravan, fortunately, arrived shortly afterwards: tents were soon put up and we had a well-deserved rest. We had been 11 hours on the march, with only brief halts to take breath but not enough really to refresh us; and this on top of a sleepless night, and including a pass of almost 18,050 feet. Poor Hashmatullah was exhausted, but the porters were smiling, as always.

Early this morning the necessary saddle-horses came up to the camp. We had an easy day. In four hours we got down to Diggher—13,780 feet. It is a wretched, treeless village, but green fields and the sun, which now again appeared through the clouds, were a relief.

We put up at a miserable little house belonging to the State, and all the porters were in the courtyard in front of our doors. It was a great event for the scanty population of the village, and the roof of the little *serai* where we are staying is lined all the time with a thick row of heads which remain there hours and hours, staring. There are some Baltis among them: they have come from the Khapalu region, some hundreds of miles away, taking a few 22-pound loads of rancid butter to Leh. No pass nearer than the Diggher-la is open to them at present, on account of the snow. What a hard life they lead, these peoples of the high valleys of the Karakoram! The coolies of my caravan may consider themselves happy, in comparison with the life they usually lead. All the afternoon they have been in the courtyard, squatting against the wall and working: some were sewing new clothes, some mending old ones, some putting pieces of leather on to their very practical 'babu', or shoes. I went to the door to look at them: they immediately got up as though impelled by a spring, saluted and, of course, smiled. Now they are sleeping their soundest: they are lying in four long, close rows, occupying the whole space of the yard, wrapped in their ample cloaks, and nothing is to be seen but their shaved heads and long pigtails.

To-day I took the measurements of 15 Ladakhis, to complete the number I had decided upon; and this is one of my days of complete rest!

Diggher, May 31st, 1930.

Diggher is a poverty-stricken village, every year for a long time under snow, devastated by the transient torrents of spring and by falls of rock and shingle which destroy houses and invade fields. Yet, when we arrived, we felt something of the joy one feels at reaching one of the flourishing oases of Ladakh proper. There were *chorten, mani, lato* with flying banners, long pennons and banners also on the corners of the houses—and the usual festive demonstrations. Yesterday morning, as we left the little *serai* where we had stayed, in order to go on down the valley, I noticed, on an enormous block of granite—which I had already seen on account of the fiery *lato* on the short ridge at its top—a large, complete figure of Chamba in bas-relief. It was done in a rather rough and primitive fashion, and must be comparatively ancient.

The long, exhausting climb over the Diggher-la seems, in a way, to have been for nothing. Though we went up so high, for two days now we have done nothing but go down; though we penetrated right into the high mountains where winter still reigns, we are now again in sunshine which warms us even with its reflection off the bare rocks. We go down, down, all the time—on horseback, of course—down the Diggher Valley, the sides of which are rugged, the bottom smooth. Other similar valleys run into it from the right—those which lead into the Tankse basin, at the extreme end of Ladakh, near the lake of Pangong, which looks like a rope of blue, so long and narrow and tortuous is it in the midst of the yellowish desolation of the first of the Tibetan plateaux.

But all at once, at a turn in the valley-bottom, there was an unexpected change of scenery. Looking down from Larsa Diggher, I had seen that the horizon ended in a massive chain of mountains with snowy peaks. At its foot there seemed to be a valley of moderate depth, and my companions had imagined this to be a continuation of the Diggher Valley. I had interpreted it differently; and I was right.

We had scarcely come to the turn when there suddenly appeared, at the foot of this massive range and also at our own feet, a valley like a vast trough. The Indus basin in Ladakh is imposing, but too wide at the bottom and too gently sloping at the sides. Here the width of the bottom, though great, is less, but the sides are precipitous. It is not a basin but a channel, an immense ditch—the Shyok Valley.

I already knew almost the whole of it, from its sources in the front of the Rimo Glacier, near the Karakoram Pass, to the point where it joins the Indus below Kiris, near Skardu in the heart of Baltistan. There was only one short tract of it which I did not know—the one which suddenly opened at our feet. Thus my knowledge became complete. One could see the great valley continuing to the left (it was impossible, owing to a spur of mountain, to see it in the opposite direction), and down there at the bottom was a little spot of green at the base of the precipice of rock; this was Seti, our objective for that day. At the bottom, grey with shingle, one could see a winding ribbon between the two banks, which at moments became so thin that it almost disappeared, and at moments widened, as though ravelled out into a broad band.

This was the river, the Shyok, the great tributary of the Indus, so intractable and violent at times that its floods have been known to sweep right down the valley like a great disastrous wave and then pour themselves into the greater river, carrying with them wreckage and corpses even as far as the point where the river comes out into the plains of India. But to us it looked almost docile and humble, seen from above and from far off, and it did not seem possible that it could put such difficulties in our way as had been predicted to us.

We descended quickly to the Shyok—that is, to its great

98

bed of shingle, where a new trial began for our unfortunate horses.

It is by no means agreeable to ride along a river-bed—but now we had said farewell for a long time to the paths, which at moments had made us shudder but which now, on the contrary, seemed to us almost like big main roads.

We came down to the river, to the first ford over the Shyok. The water came up to the horses' bellies, but, on the whole, there was nothing to make one apprehensive—contrary to what we had been told at Leh. As the Shyok here describes several loops, going alternately to beat against the rocks of the two opposite sides, so we had the variety of two more fords in succession alternating with the difficult surface of the loose shingle of the river-bed. It was amusing to see the porters crossing the fords. We were accustomed to seeing them in the immense long, flowing cloaks down to their feet, which give them a certain external dignity. To pass through the fords they took off their shoes—those comfortable native shoes —the high gaiters of white felt which they wear round their legs tied with broad black ribbons, and their wide trousers; then the long cloaks were turned right up and one had a strange unaccustomed view of two little legs—thin little legs they looked from some distance away, however sturdy they really were—moving by themselves and carrying an enormous bundle—imagine, the load itself, the whole personal equipment in addition, and then, on top, the long gown turned up —an enormous bundle in which it was almost impossible to distinguish a head or anything at all human. They entered the water to cross and the two little legs gradually disappeared in it, and then gradually reappeared, until, arrived at the opposite bank, the cloaks were let down again and the porters reassumed the full dignity of Ladakhis.

After the three fords we had lunch, near a tiny village of only two miserable houses. Even the oasis looks miserable— a few small fields and a great many dense and thorny thickets. The two landowners of the place paid us their respects, but only with smiles; there were no drums, no trumpets, no lamas, no offers of *chang* or of flowers. Indeed Rongdu has nothing to offer.

We went on again, continuing along the bed of the Shyok,

sinking in its fine sand or stumbling over the loose shingle.
The steep rocky sides do not allow of any passage which might
render progress at least more varied. The channel of the
valley was impressive all the time, even if rather less so than
it appeared as seen from above, when we suddenly came upon
it. It has high sides of granite, to which cling streaks of
slightly yellowish clay, deposited during a period long ago
when this was a lake; the ancient lake must have been beautiful
—long and narrow and twisting like a rope, and shut in by
high mountain-walls. It became empty and was succeeded
by the river—calm, almost modest, as we found it, or impetuous
and violent as it becomes at times, to remind man of its latent
power. We saw the traces of these sudden furies: at about
65 feet above the river-bed the right bank has a sort of
fringe, almost continuous and very clearly defined at the top,
of green boughs and dry, derelict timber. This marks the
level reached by a flood last year, a flood which came down
suddenly and violently, scattering terrible ruin in its path.
Even the European newspapers spoke of it, and I too shall
speak of it again when my long journey brings me near the
glaciers of the upper Shyok, which have often been the cause
of the river's sudden and disastrous floods. The one thing
which remains a problem for me is from what part of its upper
course the Shyok carried away all this mass of wood which
it deposited and left high and dry here in the valley half-way
down its length. I have been right up the upper valley and
I remember how—with the exception of a few poor clumps
of sickly bushes—it was a problem to find a little fuel: we had
to hunt for the little woody stalks of the 'burtse', and were
even pleased if a caravan of yak, or a few wild yak, had passed
that way before us.

We arrived in the middle of the afternoon at Seti, where
a lovely meadow sprinkled with shady willow-trees offered an
ideal spot for our camp. The inhabitants crowded round to
look at this great novelty—however, it was naturally not a
very large crowd.

It is a curious fact that this oasis has quite different characteristics from any other in Ladakh. It is situated, as is
often the case, on the cone-shaped deposit at the opening of
a lateral valley, and is all green when seen from a distance,

100

so as to give an impression of unusual fertility. But when one goes through it, one sees that the fields are actually very limited in extent: the rest is taken up with scanty clumps of natural bushes interspersed at frequent intervals with meagre pasturage in which grow occasional tufts of a strange grass with very long, dried-up stems—the typical vegetation of a region with an arid climate. The paths and the various properties, including not only fields, but thickets and pasturage, are not, as in the rest of Ladakh, surrounded by high walls made of stones piled up by some apparently miraculous balancing-feat, but by high hedges of dry thorn, of a slightly purplish colour, which, together with the natural green thickets, give the oasis a quite new and individual character.

The houses, too, are a little different. The best houses—that is, those of the richest inhabitants—have the usual characteristics of Tibetan architecture; but the others have an appearance of wretchedness and are often (which is unusual) reduced to one floor only or have on their wide flat roofs a kind of hut made of boughs or trellis, which evidently constitutes the summer quarters. This also is an indication, if I am not mistaken, of the dry, hot climate of the valley. Besides, there are apricot-trees here which bear fruit, whereas at Leh, farther south, they are rare and do not produce fruit.

We ourselves did not notice the dryness of the valley, partly because the season was not far enough advanced, but chiefly because of all the green which made a carpet for our camp, and, with the rich foliage of the willows, a wall and ceiling too. The caravan, divided into three separate groups, was also encamped in the willow-grove—encamped, that is, in a manner of speaking. Directly they arrive at the end of the day's journey some of the men hasten, with really amazing activity, to put up our tents, while others are at once ready to light their own fires and to boil water in the enormous copper pots which they trail along from one stage to another. Soon after they all assemble in a circle round the crackling blaze, and the longest work of their day begins—the meal. There is an exact division of labour, by turns, in each group. One measures out tea and flour, butter and salt; one boils the water and prepares the tea; one kneads the *chupattis*, and one bakes them on the broad baking-pans; and, finally, there is one to distribute to his comrades what the others have been gradually preparing. The banquet begins, and goes on for a long time, with one cup of tea after another, alternating every now and then with a handful of *satu* which, when moistened, forms a cake which makes one choke only to look at it; the banquet finishes with the classic *chupattis*, the bread of the country. Then the necessary digestion begins, still round the fire which continues to flame for a long time—so long as the fuel does not give out, which it does not here in the district of Nubra.

Yesterday evening, after dark, I went round the camp, according to my old habit, to see my men and let them see me. It is a satisfaction which I like to give myself, and is also a little piece of psychological subtlety based upon my knowledge of the Ladakhis. For me it is a pleasure to look at them; but I know also that they are pleased that the "bara sahib"—the great lord—which is me—should go and greet them after the fatigues of the day's march. This little attention, trifle though it is, is enough to make them do much more than necessary the next day, if I should ask them. In each group there was one who pulled a primitive flute from the wide scarf that is tied round the waist and keeps the cloak together, and played some cheerful little tunes which were not unpleasant even though the sounds were sharp and shrill. I gave them to understand that I liked it, and that it was real "tamasha" music. Then one rose from the circle, then another and another, and they began to dance with little steps and leaps round the great flaming fire while the others, sitting round, accompanied them with a regular clapping of the hands. At that hour, in the darkness of the night, with the fire lighting up all those faces till they looked like bronze and reddening the branches of the trees near by—it was a sight very well worth seeing.

Samur, June 2nd, 1930.

CHAPTER XI

UP THE NUBRA VALLEY

This morning we went on down the Shyok Valley, passing all the time through the same indescribably grand scenery. The majestic channel of the valley, enclosed between high walls of granite, seems to become more and more vast as it unfolds its wide and tortuous length. Small terraces, here and there, continue to mark the ancient level at which the river ran, and great slabs of clay, remaining as though stuck to the steep slopes of rock, are a witness of the time when this valley framed the blue mirror of a lake. We went rapidly on, across the sand and shingle spread all over the bottom. The sky was overcast; squalls of dust-laden wind darkened the air and raised small whirlwinds here and there, which, after circling at one spot, moved quickly over the flat ground and sometimes even mounted the sides. Signs were still visible of the disastrous flood-wave which last year came right down the valley. There is another sign—a negative one: there is no trace left of the bridge across the Shyok, which was built years ago to encourage caravan-trade from Yarkand. No trace whatever; and the rock on which it was supported looks as though denuded and picked dry of the alluvial deposit which used to cover it.

It was a pity that the dust in the air completely blurred the horizon. We could not see, but we had a feeling that the valley was widening out steadily; the opposite side seemed to recede in the yellowish gloom which made everything equal and confused. This was the mouth of the Nubra Valley, one of the longest that comes down from the Karakoram, and when it joins the Shyok Valley an immense stretch of alluvion spreads out among the mountains.

There is a village here, Tirit—a few fields, a lot of thickets, poor houses and slightly purplish hedges of dry thorn, as at Seti. We went quickly through it. Beyond, making a wide circle round a rocky spur covered by an ancient moraine, we

103

entered the Nubra Valley. I am getting nearer and nearer my goal.

In Ladakh I had always heard of the Nubra Valley as one of the most flourishing of the whole region, but thought, when we entered it to-day, that this was an undeserved reputation. The air was murky, owing to the great dust raised by the wind. We could see, with some difficulty, a bare flank of rock on one side, and on the other nothing but a wide stretch of sand which soon became lost in the gloom. In the sand, so white that when the sun beats upon it it must be blinding, could be seen here and there the gentle, delicate curves of the tops of dunes. There was nothing in the way of plants except thorny bushes, with leaves reduced to the minimum. It was in every respect —air, earth and vegetation—a real desert, except that with the grey sky, the lack of sun, and the wind which every now and then rose to a violent squall, one had an impression of cold, which is not a usual characteristic of a desert at noon.

Soon there arose rather indistinctly from the sand a long thin streak of green; one or two higher trees emerged from it, swaying under the force of the wind. It was a village— Lukjum, and a few *mani* proved that it must be near. We urged on the tired, laboured steps of our poor horses over the sand towards a house which had a fairly inviting appearance. I daresay its lawful owner was rather surprised when I dismounted at the door, and went straight in as if it was my own house; a perilous little staircase led to a little room of which I at once took possession. I was just in time. We had scarcely entered when a hurricane of extreme violence burst forth. The two little windows of the room in which we had taken shelter had, as usual here, paper instead of glass. In one of them the paper was partly torn, and this little opening, which at any other moment would have seemed quite insignificant, was enough to let in dust and sand in extraordinary quantities, so that in a moment we were as white as millers. Our greeting from the Nubra Valley was hardly worthy of Ladakhi hospitality!

Then the storm died down, the horizon became clear, and the sun sent forth a little warmth again. We were reconciled to the Nubra Valley, even though we still sank into its sand and stumbled over its shingle. But after a march of an hour, or a little more, we arrived here at Samur, when the reconciliation was completed.

Certain characteristics, clearly, are typical of the whole of the Nubra region: here, too, where the fields are extensive and partly planted with fruit-trees, the outlying parts of the great cone-shaped deposit on which the oasis stands consist of thickets with clearings of fields, and the usual purplish thorn-bushes form hedges to the lanes and paths which wind about through the cultivated area in every direction, like the arteries and veins of an organism.

The caravan was naturally late, considering the hurricane which must have struck it full, before Tirit, but when it arrived we did not worry as to where we should pitch our camp or billet ourselves, but passed right through the oasis, going right up the cone to the point where it originates at the opening of a lateral valley. Just beyond a stream there is a grove of trees —willows, poplars and apricots—which contrasts with the bareness of the neighbouring rock. This large patch of thick green was already comforting, but as we approached it we suddenly heard, coming from the grove of trees, like a triumphal march, the music of a complete lama orchestra. It is there, in fact, that the *gompa* of Samur, for which we were making, is hidden. It is indeed actually invisible among the trees until one has passed through the gate leading into the enclosure which contains the lovely green patch of trees; then only one sees the whiteness of the house through the tree-trunks. One goes on, and all at once the buildings of the *gompa* appear—verandahs, terraces, *rabsal* adorning the façade which is built along an open space, where high pennons gaily flutter their prayers.

The *gompa* of Samur looks quite new, in such perfect order are its rooms and temples. It is a dependent of Rigzon, and this is perhaps a sufficient explanation, since we know the virtues of the 'pure' lamas of Rigzon. It is rich in mural paintings, in statues of Tsongkapa the reformer, in great *chorten* of silver with friezes of gold and turquoises; all is like new and brilliant in colour—even too much so for one who likes, in Tibetan painting, the indefinable half-tones of age, and prefers them to these colours which are at times too vivid and crude.

We were given tea in one of the temples, with delicious cakes—native cakes, of course—and an abundance of red raisins and apricot-kernels. Then we went down again through the oasis, through a maze of paths bordered with thorn-bushes, under the guidance of the chief lama, who conducted us to this fine house belonging to the monastery, where we are lodged. It is a large house, but inhabited by only one monk, who oversees and directs the work in the fields belonging to the *gompa*. We relegated him to his kitchen—a fine, big kitchen, too, where I at once entered into negotiations for an ancient teapot in which copper, brass and silver are admirably combined. But the lama cannot be accustomed to being relegated thus; indeed he is no *kushok*, but a mere monklet of second, or perhaps even third, rank. He comes constantly out of his kitchen and all at once I see him in my room, which he has silently entered, standing motionless and looking at me as I write. Discovered, he smiles at me all over his face, says "ju" nicely, and disappears, gliding away as silently as he entered. I don't know how he does it; because, whenever I myself go in or out, the little door, made of branches placed vertically and badly put together, creaks in the most abominable way.

Samur, June 3rd, 1930.

The person who was most delighted to get to Samur was Tashi: he actually belongs to Kyagar, a little village almost beside the *gompa*. In the morning, at Seti, he got hold of a horse, so as to return to his native village, not as a poor coolie, but as a great lord. The welcome given him by his fellow-villagers, who crowded round his nag, must have seemed to him triumphal. I do not know if all the words of welcome were intended to express joy at his return, or wonder as well—admiring wonder, of course, at his exalted position, exalted not only because he was on horseback—and also at his really extra-ordinary 'get-up'.

When Tashi presented himself to me at Srinagar, humble and suppliant, he was still the complete Ladakhi, in a great purplish cloak, cap, and pigtail also. When interviewed, he said he did not wish to be a porter, and I engaged him, not as a servant, which he was not, but for general use. He was to follow us on the march with the lunch and, in camp, to do all

OUR RECEPTION BY THE LAMAS OF SAMUR

[face p. 106

sorts of things as required. I did not therefore fit him out as
a servant. But he at once attended to his own equipment, with
the little money he had drawn in advance, and went on adding
to it afterwards, at Kargil, at Leh, even here at Panamik, asking
for further advances and, I believe, spending everything.
Then at Leh I gave him, as I did the others, some knitted
garments and a comical fur-lined doublet I found in the bazaar,
which is so tight that the fur sticks out in all directions. With
this varied wardrobe—for the Ladakhi cloak and cap had at
once been discarded at Srinagar—Tashi has the idea that he
is a great dandy and that he will create an effect with his fellow-
villagers. He usually wears a great woollen mountaineering-
cap even when the sun is beating down hotly, as it can here;
a thick white jersey which sticks out in all directions from under
the fur-lined doublet; a pair of lilac trousers from goodness
knows where; woollen stockings up to the knee; then a great
variety of footwear—he has now acquired a pair of large
Yarkandi shoes, violet in colour, in which he slops about like
a pigmy in the shoes of a giant. But he is obviously very
proud of himself, and goodness knows what story he has told
his fellow-villagers here at Kyagar, who saw him come back
like this on horseback, in the suite of a 'bara sahib', whereas
they had seen him start out perhaps ragged, certainly poor, on
foot, with his bundle on his shoulders, to seek fortune in distant
lands! Tashi now holds no specified position, but he watches
and learns. Another time he will get engaged as a servant and
will wear, like all the servants here, a long buttoned-up jacket.
But he will be less picturesque, and his compatriots will give
him a less triumphal welcome. People often acquire fame in
this world by remaining more or less unspecified, neither fish,
flesh nor fowl—like Tashi Serin.

We left Samur the other morning under a radiant sky.
There were the usual sonorous greetings from the *mon*, and we
went off by the tortuous, thorn-hedged paths of the oasis, till
we came out beyond the fields. There is only a short gap,
however, before one comes to other fields, those of Tegur, the
largest village in the Nubra Valley, as is testified by the relative
wealth which appears in the architecture of its houses, wide,
tall, embellished with terraces and *rabsal*. Then one passes
Tegur and comes to the really flat part of the valley—for the

villages and cultivated areas are almost always on the slope of the fans at the openings of lateral valleys, that is, where it is easiest to get water for the irrigation which the fields require.

The Nubra Valley retains the grand characteristics which we had noticed all the way up from its junction with the Shyok Valley, steep, rugged sides entirely of granite, to which are attached fragments of ancient moraine often carved out by erosion into strange and wonderful pillars; the bottom is some miles wide, smooth and level. Here, however, there is no longer the blinding stretch of sand; on the contrary, the bottom is a brownish stretch of vegetation. In no other valley of the whole region (and I can say that I have been through them all) have I ever seen anything like it: there is usually nothing but the shingle left by the rivers when in flood. Here, in contrast with the sand of the lower valley, there is an abundance of quite unusual and therefore unexpected vegetation. When one comes close to it one sees it is entirely thorn-bushes; the leaves are tiny, incredibly reduced in size, and there are innumerable long thorns, but the plants are tall, like trees, and very thick and intertwined, and the bryony-plants which cling to them make the entanglement even more impenetrable: I imagine that the landscape of Western Australia, with its great thorn-jungles, is like this. Among these thickets the path is marked by sandy clearings, connected as it were by avenues which, as in the oases, are bordered by purplish hedges of dry thorn. Civilization passes this way, so to speak, in the trade-caravans which go backwards and forwards between India and Chinese Turkistan. Behind the hedges is forbidden ground for man; it is the kingdom of a certain feline creature, a large wild cat, which preys upon the hares which abound there.

Coming out of the thickets of the valley-bottom one arrives at another village and consequently passes another cone-shaped formation: it is Tirisha. A small temple opened its doors to us and gave us shelter while we had lunch. Then we went on, along the valley-bottom as before. However, we were not near enough to the middle of the valley to get back to the great band of thickets down the centre: we kept nearer the side, from which a few huge rocks jut out and break the uniformity of the flat ground. In the shelter of one of these a white expanse showed where the inhabitants would easily be able to collect soda when

CHORTEN IN THE OASIS OF PANAMIK

[face p. 108

the pools which form there at the end of winter have evaporated. A little farther on, a yellowish stain in the rocks of the lower part of the mountain-side and a penetrating smell of sulphur indicate the presence of a hot spring, on the same alignment as those other springs, also extremely hot, in the valleys of Kundos, Braldah and Basha, in the Baltistan Karakoram. A little further on again, and we were in the cultivated fields of Panamik.

Panamik, though one would not imagine it, is an important stage. It represents the first green oasis and the first village for caravans coming from Chinese Turkistan. They have journeyed through inhospitable valleys and mountains during weeks of slow and exhausting progress; have crossed rugged passes through the spurs of the Kunlun at the beginning of their journey; then, having arrived at the Suget Dawan, have traversed the desolate zone of the Tibetan plateaux, lashed by the violence of the wind; have also crossed the Karakoram Dawan, leaving on the road horses, yak, donkeys and camels unable to endure the high altitude and the fatigue of their burdens any longer: but other animals were forthcoming, purposely brought unladen to take the place of such as might die. They have come down from the plateaux into the deep channel of the Shyok Valley and have forded the swirling river; then climbed again to the pass of Saser and descended from there crossing the front edges of glaciers. And when at last they have reached the bottom of the descent and come out into the Nubra Valley, there is Panamik, the first oasis of green, the first village—rest, almost paradise.

It did not seem exactly a paradise to us, who were going up the valley. The farther one goes into the mountains, towards the glaciers, the poorer the cultivated areas become, and, therefore, the more wretched the inhabitants. Panamik proves this in its fields, its houses, and its villagers, who are indifferent in physique, badly clothed, and also indifferent in character. Only four asked to be taken on, and only ten in the rest of the Nubra Valley. I was quite right to go and look for my former men from Timosgam and their friends, who are physically strong, well clothed, courageous, eager for the new and the unknown, hardened to fatigue.

Panamik, in spite of all this, is quite an important

place, and owing to its importance has a *serai* where passing caravans can halt, and a public granary where they can provision themselves. We ourselves found accommodation—but without many comforts—in a little house which is State property.

What tremendous days these two at Panamik have been ! All my baggage, except the cases of provisions which have gone the longer way round by the Chang-la, has arrived. All the provisions which are already prepared for the caravan are also here. Every single mill in the whole of the Nubra region, requisitioned for this purpose since six days ago, is working for me from morning till night. Anyone who wants or needs flour, both now and for some little time longer, must do without. All the *lambardar*, that is, the heads of villages, are at my service, and are all collected here at Panamik to receive new orders from me: the most distant have come four days' journey on purpose. In every house, possibly, some woman is roasting barley for me. My requisitioning extends even to chickens and eggs; I already have the beginnings of a poultry-yard, with 120 fowls, and have laid down about a hundred dozen eggs to start with. The rest will come later. And in any case ordering is quickly done when one knows that the orders are carried out with military precision. What is more of an effort is making, then repeating, and then perfecting all the calculations for the rationing of the men, then expanding them in case of eventual complications, and foreseeing everything, even things which should not happen. If my companions had even a remote idea of what all this costs in labour and fatigue, they would have a greater appreciation of our meals, which, though not exactly Lucullus' feasts, are by no means so bad. For breakfast we have eggs, butter, jam, tea, and, in the villages, milk. For lunch, which we almost always carry with us, excellent *hors d'œuvres*, chicken, or occasionally mutton, with vegetables, cheese, preserved fruit, with the addition, almost always, of biscuits and jam or chocolate. For tea we have butter and jam and biscuits, and when we are not on the march, we have also the luxury of scones or a good cake. For dinner, good hot soup, chicken, or sometimes mutton, with vegetables and potatoes or rice, and a sweet or preserved fruit. And new bread every day. What could we want more? And this *régime* will have to continue even in uninhabited zones, even on the glaciers. All the men must have their full daily ration of *satu*, *ata*, tea, butter, salt and tobacco. And so the calculations—re-made, for the *n*th time, in the evening or early in the morning—have had to be put into actual practice, and Hashmatullah and I have been occupied these two whole days in checking weights and quantities in the courtyard of the *serai*, under a sun which seemed nearly to melt one's brain as one stood still for hours and hours beside the weighing-machine.

We have had a sick man in the caravan here at Panamik. The other evening, when we arrived, Rasul complained to me of a bad headache: it got better and passed off, but I noticed that whenever he could he threw himself on the ground and dozed. This was not natural, in him. Yesterday morning, when I got up, I went to see him; he had a temperature of 103. I put him into a little room in the *serai*, buried under a mountain of blankets, and gave him some medicine. Nobody here will condemn me for illegally practising the medical profession. And the fact remains that to-day Rasul was up again, declaring he felt well, and doing his job. I think the fear of being left behind alone here at Panamik had a good deal to do with it.

You already know Tashi. Rasul and Kadir must also be introduced. Kadir is our experienced cook: he sometimes makes us a certain kind of sweet, covered with a delicious cream (really only artificial cream) which might be envied by the cooks at Doney's in Florence. Then there is something else to be considered. Kadir gives us breakfast in the morning. Then, in a great hurry, he has to pack up his cooking utensils. He starts out on the march, walking with the coolies. We ride, but he walks. He arrives as soon as he can, according to the length of the march, sometimes as late as 6, or even 7 in the evening, sometimes even later, if on a longer stage. When he arrives, he picks out, with experienced skill, the most suitable spot for his kitchen fire, puts down on the ground the little haversack which he carries faithfully over his shoulder, lights the fire at once, and half an hour later—'dinner tayar', dinner is ready. If by any chance the bread is underbaked—let him cast the first stone who, under such conditions, could bake it better. Kadir was a handsome man in his time, tall and strong, and with his proud face, well-kept beard, aquiline nose, and sparkling eyes, had something of the bird of prey. Now he is growing old, but he does all the marches on foot. When I told him that I would take Rasul with me on to the glaciers and that he would remain here at Panamik with the *wazir*, he replied without hesitation: 'I am the cook, and I must follow the *bara sahib*,' in a tone that admitted of no contradiction. For Kadir is always serious; he never laughs, only smiles rarely, and in contrast to all other Kashmiri, seems to have a sense of his own dignity. At Srinagar, when I was surrounded by a crowd of petulant servants and cooks, he, though he knew who I was, remained quietly apart, and only when I recognized him did he give me the letter which he had ready, to show his desire to serve me. I stand up for Kadir, even if he does sometimes give us underbaked bread.

Rasul, on the other hand, is a more exuberant type. How much use he is as a cook I do not know, for I have not tried, but as a servant he is ideal. He does not stick too closely to his strictly professional duties, but does a bit of everything in the caravan. He directs and encourages the coolies when they strike camp in the morning and pitch camp again in the evening; he acts as interpreter with the Ladakhis,—by way of Hindustani, of course; wherever we go, he is instantly master of the situation; if we find billets, he arranges the rooms before we arrive, and generally very well; his activity is amazing, so is his practical ability in adjusting the porters' loads when they have a competition to see who can find the lightest. Rasul is indispensable, always good-humoured and always smiling. It must not be forgotten that he has half-Ladakhi blood in his veins. Perhaps this is why he is also very intelligent: he understands English at once, even though he does not know it; he even begins to understand a little Italian, and by the end of our journey I do not know what we shall do to prevent Rasul understanding what we say! He also understands one's intentions and desires. To-day he is extremely happy; my treatment has been successful and he thanks me every moment: 'bohot mervani, huzur'. His joy is mainly caused by his not having to remain alone here at Panamik!

Panamik, June 5th, 1930.

Our departure from Panamik was rather complicated, with my 70 permanent porters, 60 horses, and a certain number of

WALLS OF GRANITE IN THE UPPER NUBRA VALLEY

yak besides, also a few extra coolies taken on at the last moment, among whom were five who carried the beginnings of my travelling poultry-yard—five large baskets, out of which the hens tried desperately to poke their heads.

Our way, as usual, lay along the bottom of the valley, over pebbles and sand, and we had to cross the outer edge of a few of the cone-shaped formations. There were thorn-thickets here and there. The valley was still of imposing width, with steep rugged sides. But now I have only one longing—to arrive at the glacier. It has become an almost painful kind of anxiety.

We crossed the Nubra by a ford which was perfectly simple and caused us no agitations. Beyond it we climbed the short slope of a terraced cone, on which is the oasis of Aranu. There a lovely field and the pleasant shadow of some willows seemed to have been specially prepared for our lunching-place. Beyond the river, right in front of us, the granite cliff was cut roughly in two by a narrow, deep gorge. One could see a winding path that clambers painfully up from the river-bank and then disappears into the gorge. This was the caravan-route from the Saser-la: when we come down it in almost four months' time our great journey will be more or less completed.

We were now off the beaten track, and so, after lunch, we started collecting plants. Having made a collection of the flowers, chiefly yellow, which were dotted over our field, we started off again. It was only a short march, for in less than two hours we were at Chimi, a little oasis at the foot of a precipitous wall of granite. Here were a few fields and no trees, but the usual hedges of dry thorn. We divided ourselves between two houses, and these were the last walls which will protect us from the wind for many days.

Next day our stage was even shorter. The Nubra Valley becomes even more magnificent, the few oases even poorer-looking. But at Tzongsa there was a rarity—a rarity, at least, as far as we have seen up till now—a series of ancient juniper-trees with great twisted trunks and thick foliage, growing in a row at the foot of the reddish-coloured cliff which comes steeply down behind the village. Finally, we arrived at Gombo, the last village.

Zingrul: Terminus of the Siachen Glacier, June 8th, 1930.

Chapter XII

WE REACH THE GREAT SIACHEN
GLACIER AT LAST

Gombo is quite a special kind of village.   A lama of that
name, venturing into the uninhabited upper Nubra Valley,
found that a divinity lived on the top of a rock which looks as
if it had been cut out of the mountain-side by powerful blows
with a gigantic axe: it is smooth from top to bottom except
for the narrow gash of a chasm, which looks like a wound.
Gombo stopped here to adore this mountain-divinity, built a
little temple and founded a monastery in order to have companions in his adoration.   Round the temple appeared a few
chorten, a few *mani*, even a few fields, for the lamas had not been
ordered to remain in adoration from morning till night, nor
yet to live entirely upon alms.   Later the fields were extended
so much that a family of peasants was required to cultivate
them.   But Gombo, unlike a new American city, had no
further increase; its history is all contained here, and never
went beyond this stage—just one peasants' house, a few houses
for the ten lamas, and the little temple, small but elegant, all
white with a border of crimson, and with a thousand prayers
fluttering on its lofty pennons in honour of the divinity who
still lives on the top of the great polished rock.

I had the camp pitched on a pleasant, grassy piece of ground
interspersed with willows, and it looked very picturesque
there, owing especially to its attractive surroundings—the little
smiling oasis of fields with its gay-looking little *gompa* in a
frame of mountains of incredible grandeur and wildness.   Even
here the valley is almost as wide as it seemed at its beginning,
but the sides are different; they have perhaps been gradually
changing, but only here at Gombo have I noticed them to be
quite different and of a new type.   They are walls, veritable
walls, as though cast solid out of cement, but the cement is
granite, reddish in colour with curious dark spots.   These

walls are not very high, but so sheer that one can see nothing of any further plane. It looks as if there were nothing whatever behind them, instead of which there is a vast sea of enormous mountains. One has this same impression if one looks at the majority of the lateral ravines, which are narrow, wild, very steep, but short, because they are cut only in the thickness of the granite wall. But there are just a few which cut more deeply into it, piercing it and going right through, and then, through the narrow slit of their openings, there appears an immense peak, usually snowy, and towering high above, but not far away—quite close indeed, almost on top of one—which shows that the wall forms merely the external and extremely small border of the world of giants behind. There is one of these ravines right behind Gombo, narrow but cut deep into the rock; beyond it rises a huge mountain, topped by an immense overhanging crown of snow. This is worthy of some god: perhaps it is there that the divinity lives who revealed himself to Gombo, the pious lama. But perhaps he does not reveal himself to others. I do not know if my porters know the story, but sometimes they fix their eyes on the granite wall and examine it from end to end. When I asked them, they told me that the lama-superior of the monastery sees a great light there which others cannot see. Certainly among these mountains there is a great divine light, which one cannot but adore.

At Gombo the weather continued to be very uncertain, as during the previous days. There were hours of clear sky, broken only by a few light clouds, during which one could make out, towards the head of the valley, a gigantic, snow-covered mountain, possibly K^8: then the sky became covered with heavy clouds and mists invaded the valley and a little sleet fell, perhaps simply carried by the wind, and in the afternoon, almost regularly, the air towards the lower part of the valley became gradually darkened with a thick, yellowish gloom—the daily wind-storm which raises the fine dust of the valley-bottom.

My principal occupation at Gombo has been to collect information about the way to the glacier, which, in all its immensity, fills the head of the valley. The old "Map of India", even in its latest edition—which, to tell the truth, contains scarcely any improvements in its representation of this district—gives a distance of about 8 miles. But the owners of the horses which are bringing the provisions for my caravan from Panamik claimed a payment, for the stage from Gombo to the glacier, which is more than twice the normal, and would not give in, adducing the difficulties and the length of the march. Who was right? The old Map of India or the owners of the horses? I had to make inquiries, in order to organize this last stage in our approach to the glacier. I do not know how many men I asked: information remained quite uncertain, but, on a basis of the points of agreement in what they said, one had to conclude that the distance was about 16 miles—a stage which could hardly be considered short, in view of the fact that one must proceed without any sign of a path and through two fords in the river. Information brought back by a man who had been sent on as a scout confirmed the length of the distance to the glacier.

So we started this morning comparatively early—at 7 o'clock—with the whole of the caravan, which in itself meant a certain amount of effort and anxiety. The great snowy peak, brilliantly lit up by the rising sun, rose up behind the granite wall which was still in shadow: it looked like a great flaming torch. May the mountain-divinity who has his abode there protect me, for with Gombo I have left the last extremity of inhabited country and launched myself into the great world of giant mountains and glaciers and eternal snows! The lamas at the little monastery, though they do not know this majestic world, pray faithfully to their mountain-divinity. Last night I was already shut up inside my tent when I heard the music of the monks from the little temple. It ceased; and then it was the turn of the porters, who began the murmuring sound of their prayers. Then the music started again, though it was now late: and then again the low murmuring of the men.

Our march started this morning under good auspices— brilliant weather. The Nubra Valley seemed to me more and more magnificent, the two granite walls more and more impressive. In all my life I had never seen anything even to compare with these gigantic smooth cliffs, only slightly roughened by the ceaseless wear of time, cleft only by short ravines which do not lessen their compact solidity. They are,

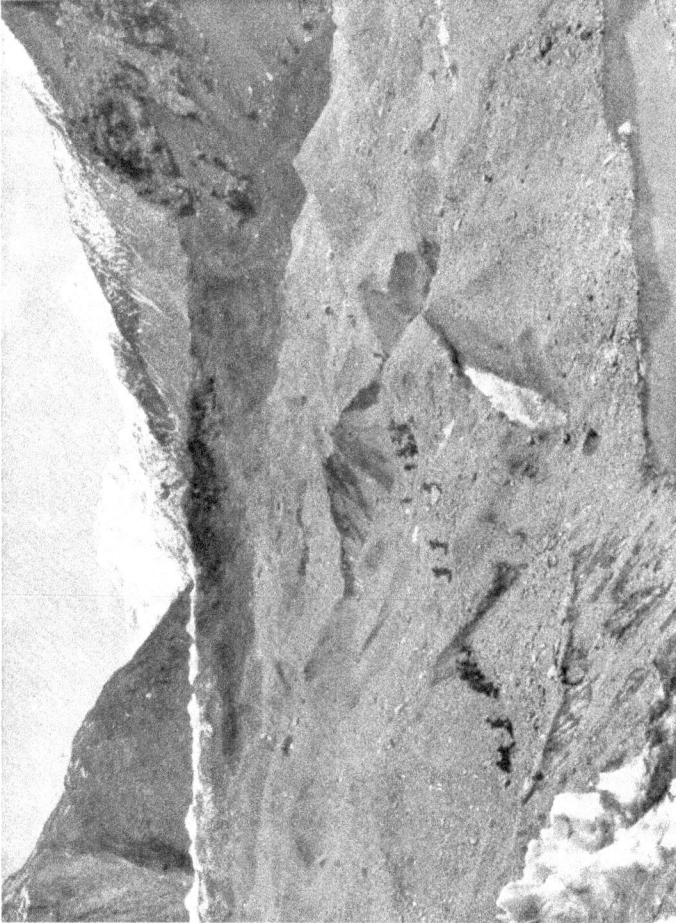

THE MARCH ON THE LOWER TONGUE OF THE SIACHEN

[face p. 116

in general, reddish, or pink, sometimes almost golden when the sun beats full upon them, but the curious dark markings I had already seen near Gombo became more and more frequent. These are caused by juniper-plants. How they can grow, how they can live thus, rooted in nothing but rock, on smooth walls and granite buttresses where there is certainly not a grain of soil, remains inexplicable. And the farther one goes up the valley, the thicker the dark markings of the junipers seem to be.

On, on up the shingly bed of the Nubra, I was spurred on by the longing to discover, at last, the glacier—which was going to be "my" glacier. One glanced up the lateral gorges, because they always gave one a surprise in the shape of some great peak, which appeared and immediately disappeared again, as though anxious to hide. But my eye was fixed mainly in front of me, towards the top of the valley, even though my view was hopelessly interrupted by a low spur of rock. We went round and past it, and shortly afterwards, right away in the distance, still a long way off, appeared a thin white streak in the midst of an indistinct dark colour. The glacier, at last, the great Siachen Glacier!

But the Nubra river played us a low trick, squeezing us with one of its loops against the side of the valley. We had to ford it and get over to the other bank, and the glacier disappeared again from view. We had to console ourselves by having lunch, clinging close to the foot of the granite wall in the vain hope of finding a little shade. Up above, a herd of about twenty wild sheep, reddish like the rocks, seemed to be laughing at us as they leapt lightly up a wall of rock which even the most brilliant mountain-climber would consider inaccessible.

After a brief halt we started again, for I was very anxious to arrive quickly at my goal. The Nubra here makes another loop, and we had again to cross the valley obliquely to get to the next ford. As we crossed, the Siachen Glacier reappeared, showing a great part of the tongue of ice at its end, slightly sloping, as a whole, but broken up into great blackish hillocks of moraine. We only saw it for a moment, for as we drew nearer the opposite side, a little spur which stuck right out into the bottom of the valley hid it from view again. The more eagerly I longed to see my glacier, the more shy it seemed of showing itself.

Nor, when it did finally show itself, was it to be in the splendour of a clear sky and framed in its surrounding mountains. The usual afternoon hurricane had arisen. Looking back, one saw that the valley was confusedly disappearing in the darkness brought by the wind. All round us the mists rose up strangely from behind the mountains, joining together to make a single vault, creeping from the ridges down the ravines, filling the air with an even, gloomy, monotonous greyness which sent a shiver through one's very bones.

We forded the two branches of the Nubra without difficulty; the water was tumultuous and looked almost livid, and now the wind was against us and made us shiver. We came to the spur of rock. It was only a moraine, left high and dry by the glacier ages ago, and we zigzagged between the mounds and depressions which broke its surface. We climbed to its top and looked over, and there was the Siachen Glacier at last, with its gigantic front filling the whole of the valley from side to side, monstrous almost, not to be compared to any other glacier in size, but dreary, almost threatening in the grey light diffused from the clouds and mists.

We soon reached the glacier-end. The horse-caravan was a little in front of me, but the porters arrived three hours late. In the meantime it rained, and sleet fell, and a cold wind came off the glacier, numbing us. There was no lack of fuel, and a good fire was soon made. But we had to be careful of the flames which darted their tongues in all directions and attacked us unawares.

This, then, was the camp to which I had so long looked forward! We are in the shelter of a bank of frontal moraine; almost immediately behind it rise the high irregular hillocks which break the front of this vast glacier, as of the other greater glaciers of the Karakoram. Zingrul—for that is the name of the locality—has certainly never seen so much movement, either of men or animals. The horse-caravan, with its unexpected additions of yak and coolies, has also stopped here for the night. The animals are scattered all over the stretch of alluvion in front of the glacier, in search of grass or at least of something to eat. The men are all in the shelter of the bank of frontal moraine, in order to get out of the wind; they are divided into several different groups, with their goods—that is, their provisions, also neatly divided. My same 70 porters form five groups, which, even though they do not actually look askance at each other (for this would be contrary to Ladakhi nature), are obviously in competition when it is a question of getting hold of the lightest loads or the most plentiful rations. There is the Timosgam group, the most closely knit of all, consisting of 24 men; there is the group from Tia, a village near Timosgam: 16 men. These two groups form the nucleus of the porters who will be with me all the time and who are equipped for high altitudes. There is a third group which I call the Leh group, because it was enrolled at Leh—17 men, all from the great Ladakh basin. Finally there are two groups of Nubra men, who for some unknown reason insist upon lighting two fires—13 porters in all.

Thus only five of these splendid fires are for my permanent caravan, but there are others for the men with the 60 horses and the men with the saddle-horses and a few odd ones. Then there is our kitchen, which has a big extra fire for hot water. It must be a picturesque sight, all these flaming fires—we are not being economical, for there is plenty of wood—at the edge of the glacier. But I did not delay long to enjoy the spectacle.

It was late when we pitched camp and we were already numbed with cold. We had dinner directly Kadir was ready. Then the "bara sahib", after a general look round, shut himself up in his tent, and took an absurd joy in being able to plunge into a deliciously warm sleeping-bag and go to sleep so near his own glacier, almost like a child who clings tightly, while he sleeps, to his favourite toy.

Zingrul: Terminus of the Siachen Glacier, June 8th, 1930.

It is two months to-day since I left Florence with all my baggage. In exactly two months I have reached the front of the Siachen Glacier in the heart of the Eastern Karakoram, still with all my baggage: there are only lacking the 22 cases of provisions which have taken the longer way by the Chang-la and will be here to-morrow. I have trailed all this heavy stuff along with me, at the same quick rate of progress as my own party, right across India to Srinagar; then over the Zoji-la, under conditions which were certainly not easy; through the whole length of Ladakh; across the high Diggher Pass, and then up through the whole of the Nubra region. I challenge anyone for an example of greater speed. I already have provisions here for a month and a half for the whole caravan, and at Panamik, only two stages off, enough for another month. These, I hope, will arrive at Zingrul in two days' time, and the mills of Nubra are at work on the rest. And all this in two months since leaving Florence. I can also say more, for my own personal satisfaction—the satisfaction of one who, being inevitably in the decline of life, had an intimate and bitter consciousness, owing to age and a long habit of engrossing sedentary study and also to having shed a few feathers by the way, of perhaps no longer having the energy of body and mind of the good old days; I can say that, after a night which was not entirely restful, being disturbed by a fiendish wind, I have conducted a party of men to make a first depôt actually on the glacier.

It is here that the difficulties of the enterprise really begin. We shall have to live for almost four months in an uninhabited zone, and for almost three months on glaciers. It is absolutely impossible to increase the number of men, and the number of men decided upon is considerably smaller than the number of loads. This is why I suddenly started off to reconnoitre, so as to take forward part of the baggage and make a first depôt, which, like the others behind, will have gradually to be moved farther and farther forward. We took 45 loads of flour to-day: each weighed 100 to 120 pounds, so I took 65 men, in order that they might to a certain extent take turns with the heavy work.

It was indeed heavy work. The huge glacier-end is not, in general, on much of an incline, and it was not therefore a stiff climb. But the whole of the front is broken up into mounds of ice covered with moraine, which means that there are continuous and exhausting ascents and descents. And not only ascents and descents, but deviations, twists, and zigzags, for the mounds are often intersected by walls of living ice, or interrupted by clefts, torrents, and pools. It makes a complete orographical and hydrographical system in miniature, but incredibly complex, and demands a good sense of direction and a certain amount of experience in order to save time and fatigue. The porters followed with admirable patience.

But this afternoon, as usual, the sky grew dark; the wind began again, cold because it blew down the glacier, right against us. Then sleet also began, at first thinly, but when, after about an hour, it became extremely heavy, I called a halt and gave the signal to return. Thus the first depôt is established at about $2\frac{1}{2}$ miles' distance up the glacier—to-day, exactly two months after we left Florence.

Someone may wonder why I chose this Siachen Glacier as my objective. I will explain my reasons.

Apart from innumerable smaller glaciers, many of which, however, are greater in size than the greatest in the Alps, the chain of the Karakoram has six really gigantic glaciers. These are the Chogo Lungma and the Hispar on the western side, the Biafo and the Baltoro in the central portion, and the Siachen and the Rimo to the east. The best known of all is the Baltoro, and it has been the frequent objective of expeditions, particularly because among its encircling mountains rises the great pyramid of K^2, giant of giants: enough for the Baltoro! Of the others, the Hispar and the Biafo have each had two European expeditions: they are tolerably well mapped and fairly well known. The Chogo Lungma is perhaps less so: there has been only one expedition to it, but, owing to the region—Baltistan—in which it unwinds its long tongue, owing to the relative unimportance of the mountains round it and the lack of topographical problems requiring solution, it could never attract me. As to the Rimo, I myself have contributed to its exploration; in any case, we shall speak of it farther on, if things go according to plan. There remained the Siachen —the Siachen, which is the largest glacier in the world with the sole exception of the Polar glaciers; which opens out in a valley of giant mountains (even if they are not actually the greatest of the giants); which still preserves a certain novelty; which has had few explorers, and has the reputation of being accessible only with difficulty. All this was sufficient to make my choice fall upon the Siachen.

This upper Nubra Valley, also, has seen few European

travellers and is known to be difficult of access, owing to the fords. Of old travellers Moorcroft in 1821, Vigne in 1835, Thompson and Henry Strachey in 1848, and a few years later Drew, were the only ones to penetrate into it. Then one comes down to quite modern times, when there have been various unsuccessful attempts and only two which succeeded—Longstaff in 1910, Visser in 1929.

Of the old travellers Strachey was the only one to venture on to the glacier, but after about 2 miles he was forced to turn back owing to the difficulties encountered. After that—the reason being that the glacier-tongue, just before it ends, forms a large bend and the glacier appears to be cut short by a great wall of rock—the Siachen appeared in maps to be quite modest in dimensions, more or less, in fact, as it looks when seen from down the valley.

After that one must skip more than half a century—till 1910—before the Siachen was properly revealed. It was revealed by Longstaff, almost by pure chance—though one does not wish to take away from the credit of his discovery. However, we must take one step back.

In 1889 Younghusband, at the end of a memorable journey from China to India across Central Asia, found his way barred by the rugged chain of the Karakoram. Although not equipped for high altitudes, he succeeded in crossing the Muz Tagh Pass, which was also crossed last year by the Italian expedition under His Highness the Duke of Spoleto. Younghusband, however, before crossing the Muz Tagh, went up the Oprang Valley in the northern slopes of the Karakoram (now more correctly called Shaksgam), and also went up a great glacier he discovered, until he came in sight of, and quite near to, a pass—much farther to the east than the Muz Tagh—which seemed to him a possible way of crossing the Karakoram range.

In 1909, Longstaff wished to find this saddle which Younghusband had seen from the northern slopes: he started from the Saltoro Valley in the heart of Baltistan (which I went up, sixteen years ago, in mid-winter) and climbed right up the Bilafon Glacier to a saddle which at first he thought was the one for which he was searching. From here he descended another glacier, in itself also a large one. But Longstaff, following it, came out upon a very much larger glacier, immense, gigantic, surrounded by wonderful, high peaks and sending out branches in every direction. It looked to him, however, as if the tongue of ice at its extremity must go in an easterly direction. He made a rapid survey and took photographs; then he turned back, partly because his caravan, though small, was not provisioned for more than a fairly short period.

The discovery of this great unknown glacier was an important one. But Younghusband, then British Resident in Kashmir, thought that this glacier might perhaps run not east, but south, and might form the upper basin of the Siachen. Longstaff was determined to study and solve the problem: he went up the Nubra Valley, but the river stopped him; he waited a few months and tried again and this time he got past it and reached the front of the Siachen. He went up it for 6 or 7 miles, not without trouble, but was forced back by difficulties of commissariat; but before starting back, he climbed up the mountain-side of the valley, was able to get a view northwards of the Siachen, and recognized far away the high peaks and ridges surrounding his own unknown glacier: it was, then, part of the Siachen. The problem was solved.

In 1911, the Americans, Mr. and Mrs. Workman, followed Longstaff's tracks from the Saltoro Valley, entered upon the Siachen from the Bilafon Glacier, looked round, and went back. But this look round sufficed to give them the idea of another expedition. They came back the same way next year, and stayed long enough to go almost all over the glacier and to make a map of it. However, they asserted that it was inaccessible by way of the front. Nevertheless, the ascent of the front was made last year, by a Dutch couple, the Vissers, but for not more than 2 or 3 miles; they then abandoned it in order to explore a lateral valley.

I had included the Siachen in a tour of exploration planned two years ago, when I was given the command of an Italian expedition to the Karakoram. But, when I resigned this command, the Siachen, with its unsolved problems, again became a field for explorers. It is not an easy undertaking: that is why it is attractive and worth while. I shall certainly encounter difficulties from the place itself, and even if these can be overcome I shall have very great difficulties with provisioning.

A week before I left Florence I met Longstaff there: our common friend De Filippi brought him to see me. We did not know each other personally, and yet could consider each other as old acquaintances. However, I was astonished when Longstaff, coming towards me with outstretched hands, greeted me with only one word, repeated again and again, "My dear Dainelli, food, food, food!" When he went away, I accompanied him to the door, and half-way downstairs he turned round and said to me again, "You must remember, food, food, food!"

I have provisions here at Zingrul for a month and a half, partly on the glacier already; another month's provisions are already on the way from Panamik; and the mills of the whole district of Nubra are working for me. Are you satisfied, my dear Longstaff, with your successor?

Exactly two months ago, it must not be forgotten, I was still at Florence.

Zingrul: Front of the Siachen Glacier, June 9th, 1930.

CHAPTER XIII

MECHANISM OF THE MARCH ON THE GLACIER

I remained two more days at Zingrul, that is, at the glacier-end, exactly according to plan. Yesterday evening I expected the 33 cases of provisions which have come from Leh by way of the Chang-la. They could not have arrived before; but I was certainly—I will not say anxious—but doubtful about their arrival. Even if they had been late it would not have really mattered either for us or for our provisioning, but I should have been obliged to wait for them at Zingrul, for the simple reason that I could not have left Hashmatullah Khan alone there without means of transport; he was to return to Panamik to await the developments of my journey. But yesterday evening, punctual as a clock, the cases arrived.

The other day I sent on another caravan-load of provisions up the glacier, with orders to make a second depôt higher up than the first one I had left. Yesterday the men had a rest. They took advantage of it to mend their clothes and shoes, and also to make their personal toilet. A barber worked in each group in turn. They all had the front half of their heads closely shaven, while the hair of the back half, loosened from the long pigtail, was carefully combed and then gathered up again into a long tress. Many of them, during the hot hours of midday, even went and bathed in the waters of the Nubra, though the water comes straight out of the glacier just near here!

The weather has remained quite good. During the night, indeed, a wind was blowing which seemed to be going to carry away my tents and all my other belongings. I had had the tents pitched just in front of the little bank of moraine which forms a clear dividing-line between the glacier and the alluvion. The ground was a sea of shingle, but I had chosen a small space where, instead of pebbles, there was fine clay, and instead of an extremely rough surface, a very tempting floor of perfect smoothness. Would I had never done so! The tent-pegs went down into the ground with delightful ease, but hardly held at all, and every morning the poor tents were all flabby and bore the signs of their struggle with violent gusts of wind during the night. And, owing to the wind, the camp at Zingrul had yet another defect; the clay which had deceived me so well on my arrival with its appearance of complete smoothness and firmness, inviting me to pitch my tents upon it, became ground up into an almost impalpable dust which penetrated everywhere, even when the wind did not actually raise it in clouds and hurl it at us and our belongings. However, I did not have much time either to notice or to bother about the wind or the dust, even though every now and then an involuntary curse would escape me as a dust-laden draught of air made complete havoc among the sheets of paper on the table in my tent, on which were my plans of campaign and also, consequently, those of my commissariat. But on the whole the weather remained fair, though every afternoon there was the usual murkiness towards the lower valley, and even a certain amount of cloud and mist where we were. Even though this made the view of the mountains round us rather grey and dull, it never obscured it entirely, and it was indeed an impressive view. There is really no other way of describing it, and yet I know that it is nothing in comparison with other views of mountains which we shall be able to enjoy later on. There was, on the left of the Siachen Glacier-end—that is, to the right of my camp—the usual wall of granite, cleft by a few precipitous channels; but, at the top, the wall was broken up into a close series of pinnacles of extreme boldness. And on the right of the glacier—that is, on my left—there was something even more tremendous. The wall, smooth, compact, almost flat, did not exactly end at the point where it broke into pinnacles at its summit; it formed, as it were, a massive base on which yet another wall was supported, but this one, instead of being smooth, flat and compact, was divided by deep scores in the mass of rock into gables of incredible size. There was one on the first level which was reminiscent of the Aiguille Noire de Pétéret, but it was bigger, more regular, sharper, extremely smooth in front, inaccessible and unassailable.

THE LOWER SIACHEN AND ITS RIGHT FLANK

[face p. 126

On the upper level, a little higher up, were other gables of similar shape and gigantic size, and right behind them rose a great superb snowy shoulder, graceful in shape and dominating the forest of pinnacles which made a double crown for it.

This morning we parted from Hashmatullah. It is impossible to imagine a greater and more complete devotion than his. He now goes back all alone to Panamik, there to wait, all alone, for three months, so as to carry out my orders and finally to come and meet me, with provisions and horses, by a different way, when he receives notice that my journey of exploration on the glaciers is nearly at an end. It is comforting to find such men in one's life: and it is also comforting to think that, to a certain extent at least, one may have deserved it. After last farewells and mutual wishes—of good luck to us, and to him, that he will not be bored—we started off, Hashmatullah with his few belongings down the alluvial flat ground of the valley, and we, with our heavy caravan, towards the first mounds of the glacier.

My very exact calculations made me certain that, having sent forward on to the Siachen two depôts of provisions and equipment which were not for the moment indispensable, all that remained at the camp could be easily transported by the 70 permanent porters: there would even be a few men who had nothing to carry, who might be loaded up at the lower depôt. What with being sure of this and with saying my farewells to Hashmatullah, I did not keep my eye on the porters: they passed by me one by one, I counted them and they were all there, so I gave the signal to start. But when they were all gone, a glance at the abandoned camp showed me 14 provision-cases which had been quietly left at Zingrul. This was the result of the cunning coolies' being left to do their own loading without strict surveillance. I caught the last of them and entrusted them with three provision-cases, modifying their loads accordingly. But 11 cases were inevitably left behind at Zingrul. I realized that my difficulties were just beginning—that there would be a daily fight, of greater or lesser importance, with the coolies.

I followed my tracks of three days ago through the maze of moraine-covered ice-mounds into which the Siachen is broken up near its end. Progress was therefore easy, as the way was marked; there were continual ups and downs and circles and twists, but on the whole we went steadily upwards and obliquely across, until we reached the first depôt, almost at the foot of the rocky side and at the edge of the glacier. In little less than an hour's climb from there we were at the second depôt, where we took a short rest for lunch in the shade of a juniper-tree at the edge of the rocks.

The Siachen here makes a great bend to the right, and it was this which made the old travellers who reached its front judge it to be of such short extent. Just at this bend two tributaries join the great valley of ice from opposite sides. I left the glacier and climbed on to the last spur of the promontory at the end of the valley which opens just here on the left—on the right as we went up the Siachen. On the top of this promontory there was a flat space sheltered from the wind, sprinkled with tufts of grass and with juniper scattered here and there—an ideal place for a camp. It was ideal, also, in the view which opened out from it, wide and clear. At our feet the Siachen curled its gigantic, monstrous tongue: in the middle there was a white band, a great bank of ice, which, however, became thinner and thinner till it disappeared a little above the extreme end of the glacier. On both sides of it, between it and the opposite sides of the valley, was the maze of hillocks, looking as if they were pursuing and trying to climb on top of each other; they were completely covered in moraine, but cleft with immense cracks, with precipitous walls of living ice, crystalline, translucent, with depressions like valleys in which flowed tumultuous streams and torrents, and with other more irregular depressions, which were enclosed and in which the water lay calmly in little clear lakes. But among the tumult of hillocks, undulating and livid as though congealed suddenly, it was possible to make out a characteristic longitudinal streak, caused by the colour of the moraine matter which covers them. Here, near the left bank, was a very dark, almost black, streak of slate schists; then a light, almost white streak of marbles and limestones; then a grey one, of dolomites. This monster coiled in the valley has its great back striped all over with different colours, and all down the middle of it a high white ridge.

Facing the little spur is the opening of a large valley, also occupied by a glacier; and a little above the opening this valley can be seen to be formed by the confluence of two branches, which owing to their windings are soon lost to sight among the mountains which feed them with snow. The flank of the mountains which closes the extreme end of the Siachen on that side is truly wonderful: it is the one which rose up right above us at Zingrul and seemed to be threatening us from right above. Now we are higher up and farther away and can see more clearly its row of gigantic gables which form a bastion to the snowy summits behind.

Here, close to us, almost underneath us, opens the tributary valley on the left. This one has no glacier of its own, but a short tongue of ice from the Siachen, consisting of a broken confusion of *séracs*, penetrates into it. This is the valley explored by the Vissers last year: it has actually a large glacier of its own, divided into several branches, but its front is some miles above the opening, and from here we can see nothing but a narrow bottom of yellow alluvion, shut in between two precipitous granite walls.

The porters would have liked to stop there at the top of the short spur. An ideal camping-ground, certainly, but it would have been too short a stage when there is such a long march in front of us. I went down on to the glacier again, after studying from above the best route to follow, and, with a sign which admitted of no objections, gave the order to follow me. We made a wide *détour* towards the central line of the Siachen in order to avoid the very broken portion full of *séracs* which goes up the lateral valley; then turned again in order to get nearer the spur of the opposite tributary valley. Near the rocks the surface of the glacier, covered, as everywhere, with moraine, took on a sort of irregular concave shape, and it seemed as if there would be sufficient shelter here from the wind, together with water close at hand and also junipers quite near on the slope of the valley-side. There seemed, in fact, to be everything necessary. This, therefore, was the spot I chose for my first advance camp on the Siachen.

The caravan arrived a short time ago. The men immediately got to work to level the ground for our tents. The pegs would not hold, but large stones to which the ropes were attached made effective substitutes. The five fires of the men are scattered here and there over the glacier, and a cairn has been constructed on top of the nearest hillock. In this way we have taken complete possession of the place.

1st Advance Camp on the Siachen, June 12th, 1930.

We stopped two days at the 1st Camp. Unfortunately the absolute necessity, initial and imperative, of trailing everything along with me forces me to a slow rate of progress when my real longing is—I do not say to fly, because I do not yet believe in the possibility of accurate observation from the air —but at all events to advance speedily at least as far as the point half-way up the stream of the glacier which I have chosen in advance for my base-camp.

In case there is by chance among my younger readers one who may be a pupil in the art of exploration, I will explain the mechanism of my advance up the glacier. My 70 men represent the precise number necessary to transport the camp with all its numerous *impedimenta* and with provisions for the whole caravan for two days. It is, undoubtedly, a heavy caravan and not easily mobile in regions which are new or even only partly known and uninhabited, and over difficult ground.

I move therefore from one camp to another: but I have to stop in each camp as long as is necessary for the men to bring up from the preceding camp all the provisions we have left there. This means delay not only for halts, but also because the stages have to be relatively short if the porters have got to do them twice during the so-called halt-days—once without any loads, and once with heavy loads. Naturally, the more halts we make, the greater the quantity of provisions consumed without furthering the object of our journey of exploration. The provisions that I carry with me—little less than 3 tons on leaving Zingrul—are so calculated that, with two halts to a stage, they should allow me to reach the base-camp with provisions still sufficient for a month—for, directly we have arrived at the base-camp, 60 men will start going backwards and forwards to Zingrul, where, meanwhile, more and more sacks will be accumulating.

This is the general scheme, within which a hundred smaller

details have had to be studied in order to avoid waste of provisions and also of man-power. For example, I leave a small supply of provisions in each camp, which, in the meantime, lightens my caravan. The men who go backwards and forwards between the base-camp and Zingrul will consume, when down below, provisions from the supplies left on the way, but when up above, from those which they themselves carry. In this way there is not the slightest waste of transport.

All this has had to be studied with extreme care and assembled, as it were, like the completed works of a watch; if one wheel stops, the whole mechanism threatens to stop also. It is a continual struggle to make everything work—which means, above all, to make the men work. And the coolies, poor fellows, are all the time doing their best to work just a little less hard. They go slowly, in hopes that their leader will pitch camp at not too great a distance; they linger over their morning meal, so that they shall not have time to go down to the preceding camp and come up again with the loads; they show one their worn-out shoes which require urgent repair; they come *en masse* in front of their leader's tent in order to voice their reasons aloud. It is almost impossible to discuss with them alone on account of the difficulties of language; it is difficult to persuade them; sometimes it is necessary to shout at them, but more often one has recourse to the talisman which is so potent all over the East and which consists of the word 'baksheesh'. But this remains the chief difficulty, and the chief danger also in a journey of exploration through troublesome and uninhabited regions.

The first day of the halt at the 1st Camp my chief occupation was the distribution of provisions to the caravan. This is an occupation which, normally and according to plan, I shall have to repeat every four days. It is not as simple as it might perhaps seem. The daily ration is half a 'seer' (almost a pound) of *satu* and the same of *ata*, a 'chatak' (16 *chatak* make 1 *seer*) of butter and the same of salt, half a *chatak* of tea, a quarter of a *chatak* of tobacco. But my men are divided up, as I have already said, into five distinct groups, and provisions have to be distributed not *en masse* but to each separate group, so as to avoid quarrels which might easily arise. The wretched weighing-machine at my disposal only measures up to 2 *seer*:

imagine therefore the amount of weighing that I have to do, and how complicated it is, at each fresh distribution of provisions to the men.

During the two days we halted at the 1st Camp I managed to collect there everything that had been left at Zingrul and at the two intermediate depôts. I had one arrival also at the camp —Rasul, whom I had left at Gombo as Hashmatullah's servant, but whose indispensability to myself I had quickly realized: so I sent Tashi down instead of him. Rasul arrived triumphant, at the head of five coolies carrying great hampers in which 80 chickens crowed—not exactly with joy, perhaps in desperation. They were at once set free in the camp, in addition to the few already there which we had brought with us. They scratch about, poor creatures, from morn till night, but, apart from stones, there is nothing but ice for them to find. However, corn has been brought on purpose for them, and when feeding-time comes it provides an amusement for the whole camp. The two sheep which came with me—others will follow, either alive or dead—do exactly as they like; they wander round and round in all directions, their heads down, in a perpetually fruit-less search, and if they have by any chance their own philosophy of life, they must ruminate upon human selfishness. There is certainly nothing else to ruminate upon.

The nights are cold, the days fine. In free moments I have walked about a little on the glacier, examining, much to the wonder of the men, the stones which form its plentiful moraine covering. It was not for nothing that they used to call me, last time I was out here, the 'patar sahib'—lord of the stones. I found some fossils—of little value, I know, because they were not in place; and yet of great value, because they have never been collected in this region and proved that the chronological level they represent must be traceable in the glacier-basin. I showed them to the most intelligent of the men, flourishing the usual 'baksheesh' talisman before them, and from that moment there has been a procession of coolies in front of my tent laden with stones of the oddest appearance and quite meaningless. It does not matter, for some day they will certainly bring me some fossils: I know this from personal experience.

This morning we were on the march again. I took a direction across the marginal bank of broken hillocks towards a

THE "JORASSES" OF THE SIACHEN

[face p. 133

belt at the side of the great bank of white ice in the middle of the glacier. Here there were no longer the same large, irregular hillocks thickly covered with moraine: there was a surface of slightly undulating ice, with very little moraine substance on it, so that progress was easy and comparatively quick. The Siachen, having completed its great curve to the right, starts upon a curve in the opposite direction; the great bank of white ice in the middle follows the bend of the valley and of the glacier, and we followed it. I might easily have gone on much farther, but owing to the complicated mechanism of my forward march, I had to turn aside about three in the afternoon from the middle belt towards the left side. It seemed a pity—from the æsthetic point of view also. I climbed up on to a high point in the great central bank of ice, which curled away both up and down the valley, vast in size, 1,000 feet or more in width and divided into several rows of parallel causeways, broken here and there by rows of pinnacles of white, blindingly white ice, pierced with the small regular cavities, elliptic in shape and running east and west, which are so rare in the Alps, where they are expressively called 'baignoires'. At each side of the great central band of white, there is a series of numerous other bands which are variously coloured according to the rocks of which the thick moraine covering is formed, ending in very dark bands at the edge. The sides of the valley become more and more wonderful, but the part which closes the extreme end of the glacier on the right remains the best of all. Now that we are higher up, its sharp gables seem to have grown lower and smaller, but the great snowy peak at the back stands up higher above them and looks down upon them, marvellously beautiful. Looking up the valley, which still continues its great curve, all we can see of the right side—apart from a beautiful glacier which leaps with a single fall of *séracs* from its basin above into the Siachen—is the spur beyond which the mighty ice-stream winds away to disappear from view. This spur rises into an extremely steep mountain which reminded me of the bold steepness of the Jorasses seen from the French side. The left side, on the other hand, slopes away much more gently, and the rocks here are almost black—slate schists where the granite ends. It is rather uniform and not perhaps very impressive in a place where we are accustomed to such very impressive mountains; it is less impressive because it represents merely the last spurs of a tremendous lateral buttress. On a higher level it rises into huge snowy shoulders.

From our high pinnacle of ice I also studied the best way to follow in order to reach the foot of this left side. It did, in fact, turn out that I had followed perhaps the best way, even when we came on to the band at the side of the glacier, which was very much broken up by crevasses, ice-walls, ravines and small lakes. I climbed on to a moderate-sized ridge of lateral moraine—a novelty, since up to this point the glacier goes right up to the rocky side of the valley. I had many other fine surprises from the thin, sharp ridge of this lateral moraine; beyond it was a ravine, and a little stream at the bottom opened out into a lovely little lake, in which all the neighbouring mountains were beautifully reflected, and on the side of the valley there were four or five big trunks of dried-up juniper trees and *burtse* in abundance.

What more could I hope for? This, at a height of 13,600 feet, became my 2nd advance camp on the Siachen.

2nd Advance Camp on the Siachen, June 13th, 1930.

Chapter XIV

ON THE MARCH TOWARDS THE BASE
CAMP ON THE SIACHEN GLACIER

The 2nd Advance Camp on the Siachen was a pretty spot and of happy memory, with its little lake and its comparative abundance of fuel. But it was certainly not in my programme to stay there four days. Even one day of unnecessary and unforeseen delay means upsetting my rather complicated plans for the month of June. If I could only explain to the men that, by obliging me to stop even one day longer than intended, they risk being without provisions or with short provisions later on, they would certainly carry out my orders more promptly. But henceforward, I hope and think everything will go more smoothly, for they have understood that I am kind, but that, on occasions, I can also be severe.

For the chronicle of the inside life of the caravan I must record that, during the first day we remained at the 2nd Camp, the men should have gone down to the previous camp and brought up half the loads left there, and the other half the day after. There is no doubt that it was a very laborious job, but I am moving by relatively short stages with the express purpose of making it not too laborious; this method of progress on the glacier is also absolutely necessary, if the distribution of provisions is to be kept regular, as it should be and as I wish it to be.

The first day of our halt at the 2nd Camp the porters went, but did not return: they returned the next day. I reproved them, but without giving great importance to my reproofs. But on the third day the men, ignoring my orders, delayed so long before starting for the 1st Camp that it was obvious that they did not intend to return till the next day again. Then severity took the place of mildness. I went for them as hard as I could with the few Hindustani words I possessed, and with

135

a few Italian ones whose tone indicated their meaning. The reply was like a sort of rebel chorus in an operetta. Then I judged that the moment had come to pick out the ringleader —a young fellow from Nubra, whom I had already observed to be a ready grumbler. I went towards him with a threatening attitude, and he found himself grasped . . . by the pigtail, and held firmly. The effect was magical, and was increased when I drew out a rope to bind the rebel. Many of them probably believed that his last moment had actually come, for they knelt in supplication and crawled along the ground till they touched my legs lightly with their hands, which they then placed to their foreheads. The end of it was that I called up each group and told them that anybody who wished to serve me must obey me blindly: anyone who did not want to must go away at once, but must give back to me the provisions and the wages I had advanced to him. Each group replied in chorus that they only wished to obey my orders. However, I left no choice to the fellow from Nubra: I gave him three days' provisions, that is, what was strictly necessary for him to get to Panamik at a good speed, and orders to restore to the *wazir* the wages he had not earned.

So ended a scene, more of a farce than a tragedy, which would have amused anyone who could have been a spectator of it. I do not know how I managed to contain myself when the young ringleader was struggling as hard as he could to escape from his predicament, with the grave risk of losing his pigtail and with it his honour.

That was a morning of great stir at the 2nd Camp, but, apart from this, everything was quiet. The nights are gener-ally very cold, and the north wind at dawn had woken me before Rasul appeared at my tent door with the *chota hazri*—that is, breakfast—of black coffee and biscuits, which I allow myself in order to provide fuel and energy for my morning's work. Actually the chickens woke me up even before the dawn. Every evening they obediently collected in an enclosure made of provision-cases and covered with a large tent-cloth; but early in the morning, at five or six, unexpectedly and, by some inex-plicable means, in perfect unison, they chanted their song of greeting to the new-born day; and then continued each on its own account. There were 70 of them, and the concert of dissonant sounds which accompanied my morning awakening may be imagined. I speak in the past tense, because every morning the concert was feebler and more plaintive: exploring the Siachen is evidently not meant for hens. It was perhaps for this reason that at our departure from the 1st as well as from the 2nd Camp there was open rebellion among the hens against being caught and shut up in the great hampers in which they travelled really very comfortably on a man's shoulder. It was really a most exhilarating sight—70 men trying to catch 70 hens, up and down over the moraines, performing feats of cunning and dexterity among the loads piled up ready for starting; they would stalk them slowly and make a sudden bound. The men were enormously amused, and so were we. But the amusement is now more or less finished, together with the sack of corn I had brought to feed my walking poultry-farm. And here, at the 3rd Camp, we have already embarked upon a slaughter of half the innocents.

The quiet of the 2nd Camp—the minute calculations required by the difficulties of the commissariat, of course, never cease—allowed me a walk or two on the top of the lateral moraine, up the little valley between it and the mountain-side and up the granite side itself. From this run out a few small ravines which have formed their fans inside the little valley which runs parallel to the glacier, and thus each fan, blocking it, has formed small lakes, or flat spaces of marshy ground. It is curious to go up the little valley, passing from one to another of its chain of lakes, without the slightest indication that, just beyond the moderate-sized bank of moraine, black with ancient schists, stretches the largest glacier in the world. But one has only to mount up a little, on to the top of the moraine or on the mountain-side, and the Siachen reappears at once in all its seemingly limitless immensity. Behind us, the whole of the tongue at the end of the glacier had now disappeared from view deep down between the mountain-walls which enclose it at the sides and form, as it were, side-barriers to it as it winds hither and thither. In front of us, in the direction to which my eyes turn with ever-growing curiosity, opens out a long stretch of the glacier which increases steadily in width and is now almost straight and almost follows the direction which it afterwards keeps right up to its head near the Karakoram watershed. But we were too close up against the left side to see the peaks and ridges at its top, except for a few snowy ridges which appear at the summit of the evenly sloping side (of an evenly dark colour, too, a little beyond my camp), and a few other ridges, also snowy, which can be seen, through the narrow opening of a valley, rising from a farther level. The really imposing mountains are not on this side, and on this side the rocks, less hard and resistant, take the form of ridges and domes rather than of pinnacles and towers. The same foreshortening also prevents one seeing the exact details of this side; one sees it stretching away into the distance, and then growing smaller and lower and coming finally to an end in two or three blackish hillocks; this, actually, is the point of confluence of the Teram Sher, the principal affluent of the Siachen, and it is there that I shall pitch my base-camp not many days hence. Beyond the small rocky spur which marks the point of confluence—the 'Junction', as the Workmans called it—and beyond the great tongue of the Teram Sher, rises a wonderful peak, an immense pyramid, flanked at the sides by two straight corner-ridges, while a third comes down from the top in our direction: this is Mount Rose, one of the giants.

If I wished to revel in the sight of precipices, towers and pinnacles, I had only to look over the tongue of the glacier at the opposite side, which is entirely of granite; but it was only a limited view, because a last curve in the Siachen prevented my seeing farther than the bold side-barrier of rock whose steepness rises finally into the peak which now seems identical, for me, with the peak of the Jorasses as seen from the French side.

The nights at the 2nd Camp have been cold but calm, the days on the whole fine, though threatening. Only last night was not cold, and it snowed for a good hour, but the snow did not lie except on the surfaces of the Siachen which were not too thickly covered with moraine, so that the glacier took on an unusually white appearance.

This morning, when we got up—more hastily than usual, throughout the whole camp—it was snowing again and the sky was hopelessly overcast and grey in every direction. This was not the best of omens for moving camp, as according to plan.

A SMALL LAKE IN THE CENTRAL RIDGE OF LIVING ICE

[face p. 138

On the other hand, there was no other course to take; every delay increases each difficulty to a quite unexpected degree. I made the men leave behind their personal belongings and the days' rations already distributed to them, so as to be at least sure that the whole of the camp would be moved, and I gave each in addition a small supply of fuel as a precautionary measure.

To-day's stage was not a long one. To begin with, the weather was certainly not inviting: better to stay shut up in one's tent than to look for a path across the immense glacier, lashed by the wind and the sleet, with a limited view of mountains shut in behind a grey curtain of cloud and mist. I climbed over the lateral moraine and crossed the outside belt of the Siachen, which is characterized by a blackish covering of lime and slate schists, and in particular by an extremely broken surface, very rough in the labyrinth of hillocks and cleft by crevasses, holes and ravines.

I crossed straight over it by the shortest route; and having quickly reached the other belt which runs along the great central ridge of white ice, found that our progress up the Siachen immediately became quicker and more secure. But it must be understood that this, like everything else in the world, was a relative matter. However, we had to be content with it; here, at any rate, the surface of the glacier was no longer broken by hillocks, often steep and sharp, or complicated by crevasses and formations due to erosion; there were only gentle undulations, which again forced us to be continually going up and down, but at least without the preoccupation of a continual search for the best way. The way is easy and clearly marked, for one had only to keep to the side of the great ridge of white ice.

After four hours' march, with wind almost all the time, and sleet, and a dull, heavy, completely grey sky, we took a short breathing-space—short, because there was nothing whatever to invite one to prolong the halt. After this, I judged it advisable to go close again to the side of the great ice-valley in order to look for the three customary requisites of a good camping-ground—shelter from the wind, water, and fuel. As the valley here makes its last great curve—the great precipitous flank of the Jorasses was now on my left—I did not turn sharply, but simply cut across gradually to the right, making for the side.

But alas! we immediately found ourselves on the broken ground of the marginal belt, which was here, owing to the bend in the valley, much wider and much rougher than before. Patience was needed, and we had to work our way forward, finding a way through this veritable labyrinth which became more and more complicated with crevasses, deep ravines, holes and ditches and ramifying lakes. We went continually up and down without respite, and also without seeing anything, as there was always at least one new hillock blocking one's view of the way in front. I saw one higher than the rest and immediately made for it in order to study our course better and decide on a definite objective. Taking out my field-glasses, I could see that the side, fairly close now, came down in rocky precipices or smooth surfaces of detritus, without a sign—I do not say, of trees—but even of *burtse,* the modest little plant whose woody roots are the greatest resource of travellers. I came to a rapid decision; it was useless to plunge again into the tumultuous sea of ice-hillocks so exhausting to cross, and also useless to reach the side of the valley. I caught sight of a small depression in a higher belt of the glacier—the lower portions, even if more inviting, are always to be avoided for the dangers they may conceal in the event of the sudden emptying of a glacial lake; it was fairly well sheltered from the wind, there was any amount of water, and I had brought a little wood with me, as a precaution, so this, at an altitude of 14,700 feet, became my 3rd advance camp on the Siachen.

3rd Advance Camp on the Siachen, June 20th, 1930.

The caravan was prompt in arriving the other day. A few of the men performed wonders in adapting the ground, with surprising speed, for the pitching of our tents; they then went off after their companions. The new system is working perfectly. I make the coolies leave their provisions and personal baggage at the previous camp, so that they have no *impedimenta* to speak of; they carry more of my camp equipment, they carry for a shorter distance the provisions which they are gradually consuming, and the idea that they have got to do the journey back to the previous camp where their meal is awaiting them makes them quicker on the march.

It must not be thought that the coolies' own baggage is small in quantity. The mere fact that they continue to eat for two days in the lower camp gets rid of five loads which they would have to transport to the next camp (my own camp), if I made them spend the night here. It is difficult to get an exact idea of what constitutes the actual personal baggage of these people when they are on the march. I provided them with little tents so that they might pass the nights, which are already pretty cold, under shelter. They were pleased with them, but they do not use them—just as we ourselves, sometimes, want some lovely object and then, having obtained it, put it aside or in a box, because it is a luxury and not part of everyday life. They are accustomed to sleeping in the open, so they continue to sleep in the open even when they might be in shelter. At least, they have done so up till now. The tent-cloths have served as a chicken-run, as coverings for flour or butter or fuel, but not yet as shelters for human beings.

It is obvious that these men, in order to show such a complete independence of the luxury of tents, must have resources in their own customs which permit of such independence. There is no doubt that the Ladakhi costume is specially devised for protection against the cold. They wear a kind of ample woollen shirt, trousers of the same heavy white material (which the women weave at home in long, very narrow widths), high leggings of felt tied round the legs with strong woollen laces, then an ample robe which folds over in front and is held simply by a belt at the waist. This is the usual costume. But when they travel, they generally wear a second robe and on top of it —most important of all—the 'postin', a big fur cloak down to the feet, with the fur inside and leather outside. At night, when any other mortal would put on one sweater or jacket on top of another, the Ladakhis undress completely and then wrap themselves in their abundant travelling clothes—their robes and *postin*. Then they lie down on the ground. It may rain, snow or freeze, for all they care! The tents I brought can perfectly well be used for the chickens and the fuel!

In the meantime the personal *impedimenta* of the coolies are both heavy and voluminous; there are, besides, big pots, great ladles, cups, a mountain of bags in which there is a little of everything—wool, needles, pieces of leather, spindles (for the Ladakhi can justly repeat, in Tibetan, 'omnia mea mecum porto'); finally, most of my porters have the high altitude equipment which I issued to them, but which up till now is simply an equipment *de luxe*, just as the tents are. Only a few woollen helmets have appeared in use so far.

The new system adopted on the march up the Siachen has had other advantages, for there would not have been room for the whole caravan at the 3rd Camp. I had the main part of the baggage brought up during the two days after our arrival, and deposited on the smooth belt near the bank of white ice —which also avoided an unnecessary *détour* over the difficult part which is covered with jagged hillocks; and the coolies also stopped last night near the baggage-dump. There is another considerable advantage: the caravan has been able, for two extra days, to benefit by the good juniper-wood which is comparatively abundant at the 2nd Camp, whereas, at the next camp, only a little *burtse* could be collected by the men whom I sent to explore the mountain-sides for the purpose.

It was, indeed, a wretched camp, our 3rd advance camp on the Siachen. The tents were pitched in a very irregular line along the bottom of a very small depression among the mounds of moraine-covered ice. The ground had to be levelled as well as might be and little walls built, so as to make sufficient space for each tent. A series of crevasses crossed the little depression; there was one which passed just where the ten coolies who are with me established themselves, and another at the spot where Kadir placed his fires. They were, of course, filled with stones and lumps of rock, but if a slight widening had occurred our kitchen and the men's pots would have run the risk of making the acquaintance of the unexplored depths of the Siachen.

Nor was this risk an entirely imaginary one. During the night—for I slept badly at the 3rd Camp—I really 'felt' how alive the glacier was. The dull plunge of big lumps falling into some lake; a rolling sound of flints in some crevasse, which seemed to go on for ever; then, suddenly, almost underneath my bed, a deep mysterious crash—a new cleavage in

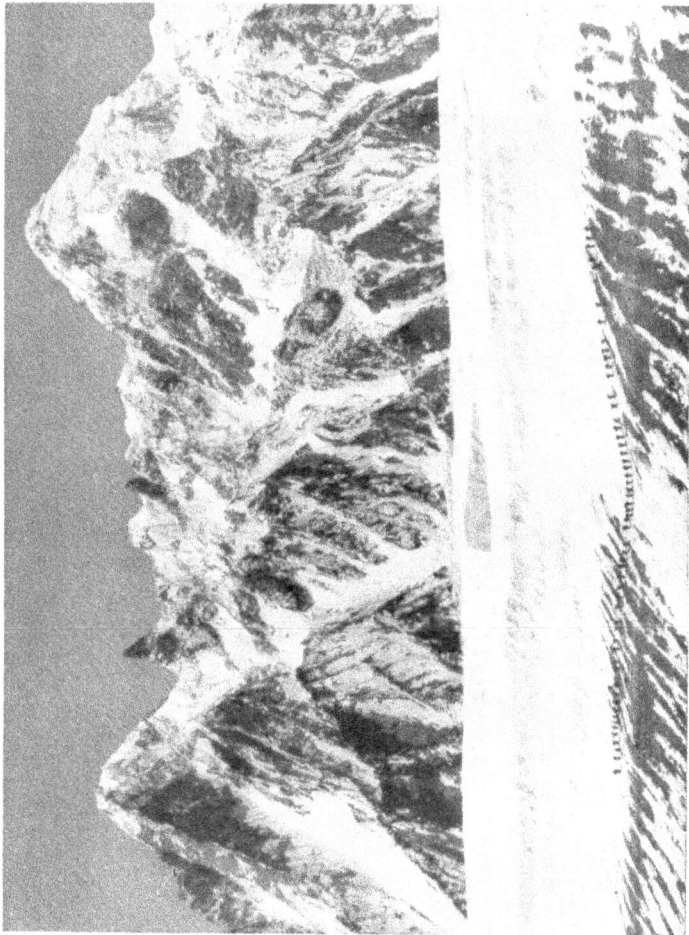

THE CARAVAN ON THE MARCH TOWARDS THE BASE CAMP

[*face p.* 142

the mass of ice. This was at night, when all life, even that of the glacier, seemed to be suspended by cold and frost. But by day, one had only to go a little distance from the camp, with its chattering servants, the murmuring sound of some porter at his prayers, and the petulant crowing of cocks, then stop on the top of a mound and listen attentively, to hear innumerable unsuspected noises and rumblings. These are the thousand voices by which the multiform life of the glacier shows itself.

Yes, it was a wretched camp, my 3rd advance camp on the Siachen, but so picturesque in its wretchedness! And then, it placed us in direct contact with this immense world of ice, and more completely in the midst of the high mountains —magnificent, incredible. It was a joy to climb one or other of the higher hillocks by which we were surrounded and revel in the beauty of the mountains. The side opposite me attracted me most of all. It was so close—separated only by the width of the Siachen, that is, by a few miles—that no detail escaped one. It is cleft by a few valleys, which would be large in the Alps but look small here, and these are filled by glaciers which come down steeply in fall after fall, enclosed at the sides by walls, still of granite, that rise straight up as though the rocks had been sharply cut, and, up above, break into pointed crags from which rise a row of quite thin, sharp, dizzy spires. The Jorasses, seen from here, had completely changed their appearance: they looked like a single gigantic spire, rising from a moderate-sized base at the level of the glacier, growing thinner and thinner and ending in a peak of incredible sharpness. To the north of it opens a large valley, with a wide glacier consisting of alternate falls of *sérac* and wide, flat spaces of snow which then rise, gently almost, towards a distant line of ridge, dazzlingly white in the sunshine. Then I looked towards the upper Siachen. The high, regular pyramid of Mount Rose has disappeared, but from certain of the hillocks one can just see its extreme top appearing above one of the dark precipices of the valley-side. In the background there is a really supreme group of mountains—the King George chain, which runs straight in our direction, piling up one vast peak above another. There are two extremely bold, quite distinct, peaks, and behind

143

them rises the enormous mass of K²³, the Hidden Peak, over 26,000 feet high. These are the real giants.

This morning I started again on the forward march. I employed the usual method: the whole camp moved forward; only ten men remained permanently with it; the majority went back at once to bring up the baggage-dumps during the next two days.

We had a splendid march, the weather brilliant and clear. From the camp, passing through the usual hillocks which make progress so exhausting, I quickly reached the grey strip of moraine which stretches along the central belt of white ice. The surface forms of the glacier are continually changing, and now this strip is only slightly undulating; it forms a great high road for our march forward, between the belt of often impassable hillocks on one side, and on the other the high ridges and banks of white ice

However, as we advanced, our road seemed to be gradually rising, and at the same time the level of the ridges and banks of uncovered ice seemed to be getting lower. There was more snow lying even on the moraine-covered surfaces; the Siachen, in fact, tends to become more uniform in shapes, appearance and colour the farther one goes up it. So, at least, it seemed to us, though if we could see it from above, its great series of belts would still be there and still obvious.

Towards three in the afternoon I judged it to be time to halt; I went down a little way from the "high road" on to a little flat space enclosed by the loop of a stream. A stream on the glacier? Yes, and wide enough to be impassable. We have ice on all sides, rising in lovely shapes in walls, pinnacles, high ridges and banks. In places it sinks into huge depressions, occupied by lakes; and where the water, either of streams or lakes, has hollowed out the base of the walls, there hang long festoons of icicles, which look like shining, iridescent fringes. As we are a little lower than the level of the glacier, we can see nothing but an apparently endless whiteness and gigantic mountains in every direction.

When the sun had already set and the uncertain light which succeeds the short twilight was already invading the whole valley, I climbed up on to the top of the first ice-bank of the great central belt: the solemn silence of the evening already lay heavy over the glacier. Up there, there was a wind and a cold which numbed me.

The cold is intense, also, in this 4th advance camp in the midst of the ice world. I am encamped to-day at a height of about 15,070 feet.

4th Advance Camp on the Siachen, June 23rd, 1930.

Chapter XV

ARRIVAL AT THE OASIS OF TERAM SHER

We have had brilliant days and cold nights at the 4th Advance Camp on the Siachen. The moment the sun set, every rivulet, every drip or trickle of water which, when the sun was high, intersected the space where the camp was, began to freeze: it must not be forgotten that we were encamped on a glacier. The nights, therefore, were cold, and the feeling of cold was further increased by a very strong wind, which, though it might scarcely affect anyone who was sleeping in the little hermetically sealed "Whymper", yet penetrated with a whistling sound into my large tropical tent. But, to tell the truth, I also remained unaffected by it, lying hidden in my sleeping-bag, into which I disappear early in the evening, not to reappear until early next morning.

How lovely it is here, at this 4th Camp of mine! Ever since the 1st encampment, each new one had seemed more picturesque than the preceding ones and had brought me further into this majestic world of giants, yet the 4th Camp seemed at the time quite insurpassable, because nothing was to be seen from it in any direction but the immaculate whiteness of the glacier, no longer stained, no longer sordid—as it had really looked so far, owing to the long, wide belts of moraine.

From the 3rd Camp onwards, the tongue of the Siachen, monstrous and immense as it had looked before, had been steadily widening and growing, in consequence, even more beautiful. The central band of white ice tends actually to become broader and broader; and two lateral bands, one on each side, have crept in, thin at the beginning and as though squeezed between the moraine-covered strips, but afterwards becoming, little by little, steadily broader. At the height of the 4th Camp the huge extent of the glacier is already mainly white, of living ice, and the moraine-covered strips are thinner and more clearly defined, like slight dark markings on the white back of a great snake-like monster.

The unevenness of the glacier-surface had also become gradually more uniform, and the banks and ridges of ice, the mounds covered with lumps of rock and flint, tended to come down to the same uniform level. The irregularities in the surface of the Siachen were produced mainly by the erosion and melting caused by running water; there were regular valleys, with rushing, noisy torrents at the bottom of them, and real basins filled by lakes which generally had their outlet through large cracks of glassy, transparent, slightly greenish ice.

My 4th Camp was particularly beautiful, because, in spite of being right on the glacier and in the middle of it, one had no feeling of monotony; on the other hand, the surface of the ground—though it may seem rather odd to speak of the ground, when it was composed entirely of ice—was uneven, varied, hollowed out by a stream into a little valley with many windings; and the sides of this little valley were now smooth, now, on the contrary, formed of steep, perpendicular, or even overhanging, walls, from the upper rim of which, in the latter case, hung a beautiful fringe of icicles sparkling in the sun and looking as if so many iridescent pearls were dropping from them with the drops of water left upon them every now and then by the tumultuous stream.

The nearer view was beautiful in a picturesque way, the more distant view—that of the mountains—both beautiful and impressive. Less so the valley-side on the left, almost at the foot of which lay our camp. This was formed by the flank of a lateral buttress, which a little farther northwards comes to an end in a small spur at the point of confluence of the Siachen and its largest affluent, the Teram Sher. There were, therefore, no big valleys, only short ravines, generally cut out of the usual dark, almost black schist, which tends to make any feature of the landscape less rugged and therefore less imposing. But the head of the ravine which opened just opposite our 4th Camp was again composed of granite, and therefore formed a high, precipitous wall which renewed the impression of grandeur.

On the other side of the Siachen one could see that the

valley-wall went farther back and that the valleys were therefore deeper, with a variety of precipices, ridges, and peaks,
and great glacier-streams descending with a tumult of *séracs*
into the larger glacier. Thus there was a whole series of
glacier-basins, any of which, in the Alps, would deservedly be
a place of pilgrimage for mountain-lovers. There were so
many here, and all so beautiful—on the valley-sides and the
ridges, on the flat snowy spaces and the falls of *sérac*—that we
hardly knew which to admire most, and one's eye passed quickly
from one to the other with a sort of avidity—like that of a
child who wants to eat all the sweets on the table at his birthday
party, and all at the same time.

We had a different reason. Does one stop often, as one
goes up the Val d'Aosta, to look at and admire the rocky
crags of Monte Emilius and the snowy tops of the Rutor?
No, for one's whole anxiety and longing is to see Mont Blanc,
and one hardly dares take one's eyes off the opening between
the two sides of the valley in front of one, in expectation of
the giant's appearance.

Here the giants have already appeared. All the rest—
precipices, towers, spires, glacier—which in the Alps would
seem so amazing (as indeed it is), here forms only the frame,
the foreground, as it were the advance guard of other much
grander and more imposing mountains. They are all over
there, at the head of the Siachen. The wonderful thing about
them is that one would almost think they did not form a
continuous ridge, even though, just over there, is the highest
ridge of the biggest mountain-range on earth. Each mountain
seems to rise all by itself from this lofty base of over 16,400
feet; each seems to refuse to have any connection, to allow
its sides any relationship with the neighbouring mountains,
and rises alone, independent, as though in a competition of
height and grandeur. It merely throws out at its sides a
few low spurs which join it on to other mountains or become
lost in the wide, icy stretch of the Siachen, but there are only
a few of these low spurs, as though to enhance the majesty
of the mountain itself. Each is a colossus, a giant, a king
among mountains. Gombo, the pious lama, ought to have
come as far as this: who knows how many divinities he would
have seen, shining and diffusing their own divine light, in-

visible to infidels, from these peaks which are noble, solemn, divinely beautiful even to those who have not the piety of the old lama? There is one on the left, the Hawk, which towers above its surroundings and ends in a snowy hump shaped like the beak of a bird of prey, giving it an appearance of rugged strength and pride. Then, right above the central line of the glacier, are the peaks of the so-called King George chain which we see almost in file one behind the other, yet without their losing their individual character of bold magnificence. And, behind all, is the last giant, the Hidden Peak, with its vast snow-covered shoulders. Towards the right is the pyramid of Mount Rose, sharp and steep with its regular faces and corners. But in the background, between the Hidden Peak and Mount Rose, one can see smooth slopes of snow coming down almost to the level of the Siachen: this is the opening of the Indira Pass which cuts through the main ridge of the Karakoram, and of which Younghusband caught a glimpse from the northern slopes at the end of his long and adventurous journey across almost the whole of Asia; it was also the essential cause why Longstaff, when he went in search of it, finally discovered this giant among the glaciers of the earth.

I was tremendously busy at the 4th Camp. There was the distribution of provisions to all the men, which I make at short intervals so as to oblige them to return to the fold in good time, even if they do not very much want to. In the meantime, all the baggage-dumps have been brought up during the two days we have halted; I have even sent on a few sacks of provisions in order to facilitate my plans, which were beginning to be even more complicated.

This morning, in fact, I have moved the encampment for the last stage of our advance towards the Base Camp on the Siachen. As usual, only 10 men came with me as permanent staff; the others, having transferred the camp and being without their own personal baggage, had to return to the 4th Camp— not, however, as before, to bring up what had been left behind, but to go down to Zingrul, where three more tons of provisions for the porters are waiting. I distributed eight days' rations of butter and salt and tea: flour they will find on the way down, left behind in small deposits; and on the way up they will consume some of what they are carrying on their own shoulders. Three days to go down, five to come up; on July 4th they should be here at the Base Camp with a little under 2 tons of fresh provisions. But meanwhile all that I have managed to bring along with me remains at the 4th Camp and my 10 men have just enough to eat till the evening of the 4th. This shortage is due to the day they caused me to lose on the way up, which upset my carefully worked out plans. Moreover, it will have consequences later on too, as it will force me into delays and complicated expedients in order to carry out my future excursions on the glaciers. In the meantime we have plenty of provisions for ourselves, and here at the Base Camp we are almost in a sort of paradise.

This morning's march was almost like taking a walk, but an extremely beautiful walk. Leaving the little flat space of the 4th encampment, bounded by the loop of the stream in its deep furrow, one had merely to cross straight over on to the moraine-covered strip which runs along the great central belt of white ice. Actually it is becoming more difficult to distinguish between them: the central belt of white ice becomes wider and wider, but also flatter, and the strip of moraine rises gradually to the same level, becoming narrower until it finally loses all irregularity of surface and is covered for the most part in fresh and as yet unmelted snow. Thus the Siachen, as one goes up it, becomes steadily wider and more impressive, but at the same time more uniform in its surface, which is now almost completely flat and almost all white with ice or snow, the moraines upon it being now reduced to nothing more than slender longitudinal bands, uniform all along their course both in prominence and in colour—just like stripes on the back of a monstrous serpent.

Meanwhile, as we advanced so easily along the flat, striped back of this apparently calm, domesticated monster, the mountains became more and more imposing, both in fact and in appearance. Not yet those on our right: on that side they came to a sudden, almost sheer end, and then continued in a narrow, low band of dark rocks, above which could just be seen another band, a white one—the Teram Sher Glacier—which sends out a few lateral branches, breaking the uniform continuity of the low band of rocks. At the point where the latter begins, where it joins the side of the valley with a short

MOUNT HAWK

[*face p.* 150

re-entrant curve, was the place where my Base Camp was to be established. On the opposite side the mountains were more and more marvellous: when we turned round we could see—as we see from here too—the slopes which face north and are therefore more thickly covered with snow; so one gets the contrast between the rugged rock of precipices, ridges and peaks, and the whiteness of little glaciers hanging as though ready to fall at any moment, of larger glaciers flowing tortuously down the valleys, and of mantles of snow which introduce here and there into the landscape lines of a softness which is very unusual here. K⁸ is extremely beautiful; its long ridge, made up of snowy shoulders and angles and rising into a broad majestic pyramid of rock slightly sprinkled with snow, rises up higher than any other mountain in that direction, although it is in the background, right on the horizon. In the foreground, as we continued on our way up the glacier, we had a clearer view of the huge giants which surround the head of the Siachen, as though to protect it from profane assaults. The Hawk, with its beak-like top; the Twins, joined in massive strength; the Ghent, with its snow-covered peak shaped like the bows of a saddle; the Hardinge and the Queen Mary in the King George chain, bold and pointed; the Hidden Peak, a gigantic mass; the last bastion between the Baltoro and Siachen glaciers, Mount Rose, with its perfectly regular pyramid; then, more to the right, Teram Kangri, which has only just appeared, with the many peaks of its long ridge—these are the giants of the Siachen, which become more and more clearly visible to us, more and more imposing in the mighty formations by which each is characterized and actually detached from the others. Near us and all round us, on the other hand, was the vast, uniform, flat expanse of the glacier, as though to give us the illusion that approach to the giants was humanly quite an easy matter. Approach, perhaps, but no more; one may admire, but not desire, and only admire from down below: these are heights not made for men.

When I arrived at about half-past twelve, followed by the whole caravan, right in front of the little bay by which the mountain-side on our right joins the low spur of dark rock, I judged it a suitable moment to halt, partly in order to draw breath. It was a question of establishing our Base Camp, not a provisional encampment which might be placed more or less haphazard, as our previous camps had perhaps been. This, on the other hand, was to be our centre of activity for at least a month and a half; it must be properly arranged, the tents must not be pitched hastily, but with calculated care and with at least a sufficiency of space. To get here early I had hurried a little over lunch; besides, I could see the dark rocks not far off, perhaps not farther than 5 furlongs, or even less; they were so clear in every detail that it looked almost as if one could touch them with one's hand. But easier said than done. To cross that half-mile of the glacier took us no less than $3\frac{1}{2}$ hours. When one goes up or down a glacier, everything depends on choosing, or finding by luck, a good (and if possible the best) longitudinal belt or strip. But when a glacier—and a glacier such as the Siachen—has to be crossed, one must be prepared to make one's way over belts that are good, indifferent, and also bad.

We did not come across any really bad belts. However, we had at once to cross a small valley cut out of the ice, with its stream, the same which wound so picturesquely round our 4th Camp; after that we climbed straight on to another greyish strip of moraine—quite easy going. Then another strip cut across it, black, full of high, sharp hillocks, intersected with precipices and cavities filled with pools—unpleasant, but short. Then the living ice again—a piece of good luck, we thought. But it was anything but good luck. It was a very wide belt, all broken up into banks, causeways and pinnacles. We turned into a small valley, but the bottom was a regular bog, owing to the intense melting of the snow, and it was crossed frequently by crevasses, covered or otherwise, which forced us to make frequent *détours*. Then we realized that the valley was taking us in the wrong direction: we had to cross banks and causeways and pinnacles to get to another, and so go forward again. This game went on much longer than I had expected. But at last it ended: at last we were quite close to the rocks, and had got over the last line of banks and pinnacles. All at once, at the foot of a regular wall of ice, between it and the rocky side, opened out a lake, in which large slabs and picturesque lumps of ice floated on the water, which was slightly ruffled by the wind. Beyond this a broad stream of ice, a lateral branch from the great mass of the Teram Sher, all broken up into *séracs*, comes down almost to the lake, into which it sends its foaming, noisy waters. But on both sides of this—on one side, where the side of the Siachen Valley appears to be interrupted, and on the other, where there is a short succession of low rocks as far as the point of confluence of the Teram Sher—on both sides an unusual, unexpected sight made me almost doubt whether all the brilliance of ice and snow which I had seen during the day—even though modified by big smoked glasses—had not affected my sense of colour. No, there was no doubt: it was real green which we saw on each side of the frozen overflow of the Teram, the very pale green of a kind of short grass which covers the flat places and the more gentle of the slopes to which the wildest and most rugged mountains in the world suddenly descend—like a giant stooping down to play with children, or a cruel tyrant whose face breaks suddenly into a smile. This green is all the more unexpected, right in the middle of this immense world of ice, if one thinks of the bare aridity of the valleys and mountains of the whole region, even where man lives and is able with patient toil to produce, with the aid of water and a meagre soil, a vegetation which even so is confined strictly to the oases.

For years I have longed to traverse this great world of ice; for almost two months we have been crossing mountainous districts almost without a tree; for weeks, ever since Sabu, we have seen no natural grass; for weeks, also, we have been coming up the endless glacier—and suddenly, right in the middle of it, appears all at once a perfectly green oasis.

Followed by all the men, I went off the glacier on to the rocks, skirted half the lake, going along its shore, climbed a short slope near the torrent which issues, noisy and tumultuous, from the great mass of the Teram: here there was a flat space which seemed made for a camping-ground. The tents were soon pitched, in full view of the little lake with its slabs and lumps of ice wandering from one side to another according to the changing play of wind or current; in view also of the great wall of ice with which the Siachen encloses the waters of the lake, and of the rugged, snowy mountains on the right-hand side of the great valley, behind which, right in the background, rises the vast ridge of K^8, highest of them all. But all round

153

us there is grass, green grass, and hundreds of flowers. It seems almost a dream.

When we arrived a short time ago, there was a strange sight to be seen. The men from Tia, the moment they had put down their loads, started off, laughing and shouting, on a mad race up the slope. Their laughing and shouting was caused not only by the thing which had set them off on this sudden race, but also by the fact that they easily outdistanced the men from other groups who were also taking part in the strange Marathon. Suddenly the men from Tia stopped in the middle of a pile of rocks, stooped down, and then came down again towards the tents, slowly and in a close group, as though in solemn procession. Then they stopped again, and looked as though they were occupied with some serious matter, in contrast with the shouts and laughter and the mad race of a few moments before. I went to look, and found that they had taken possession of two enormous skeletons of Himalayan ibex, which had been preserved with the skins almost entire, and the men were taking off and collecting the large amount of skin which was left, with an almost religious care. I knew the Ladakhis, and remembered the joy of my men at the discovery and conquest—not, indeed, difficult—of a newly-dead gazelle on the Tibetan plateaux of Lingzi-Tang. But I really could not understand the mad race, the rejoicing, and then this serious concern over two skeletons of ibex which had been dead goodness knows how long. But with the Ladakhis there is always something to learn.

All the men except 10 will have to go back to the 4th Camp, and go on down to-morrow towards Zingrul, at the glacier-end, where in the meanwhile a large new depôt of provisions has been accumulating. They asked to be allowed to spend the night here, in the green oasis. I pointed out that they had neither provisions nor *postin*, since these had been left at the 4th Camp. It did not matter, they replied: as for eating, they could make up for that to-morrow morning, and as for sleeping, there was plenty of *burtse*. But when night came on, quite clear, the north wind must have been too penetrating, for they disappeared silently, in groups, into the darkness, across the great glacier towards the 4th Camp.

But how beautiful it is, this calm, starry night! And how

154

beautiful it was, too, just before sunset, when everything was already in shadow, and only K^8, the giant which rises above all the other mountains, still shone with the last rays of a tropical sun glinting on its ice and snow!

Base Camp on the Siachen, June 26th, 1930.

CHAPTER XVI

LIFE IN AN OASIS AMONGST THE ICE

Every day that passes in this Base Camp of mine brings me some new marvel. We are actually in an oasis, a real oasis in the midst of a world of ice.

Not far from here, a little above us, the Siachen is joined by its largest affluent, the Teram Sher, which runs from a due easterly direction. This is one reason why I am particularly interested in it and have chosen it for special observation, for just beyond its head extends the great Rimo Glacier, in the first exploration of which I took part sixteen years ago. The wide ice-stream of the Teram Sher runs westwards; and as the Siachen runs south-eastwards, it comes about that the buttress of mountain at the point of confluence narrows down to an extraordinary degree, into a long, low ridge of rock, breaking abruptly off from the superb heights to which it attains. At the foot of this long, thin, low ridge of rock runs the Siachen; and over the top of it, flowing in the opposite direction, appears the Teram Sher, which, swollen as it is, seems in a hurry to throw itself into the larger glacier, and sends out three or four lateral overflows down across the dividing rocks. The largest of these lateral overflows is precisely at the point where the buttress of mountain is abruptly broken off and the narrow band of rocks begins, and the point where the two join is marked by a little bay. From above, precipitous and full of *séracs*, falls the lateral tongue of the Teram; below, the mighty mass of the Siachen completely shuts in the rocky bay and causes the formation of a lake.

My Base Camp is on a small flat space on the slope which descends to the lake, between the two glaciers, in the midst of a world of ice which, in immensity, has no equal on earth, except possibly in the ice-caps round the Poles. We are barely half-way up the length of the glacier: it would take at least five days' march to reach its head, at least five days to get off it at

its end, five days also to get off it in the direction of the
Saltoro Valley, whence came its first discoverer, Longstaff
(but without reaching my oasis), and whence came also his
successors, the Workmans. This had been the only way of
approach, by the Saltoro Valley and over a pass, the Bilafon-la,
of over 18,000 feet. All other ways of approach were closed,
and, more so than any of them—if one were to believe both old
and recent travellers and explorers of the region—the one which,
of all of them, should be the most natural, that is, by the
front of the glacier. We, however, have proved that the
Siachen is not inaccessible by way of the front: here I am,
with a large caravan, heavy baggage, tons of provisions, without
having looked for side-doors (or back-doors), but having come
straight in, honourably, by the great front-door itself. However, here we are in the midst of the ice, in the largest and perhaps the most difficult ice-region in the world.

I am sometimes tempted to forget this, when I am busy in
the camp with boxes and bags, and especially when I stay
inside my tent to write or to check my endless calculations.
Oh, these calculations, what a torment they are! I think I
have already spoken of the difficulties an explorer has to contend
with when he has to transport everything by means of porters,
who themselves also have the right to exist, that is to say, to eat,
and therefore require still other men to carry provisions for
them. I remember I also explained how, not wishing that the
calculation should go on multiplying itself *ad infinitum*, I had to
have recourse to drastic measures in order to cut it short. But
here things are greatly complicated, because fuel also has to be
transported. It must be understood that each group of men
consumes, every day, not less than five loads of *burtse*, the little
plant which creeps along the ground, whose woody roots give
a fine flare and also a little heat; luckily there is plenty of it
here. Well, on the march up the glacier I am reducing to one
load only the daily provision of *burtse* for all the men, whatever
their number may be—which is a real hardship, when one has
to live, and also sleep, on the glacier.

To lessen the numbers of the caravan, and hence also the
necessity of provisions, I have sent the Nubra men back to their
own homes. Thus there remain with me 57 men, the three
groups from Timosgam, Tia, and Leh. But this number is

diminished by the couriers who come and go between the camp and Gombo, and by the sick, of whom there are always some in a caravan, because someone always gets wounded or bruised, or suffers from the high altitude, or eats too many *chupattis*, or just wants to make a good excuse and take a day or two of rest. So the 57 men are merely on paper, and the lesser number which actually exists has to be used by the unfortunate commandant to solve problems which almost always appear insoluble.

When I am racking my brains in my tent over such problems, however, I have only to look out to get consolation and fresh energy for my difficult tasks. On one side descends the vast mass of the Teram with its livid, moraine-covered *séracs*; on the other side is the white wall of the Siachen, topped with pinnacles, forming a low foreground for a series of lofty mountains, snow-covered, bold and impressive. In the middle I see the little lake, always slightly ruffled by the wind and itself also rather livid in colour, since the waters which feed it are laden with the fine dirt of the glacier; but when we arrived it was covered with great white slabs, and large irregular blocks of ice which had fallen from the broken wall of the Siachen were floating in it. Every morning without fail the slabs and blocks of ice were to be found collected at the foot of the ice-wall of the Siachen, and during the day, just as infallibly, moved away very, very slowly in the opposite direction, until they were all reassembled against the bank on the side nearest the Teram. However, during these few days, both are so much reduced in size that probably they will have soon disappeared completely. The melting all over the glacier increases every day, so much so that the couriers going to Gombo already have serious difficulties in fording the Nubra; they tell me that we shall soon be entirely cut off from the outside world—the front-door of the Siachen will be completely shut till the autumn.

Never mind: we have come in—and by the main entrance —without extreme difficulties. Now we are revelling in the fantastic grandeur of the enchanted palace, the garden of which is here.

Below the Teram Sher, between its lateral overflows, are steep slopes of rock—bare walls, precipitous farther up, that is, farther towards the point of confluence of the two great glaciers. But here there are rounded summits which descend in platforms and gentle slopes, only interrupted by a few short cliffs. On two of the platforms a little above the camp, are two little lakes, but not so picturesque as the one we call "our" lake. The more gentle slopes of these rounded hills—as though to emphasize the contrast with the surrounding grandeur and ruggedness—are covered with smooth green grass, sometimes sparse, with little parched-looking stalks, but in most places thick, so as to constitute a meadow, a real meadow, and often even a kind of deep, soft quilt such as is seen in certain hollows in the Alps, the bottom of which has been the bottom of a lake or a marsh.

Imagine finding meadows, proper meadows, right in the middle of the Siachen! Especially when the whole region, even outside the glaciers, is characterized by an almost entire lack of green or of any vegetation. And these are meadows in which green is not the only colour. There are pieces of ground where the soil is scarce and the lumps of rock scattered over it are consequently more frequent: here the grass is thinner, but there is an abundance of flowers instead. Then, as one walks over these hills of deep black schist or pink granite, there are moments when one does not see the ground green with grass, but purple or bright yellow or pale pink from the masses of flowers which, so it seems, are careful to avoid the mixing of different kinds and prefer to grow in groups, here or there, according to each separate kind. Primulas are the most plentiful—a circle of small leaves like rays, then a tall straight stalk, and on top a colony of flowers, which sometimes grow so close together that they seem to form a little compact sphere of a pale but bright violet. Whenever the soil appears to be drier, there are no primulas; here supremacy is divided between a kind of bright yellow flower of the pea family, which in the Nubra Valley (the desert-like character of the Nubra Valley must be remembered) is surrounded with a multitude of long treacherous thorns, but which here, on the other hand, seems to grow gentler, being surrounded only with little soft leaves —and a kind of flower like a small, round, white cushion crowned with a circle of pink petals.

Miss Kalau, when she returns from one of her little excursions on the rocks between the two glaciers, always brings with her a large harvest of flowers, which immediately go to increase our collection. And as the season appears to develop in a much more rapid cycle here than it does down below there are new flowers coming out every day, adding the brightness of their colours and the gracefulness of their shapes. It is interesting to notice their preferences; some prefer the drier and more rocky slopes, others the diffused dampness of the thick, soft meadows. One kind grows all alone, rare but vigorous, in the lumps of earth which chance has placed between two branches of a stream, so that its roots are always in soft ground and always wet. The forget-me-not, on the contrary, only grows at the foot of lumps of rock with a south exposure—actually, indeed, at the very foot of the rocks; its tiny leaves and long, flowering stalks are not scattered about in more or less irregular clumps, but grow upwards, all on the same level, clinging to the side of the rock almost like an espalier, so as to get the full benefit of the sun's warmth and also the warmth given back by the rock.

I believe it would be difficult to find anywhere a greater variety of flowers and a gayer brilliance of colour. I always have some of them in my tent—not, of course, of those we are collecting, for they soon end by being pressed between sheets of blotting-paper, where they lose their grace and their colour, even though one day they may be a delight to certain colleagues of mine. But every time the coolies return from work or from cutting *burtse* in the neighbourhood, they come up to my tent and pay their respects with a little bunch of flowers, accompanied by a "ju" and a smile. Thus, right in the middle of the greatest ice-region on earth, I am always surrounded with the charm and colour and the subtle scent of a thousand flowers.

It is really marvellous, this oasis in the midst of the ice! It is not only we who appreciate it; there is a whole world of living creatures who hold undisputed sway here until some horde, like ours, of conquerors from afar descends upon them. It was a surprise indeed, after so many days' march up the glacier, to find this green and flowery oasis, but perhaps an even greater surprise to find its population of living creatures. There are butterflies—white, yellow, sky-blue—grasshoppers and locusts, caterpillars and spiders, which would be the delight

CROSSING A BELT OF PINNACLES

[face p. 160

of an entomologist. They are certainly a delight to my two remaining chickens. A general execution of poultry was decreed at the 4th Camp, but when, later, the tents were removed, two cockerels appeared which had escaped the slaughter, hidden, probably, among the heaps of provision-boxes and bags. They were spared, and did the last stage in triumph, tied on the top of two coolies' loads. These two chickens appreciate the Teram Sher oasis: they scratch about from morning till night and no longer have the starved appear-ance they had when they scratched hopelessly in the rocks and the ice at our camps during the march up the glacier.

Nor need they feel lonely at the Teram Sher oasis, for there are little birds of a yellowish pink colour like the surface of the lumps of granite among which they lay their pretty eggs, of a clear, bright green like the grass near by. There are also pale grey pigeons which fly in faithful couples, terrified, over the camp, and blackcock which pass over sometimes, higher up, with their rather heavy flight, calling to each other. The crows are more faithful to us; big, raven-black, with their sharp cawing sound, they circle slowly round in wide spirals and always end by settling near here, in hopes of picking up some remnant of our daily food. Great birds of prey sometimes soar high above us, with a majestic, almost contemptuous air. The centre of attraction for all of them is the Teram Sher oasis.

But there are other living creatures besides these. The other evening I discovered a very, very small mouse which had had the impudence to worm its way in amongst my sacks of flour—which must have been a novelty and a piece of luck for an inhabitant of the oasis! And a few days ago someone caught an enormous rat, long and grey, which would certainly make a most sumptuous fur. But there is no doubt that the most numerous inhabitants are the ibex, the real lords of the oasis. When I go about near here and stop to look at and admire my glacier, the ibex who are lords of the place are much interested: they look intently at the intruder, even from quite close, and then, in a dignified manner, go off at a gentle trot or a gentle gallop up the slopes of snow or rock, in such a way as to make the most experienced moun-taineer envious. Sometimes they are in herds of as many as

forty, but they have never come down towards the camp.
Their remains are a proof of how numerous they must be.
It is no exaggeration to say that the remains of ibex are so
plentiful and heaped up in such quantities, especially against
the rocks (though why that should be, I do not know),
that often the coolies start out with large empty sacks and
return a few minutes later with the sacks full. It is so much
more convenient than pulling up the little *burtse* plants one
by one, stretching them out to dry a little so that the earth
may detach itself from them, then collecting them again one
by one, laboriously making a bundle of them in such a way
that they may be tied up and carried without too many being
dropped on the way. On the other hand, with the material
provided by a dead ibex, one has only to put the open sack
on the ground and stoop and fill it hand over fist, and there
is the fuel, excellent and all ready collected. Though the
burtse may give a fine flame which is cheerful but gives little
heat, this other fuel glows and gives a splendid heat—especially
welcome when we are surrounded with ice, even though on
an oasis where there are grass and flowers and living creatures.

These are not the only remains of these numerous lords
of the oasis, the ibex. One has only to walk about a little
in the neighbourhood to find, between the great blocks or
on the grass or among the rocks, the badge of royalty of
some of them, mighty horns, long and knotty, which give
them a real appearance of dignity and pride when they stop,
in single file, to look at the new intruders, outlined sharply
against the sky on a shoulder of the mountain and standing
firmly on their agile feet, necks and heads erect. We collected
as many as we wanted of those horns: the best are already on
the way to Panamik, and at least one pair of really colossal
ones will make the long journey to Courmayeur, to be placed
with the other similar remains of large Himalayan animals I
have collected in my house in the mountains—owing to which
people who do not know me must imagine me a keen follower
of Nimrod. In the meantime the inferior horns have become
ornaments of the camp: they have been placed on the top of
a large *lato* built by the men, and from them hang or flutter
little pieces of cloth, printed all over with prayers. May all
the Buddhist gods therefore protect my undertaking right to

its end, since we have given them their first altar in the midst of the Siachen!

According to the Workmans, who encamped near here in a meadow beyond the stream which comes out of the overflow of the Teram, there was, near their tents, a circle of stones, 4 yards in diameter, in which were heaped up an extraordinary number of ibex' horns. These travellers add that both the circle and the pile of horns were certainly made by natives who frequented the glacier in times now past and forgotten. That subject had already attracted and interested me. Having collected all the scattered information given by old travellers and co-ordinated it with a few reliable signs I had myself observed and with other information collected by myself from old men and notables in the high valleys of Baltistan and carefully sifted, I have tried to reconstruct the routes followed in the past by the natives, almost exclusively Baltis, over the chain of the Karakoram. That some of these ancient routes—for example the Muz Tagh Pass—were used is proved by the testimony of travellers who met and saw natives coming from them, and in the case of others, both signs, information, and actual proofs make it certain that, up till 60 or 70 years ago, the natives, in order to get over the Karakoram chain from the valleys of Baltistan towards the important centres of Chinese Turkistan, made a more or less normal use of routes which have since appealed to the enterprise of modern European travellers and explorers. This has something almost miraculous about it, when one thinks of the wild mountain regions and the natural conditions there, and also, one may add, of the fact that experienced mountaineers have often failed in a feat which natives have accomplished unequipped and, in addition, loaded. One of these ancient routes (according to observations and information I collected last time) must have led from the Khapalu district right up the Saltoro Valley across the Bilafon-la, and thus come down on to the Siachen. It perhaps forked on the Siachen, one way going right up the great glacier to its head, and, not improbably, crossing the Turkistan-la; the other touching our oasis, going right up the Teram Sher Glacier, crossing the Rimo Glacier which we have "explored", and leaving it again by its northern tongue, which we have "discovered" to be the source of the Yarkand.—"Explored" and "discovered", that is, only in comparison with our previous knowledge.

That is why I was interested in the circle of stones full of ibex' horns, near the Workmans' old camping-ground. But it so happened that, though these ibex' horns were so plentiful all over the oasis, there was no sign of them there, nor was there any circle of stones 4 yards across: there were merely the traces of two rough semicircles near by, 2 or 3 yards in diameter, but so vague that I would not dare to assert them to be the work of man. In spite of this, my theory of a route from the Saltoro Valley to the Yarkand Valley still holds, as it is founded on reliable information collected by me in the former valley, and on observations made by me in the latter. And my admiration remains for the enterprise of the Baltis of past generations, who lightly faced natural conditions which often seem to us to be impossibly harsh.

How many subjects of interest there are in this oasis of ours in the midst of the ice! The lake also has begun to excite my curiosity. After we had been here two days I realized that it was no longer the same. Certain points of rock which jutted out along its banks were tending to become shorter and rounder, and a fine moraine which broke its surface gave me the impression that it had become lower. As my natural habit of observation had not allowed these signs to escape me, I was now anxious to find others. It was immediately evident that the lake was rising, submerging the rocks which jutted out; it has already reached and covered the path not far from the bank which we followed when we arrived; it is slowly approaching a path higher up, which has been made by the men going to get water from a neighbouring stream; little by little the whole moraine is becoming submerged, and the grassy slopes of the oasis are being slowly but surely invaded. When we arrived, its surface was at an altitude of exactly 15,480 feet, and our tents 72 feet higher up. I can already foresee the moment, perhaps not very far off, when we shall have to move. Evidently the sub-glacial outlet of the lake is no longer sufficient to drain off the large quantity of water, due to melting, which comes into the lake from the Teram Sher and perhaps also from the

Siachen. The lake is rising and will continue to rise till, one day, the water succeeds in forcing an outlet for itself.

We are having a period of rest, however, at least in appearance, inasmuch as nobody leaves the "base" for more than a day. There would in any case be a lack of men, since they have almost all gone down to Zingrul. We had only nine left, of the Timosgam group, commanded by one of my old porters of 16 years ago, who, owing to this previous experience, was elected by his compatriots as the "jemadar"—a sort of corporal—of the group. A good man, but lazy, exactly as he was before—which is rather exceptional for a Ladakhi.

I have been able to utilize these men, however. I have sent them down once or twice to the 4th Advance Camp, in order to diminish the dump of boxes and bags which had to be left there.

But yesterday there arrived, with mathematical punctuality, the main part of the caravan with the loads brought up from Zingrul, at the end of the glacier. I had given the command and the necessary instructions to Zewang Tashi, *iemadar* of the group of men from Tia. There were, of course, also men from Timosgam and all the men from Leh and Nubra. Zewang Tashi could not have carried out my orders better, complicated though they were—especially when one thinks that he knows Hindustani even less than I do, which is saying a good deal. I had kept my eye on him ever since Timosgam, when I had had to make the laborious choice of my 40 permanent porters. He had "chits", or references, from the Vissers and from Mason, who have both made journeys of exploration in these parts. Actually the "chits" did not much impress me, but I liked the appearance of forceful energy which showed itself in the whole of his robust, thick-set person. After leaving Seti I made Hashmatullah tell him always to take his orders direct from me, and from that moment he began to superintend the pitching and the striking of my own personal tent. I soon appreciated him from actual knowledge, no longer simply from my impression of him, and since I started coming up the glacier, he has become my right-hand man. The *jemadar* of Timosgam, who, officially, is superior to all the men, amuses me

with his subtle artfulness in avoiding fatigue. But I entrust
Zewang Tashi with any difficult job in which his energy and
his influence over men may come in useful. Contrary to the
opinion of most people who say that the Ladakhis are Mongols
merely because they have a civilization which comes from the
Mongol East, Zewang Tashi, who is very fair and has bright
blue eyes, might well be an Irishman, in spite of his long
pigtail. Short but broad and extremely solid, he must have
a quite extraordinary physical strength—but also strength of
character. Generally serious, unlike most Ladakhis who are
always ready to laugh and smile, he looks me straight in the
eyes as though to drink in the orders I give him, which
almost always, I can vouch for it, must seem to him extremely
puzzling. The word "huzur"—my great lord—preceded by a
kind of deep sigh as though he were taking breath again after
the terrific tension required to grasp my wishes, is the sign
that he has understood. Then he executes—marvellously well.
Every now and then, without the others seeing, I let him have
an extra few rupees, and his men from Tia also. In this
way I have a reliable man, and also a reliable group, which
should be an example and encouragement to the others. For
there is obviously a certain rivalry between the various groups.

There was undoubtedly rivalry when we arrived here and
all the men started off on that mad race to get possession
of the skin-covered skeletons of the two ibex. The men
from Tia won. It was only yesterday that I understood the
reason of their Marathon race. When the caravan arrived
yesterday, laden with heavy sacks of flour, the Tia men—as
they walked, and with the heavy loads on their backs—were
all taken up with other occupations as well: some were spinning, others knitting with needles which they had made of
juniper-wood. This was the fleece collected from the two
skeletons. And when they told me about it, the men of Tia
laughed with satisfaction, still, perhaps, enjoying their victory
over their fellow-porters.

Base Camp on the Siachen, July 5th, 1930.

166

CHAPTER XVII

OCCUPATIONS, SURPRISES AND ANXIETIES OF LIFE ON THE SIACHEN GLACIER

It is now more than a month since we pitched our tents in this wonderful oasis in the midst of the Siachen, a little less than two months since I attacked the great glacier. It will be at least another fortnight before I get off the glacier and leave it for good. Contrary to all expectations, all reports, and to its own usual behaviour, the glacier has received me with unwonted kindness. Everyone has always agreed in abusing it: 'Beware of the Siachen! It is unassailable. Almost everyone has failed [which is, indeed, true!]. The Nubra will certainly stop you. The tongue of the glacier [also wrote the Workmans] with all its crevasses and *séracs*, is like a rampart specially made to prevent access to the glacier.'

Well, it is true that the Siachen seemed to get into a passion and, so to speak, show its teeth, and was apparently anxious to prove itself worthy of its reputation: yet in the end it allowed me to enter by the front-door, without putting difficulties in my way, nor did it object to my bringing in, also by the front-door, a whole crowd of servants and a large and varied quantity of baggage. Then, however, it repented and shut the front-door with considerable firmness. One could get out by the little side-door, the service-door, but I am not going to look for this. I wish to go out honourably, as I entered, and intend to try another door which is, indeed, a side-door, but not a service-door—at any rate up till now no one has used it. But I must not get ahead of events: I do not want the Siachen, which is still rather angry, to shut this door too against me, when I have yearned after it so long.

This has been a time of great bustle and hard work, except for the first week, during which we were taking possession of the oasis: the whole caravan had then gone back down to the glacier-end to bring up the flour, and I had here only a few men, not enough for any excursions. The camp was pitched: a complete meteorological observatory was established; I took a few short walks round about here, on the rocks at the point of confluence of the Teram—a wonderful spot, because there can be seen from it, one behind the other, the lower and upper Siachen and its chief affluents, the Teram Sher, of course, which comes from the east, and the Lolofon which comes down from the west, from the Bilafon-la (which would be the little . . . service-door); Miss Kalau collected flowers; the poor commandant, between his walks, racked his brains more and more to find a solution to the problems of commissariat, which seemed more and more insoluble.

I do not know if my readers have any idea of what the Siachen is like. I remember that I explained how it was, so to speak, discovered: I remember that I have repeated more than once that it was reputed to be inaccessible; I remember that I have more than once stated that it is the greatest glacier on earth, with the exception of those in the Polar Regions. But my readers would probably also like to have some concrete indication, to fix their ideas and give them shape, so I will give it them.

Imagine that the Miage, the largest glacier on the Italian side of the Alps, coming down from its valley at the foot of Mont Blanc, did not stop in the middle of the pastures and woods among the huts of Le Frésnay and La Visaille, but went on down as far as Entrèves, as far as Courmayeur. It would then be a much larger glacier than it is now. But to get an idea from it of the size of the Siachen, one would have to imagine it coming still farther down the valley, twisting and winding and forcing its mighty mass between narrow, overhanging rocks or broadening out with the broadening of the valley, and finally spreading its gigantic front at least beyond Châtillon. About two-thirds of the Val d'Aosta would be occupied by its monstrous tongue.

As far as is known at present, in fact, the Siachen is about 50 miles in length: the Teram Sher, a mere tributary, is about 18. The area of the glacier, which is still uncertain owing to its not having been completely mapped, has been calculated at something between a minimum of 618 and a maximum of 928 square miles: however, the principal tongue alone, which has a width, in places, of over 3¾ miles and is less than this only in its final portion, where, near the front, it is compressed between massive walls of granite, is certainly about 83 square miles in area.

It is a vast, wide avenue of snow and ice which, from above, appears to be of an extreme regularity. The average slope, between the end and the head, is 3·7 per cent., and only 2·9 per cent. if the head is counted as beginning, not at the Indira Pass, but at the foot of the brief snowy slope which goes up to the pass at the top. It is an immense, white avenue, striped lengthways with moraines, looking on the whole almost flat, but at the sides of which rise, by contrast, high, boldly-shaped mountains, more or less independent of each other, almost always over 23,000 feet, and culminating in one of the two Twins, K[36], 25,410 feet high. It is a valley enclosed by giants; even though they do not reach the height of the peaks round the head of the neighbouring Baltoro, they are giants nevertheless, in shape, in boldness of outline, in the very independence with which the greater of them tower in isolation from their neighbours, with shoulders and ridges and peaks which seem striving to touch the sky.

But even the gigantic tongue of the glacier is not uniform and really flat, as it appears if one sees it from a little above and takes in the whole of its vast extent—as one can, owing to its general course: it can be said that, from the rocks behind my Base Camp, it is only the extreme end of the tongue which is invisible, owing to the curves it describes between the precipitous sides of the great valley. All the rest unfolds itself in all its grandeur and wonderful beauty below us, enclosed by a double row of mountains which, wherever they are not of naked rock, owing to the ruggedness of the precipitous walls, are blindingly white with snow and ice.

If one crosses it or walks about upon it, however, the great tongue of the Siachen shows itself to be by no means so uniform as it appears from above and from comparatively far off. It is uniform only near its head and near that of its chief affluents, because there one is above the line of the eternal snows, and the snow covers everything with its mantle of white—often hiding crevasses which are sometimes deep chasms. But as one comes down the tongue, the uniformity of shapes and colour gradually changes: long, slightly convex ridges begin to take form, especially at the sides of the glacier, and on the top of them can be seen among the snow the black or grey colour of curious lines of stones and flints. These are the moraines: they start from the more important lateral spurs and buttresses, which terminate in the vast tongue of the glacier.

As one goes still farther down the glacier, the covering formed by the eternal snow, which is excessively soft to walk upon in the middle of the day, becomes gradually less thick; the stones and flint of the moraines show up more visibly, like long, regular stripes running along the great back of the glacier. They become even more numerous, because others, starting from each new spur, each new buttress, each new lateral valley-mouth, are added to the first ones; they are quite close at the sides and rarer in the middle. They seem to be floating on the glacier, to be floating on the top of the longitudinal ridges, which meanwhile become more and more clearly marked and are separated by long depressions between them.

Then the eternal snows come to an end: we are at their lower edge. They no longer cover the living ice, which shines with the beauty of crystal or is opaquely white, or pierced all over with those singular elliptic cavities running from east to west, with vertical sides and filled at the bottom with melted snow-water. The moraines are clearer now, easily visible and almost perfect on the longitudinal ridges which are still slightly convex; but the long depressions between them begin to be proper valleys, with tumultuous streams or calm rivers (according to the slope of their bed) running through them. These rivers and torrents are very often impassable in the middle of the day, when the melting of the snow and ice is at its height.

We are, in fact, coming into the zone of the glacier in which the melting of the snow and ice during summer is extremely intense. It must be remembered that this melting takes place during the three months of summer in ice about 33 feet thick. What happens then? The lines of moraine form a protection for the ice underneath them, with the result that they get higher and higher till they take on the appearance of rows of high hills like monstrous stripes on the surface of the glacier; the unprotected belts of ice between them are shaped by the melting into gigantic banks and dikes and rows of pinnacles and spires, and in the middle of them are cavities in which the water collects in lovely bright crystalline lakes of a colour which is often indefinable.

As the melting intensifies and the number of moraines increases the farther one goes down the glacier, so, little by little, the belts of ice which form the white stripes are forced to become narrower and finally end by disappearing, as though submerged by the increasing prevalence of the ridges of moraine. Finally, near the glacier-end, where the melting is extremely intense and the glacier is constricted between narrower limits in spite of the continual influx of new affluents, the moraines also lose the individual distinctness of independent longitudinal threads, and unite, or rather break up into a fantastic labyrinth of irregular hillocks, interrupted by holes and perpendicular walls.

And so the appearance of the glacier is continually changing, from its uniform, snow-covered head to its broken frontal extremity, black with moraine, out of which comes the tumultuous, raging Nubra, the real obstacle in the approach to the Siachen.

Such is the glacial region which I have chosen as the field of operations of my Expedition, a glacial region of such imposing grandeur that it both fascinates and enchants. An attempt upon it was well worth while.

The work proceeds. When the caravan arrived from Zingrul and we had therefore a sufficient number of men at our disposal, we at once started excursions—the first, up the Teram Sher in the direction of its head. The organization of this was easy, for the Teram Sher is just behind us here, and it was simply a question of going up it and coming down again. All we needed was a small nucleus of supplementary coolies, to make a depôt of flour and *burtse* at the first place of encampment and return immediately to the base, all in one day.

Later excursions proved much more complicated, because they took us farther away from this central camp. It was useless to think that we could carry all necessities with us. Should one increase the number of men? So a person unskilled in logic might think; but it would have to be increased *ad infinitum*, as I have already shown. The only solution was that the travellers' caravan should be preceded by another caravan, which should make depôts of flour and *burtse* at all the points previously

arranged for camping. This caravan—which I am tempted to
call the 'altruistic' caravan, because it is organized exclusively for
the good of others—would be necessarily more numerous, and
at the same time—in order to avoid the maddening necessity of
having to multiply men *ad infinitum*—would have to be extremely swift, would have almost to fly: so that the altruism, as
can be seen, was double. Luckily I had Zewang Tashi at hand,
always ready, like a noble horse, for any call I might make upon
him.

In the meantime (and this was the secret of the organization
of my commissariat: to make the greatest possible use of the
smallest possible number of men) I dismissed the twelve Nubra
men, sending them to Panamik with two of the Tia men who
were to be couriers, and I sent down the rest, on three successive
days, to the 4th Camp to bring up the last of the stores which
remained there. I had nothing left in my rear but a ton and a
quarter of provisions at Zingrul and the small balance of the
stores which had been left at all the intermediate camps for the
use of the men who were going up and down. I felt I could
almost breathe again.

So on the 8th I started, with Miss Kalau, at the head of
a flying caravan of 36 men, all well laden. Do my readers wish
to know the exact mechanism of a 'flying' caravan? The first
day, having crossed the Siachen, we encamped at the mouth of
the Lolofon glacier: nine men returned at once to the base, so
that they should not depend on the caravan either for provisions
or *burtse* or *postin*, but they would have done a double stage.
The second day we moved on to the point of confluence of the
glacier called by the Workmans the 'Peak 36 Glacier': I sent
back nine more men, who thus also did a double stage, but had
depended on the caravan for one day's provisions only. On the
third day, after a completely sleepless night, I thought it better
to stay where I was, but Miss Kalau, with the men, went on
up the glacier, made three more depôts and returned to the tents
when night had already fallen: they had covered four stages
since the morning. On the fourth day a double stage for
everyone, in order to get back to the Base Camp. That is how a
flying caravan works.

It was a wonderful trip, however. Even the crossing of
the glacier was interesting: it took us a whole morning to find a

way through the maze of pinnacles and ridges—all of ice, of course—intersected by little valleys and lakes. However, there was nothing very exciting about it; a little delicacy was required in cutting steps and climbing up a short wall of snow which formed a bridge over a torrent. Then, having crossed two moraine ridges, our way was clear, if not always unimpeded, towards the Lolofon. The impediments were caused by the numerous watercourses which we had to cross, but the difficulties were not excessive.

At the mouth of the Lolofon I placed the camp on a moraine, that is, on a hilly ridge entirely composed of ice and covered only by a thin veil of moraine. Towards sunset, while I was in my tent (I was getting the dinner ready!) I became aware that the floor was glowing with a fantastic pink light: it was the golden sunset light which, filtering sideways through the ice, was reflected by the ice to me, as though I had been standing on the floor of an enchanted palace. Next morning at dawn a strange yellow light filtered through.

The Lolofon, which leads, snowy white, right up to the Bilafon-la, is extremely beautiful. I thought of the time when I was on the other side of the pass, in the middle of winter, and of poor Chenoz from Courmayeur, who fell into a crevasse, also on the other side, and came out almost entirely unhurt, but shortly afterwards passed insensibly from the calm of sleep to the calm of death. He was a guide attached to the Workman Expedition.

The next camp was less beautiful: it was on a moraine-covered ice-mound hemmed in between two lakes and full of crevasses. I did not feel we were entirely safe there. The men took up their position in the shelter of an enormous 'table' which stood balanced on a slender support of snow: if this had moved even a little, they would have been completely squashed. But, to take my thoughts off, I had a view of the Hawk, incredibly fantastic.

Our return down the glacier was speedy, apart from the inevitable delays in crossing the final belt of pinnacles, ridges, and lakes.

Miss Kalau should have left again at once, to conduct a flying caravan to the upper Siachen. As for me, it was now impossible for me to move, so complicated has the commissariat become during this last period; I have to remain at the Base

Camp and direct every movement. But alas! on the morning arranged for her departure the sky was completely overcast and there was a heavy rain which soon changed to snow. It was impossible for her to start. And as, in such circumstances, one must make a rapid decision, so that not even one day shall be wasted, I at once sent off the majority of the caravan to bring up more provisions.

We had no more completely fine weather. It stopped snowing, but the sky was threatening every now and then. I followed the barometer with a care which seemed almost exaggerated.

The caravan returned from Zingrul with a ton of provisions, having also raked up on the way all the last remains of the little depôts which I had left at the various encampments. But, as soon as the men have arrived, off they go again at once, with the flying caravan conducted by Miss Kalau. What a quiet life I lead, in the green and flowery oasis of Teram!

.The lake also has taken upon itself to make my life less peaceful. Its level has been continuing to rise with ceaseless persistence. One fine morning, the 23rd, the water reached the kitchen, Kadir's undisputed realm. It was no use delaying: I made a first move and took my tent 33 feet higher up. However, I foresaw the necessity of an even more drastic move, but for the moment was not able to do anything, having only four sick men in camp and the lazy *jemadar* from Timosgam.

The water continued to rise that day and the next, and Kadir, who had established himself a little lower down than my tent, again trembled for his kitchen. In one month the level had risen a good 72 feet—during the first days, in fine weather and restricted in a much smaller circumference, as much as 5 feet a day; during the last period only 20 inches. Now that the fine weather has returned, it seemed as though it would return to the previous rate. The whole landscape has been changing: the green meadows have been disappearing beneath the water, the ice wall of the Siachen has become lower, the surface of water has widened steadily, more than one would have thought possible. Naturally, I kept a close watch on the lake. The evening of the 24th, just after dinner, I returned to the bank and realized that the water had gone down a little, in just an hour—perhaps 2 inches.

This was an interesting piece of news! Next morning, when I woke up, I was surprised to see that in 10 hours the level had sunk by about 33 feet: the wall of the Siachen had become more imposing again, meadows and rocks were reappearing, and the surface of the lake was again restricted to smaller limits. The water went down another 13 feet during the day, and another 6½ during the next night, then at a slower and slower rate. The Siachen is full of surprises!

I thought of the flood-wave which there has perhaps been down below in the Nubra Valley, and of the terror of the inhabitants in spite of being accustomed to these sudden jokes on the part of the glaciers. Here, on the other hand, all is calm. The Teram Sher oasis seems even greener, more flowery, more full of life than before. Every day I collect new flowers; every day new animals appear; insects seem to multiply and birds also. There have appeared certain little birds with black and orange bodies and white wings, also woodcock. What splendid game for a keen sportsman! And what splendid game the ibex would be, which feed every morning within easy range, in large herds, knowing that they have nothing to fear as far as we are concerned. But I do not deny that I now look at them with a certain longing, not exactly from the sporting, but from the utilitarian point of view.

There are complications, and consequent anxieties, on the horizon. When I sent back the Nubra men, I sent with them two of the men from Tia, with orders to collect the post at Gombo and also a few sheep which I had ordered some time ago, and which would have varied our diet and that of the coolies. These two couriers should have been back here on the 18th. Instead of that, they did not reappear till some days later, with the caravan which was bringing flour from Zingrul. They were in a terrible state. Their faces were pitiable with fright, and they had nothing on but their *postin*: underneath, they were naked as God made them. This very summary costume allowed one to see that their legs were covered all over with bruises and cuts.

It was a brief story. They had found the Nubra incredibly swollen. Going down (perhaps because there were so many of them and they could help each other) they managed somehow or other to get across. But coming up, the violence of the current almost swept them away, and reduced them to this wretched state: it was fortunate that they had their *postin* at Zingrul. They escaped, which was the main thing as far as they are concerned.. But they also reported that the Nubra is no longer fordable: the porters I dismissed had been obliged to stop opposite Panamik, in a small oasis, where my two couriers from Leh are also kicking their heels, while at Panamik itself both the post and the sheep are waiting in vain to reach me on the Siachen.

The moral of the story is this. When I move from here to leave the Siachen, I had intended to lighten the caravan by sending down by way of the Nubra all the porters belonging to Leh, with such baggage as had become useless and super-fluous. I shall send the baggage to Zingrul and recover it later from below, when the Nubra has become more tractable. But at present I am completely closed in, cut off, from below. Therefore I shall have to keep the 17 men from Leh, who are not equipped for high altitudes, on the provisions which, if plentiful for my 40 permanent porters, become rather short with the addition of these extra 17 who are forced by the Nubra to follow me, at all costs, right to the end.

It is therefore necessary to be economical with provisions, and the most effective means is to start a bit earlier. So I shall leave some days earlier, also because the march will neces-sarily be slow: I shall have with me about 100 loads, and 31 men, if none are ill.

At the moment I have six who are ill here at the Base Camp, as well as the two who ought to have been couriers, who are bruised all over. My generosity went so far as to allow them a few empty flour-sacks to replenish their wardrobes; they are working from morning till night to make themselves jackets and trousers. But they will feel the north wind, when we leave the Siachen!

Base Camp on the Siachen, July 28th, 1930.

I do not say that the closing of the Nubra, which has now cut me off completely from the world for a month and a half and will in all probability continue to do so till the middle of September, was entirely unexpected. However, I felt that the kindness shown me by the great river till about the middle of June should have continued; but it is well known that man is often rather selfish, at any rate in his desires.

There is no doubt that my circumstances have changed, and changed, of course, for the worse. It is no good dallying with the illusion that, because one does not look difficulties straight in the face, the difficulties do not exist. On the contrary, one must weigh them dispassionately and be extremely rapid in making the decisions which are required to overcome them.

One general principle with regard to men, which I apply and which should always be applied, is that they should always be treated well. But it must be realized that, in applying this elementary principle, there is a whole series of minor subtleties. Some people think that treating Ladakhi porters well consists in showing the greatest possible exactness in the distribution of provisions and wages, and after that considering and treating them as inferior people. But this is not enough—or, rather, it does not work. The Ladakhis are a people of superior intelligence, with a by no means primitive culture, an extreme delicacy of feelings, and a great charm of character, jovial, cheerful, frank. They are not satisfied to be paid and fed with exactness, according to agreement. They are rather like children who want to be soothed and caressed. They must feel the unceasing fatherly care and confidence of their 'bara sahib', but such a confidence as naturally does not show itself in the same way on both sides—in fact a fatherly confidence on one side, and on the other a confidence resulting from devotion. I know travellers who think that they treat their Ladakhi porters well, and who even go so far as to joke with them. But they have no sense of proportion in their jokes; they laugh at them when they repeat their interminable prayers, and address them, not by their own fine-sounding names, but by elegant epithets such as donkey and the like. The Ladakhis laugh, even at this, but they immediately lose respect for such travellers, and, with their own subtle sense of humour, give them nicknames and get an infinity of amusement out of making rhymes about them. This is not the sort of confidence that I bargain for.

The confidence that I mean and which one ought to obtain must be the result of devotion and unbounded trust. The men must feel their 'sahib' to be their father, superior to them in every way, but interested in everything that concerns them. He must praise them when they do well; must go and see them when they are all gathered round the fire, busy over their endless meals; must ask them about their village—or, better, show if possible that he knows it; must also give them some idea of future plans, for they are people who like to understand and to know, and who like the unknown and a certain degree of adventure; he must also look after them in any calamity, whether great or small, and show interest in the progress of an illness, a wound, or a cure, without waiting for them to seek further help from his medical knowledge, which they believe to be infinite.

In this, too, they are rather like big children. Children, as one knows, come almost with pleasure to their mothers or fathers to show them little hurts which are often non-existent. So do the Ladakhis to their 'bara sahib'. The slightest, most harmless scratch is enough to bring them to one's tent, seeking help, and one must satisfy them, even if there is no real need. One must not give the impression that one is driving them away or unwilling to be interested.

What was it that the *jemadar* of Timosgam reminded me of, the moment he saw me again? Not of our struggles to reach the Lingzi-Tang plateaux across an unknown and therefore unexpected range of mountains; not of the dangers of the Shyok ford, deep and turbulent, just below the end of the Rimo Glacier; not of the really drastic rationing of provisions when, having come out at the northern extremity of the Rimo, we realized that this must be the real source of the River Yarkand, and followed the valley down, though we knew we were at the end of our resources, the coolies also, when consulted, being of the same mind about continuing on this unknown route, such is their passion for newness and adventure. It was not of these things, nor of anything like them, that my former porter reminded me. He reminded me that one morning he had felt so ill that he could not walk. We had got rather lost in unknown country, because we were following a new route, but I gave him some medicine, left one man with him and a week's provisions, and punctually in a week's time came back to relieve him. I doubted at the time, and have always doubted, whether his illness was not at any rate slightly exaggerated. That does

178

not matter: when in doubt one should always accept a declaration as being true, without being afraid of the men, as a result, considering us mere simpletons: it will be more likely, on the other hand, to strengthen their persuasion that the 'sahib' is ready to help them whatever may happen, and to confirm their devotion and attachment, and even— why not?—a real affection. But if—which God forbid—the 'sahib', in the fear of being deceived, fails to take notice of a genuine sick man, then he can no longer hope to have his men ready to do his bidding. One of my colleagues on a journey of exploration—not an Italian, however—found one of his men lying on the ground one morning, saying that he could not walk. He did not believe him, and, in order to show him his own energetic method of handling men, gave him a good kick. The Ladakhi got up, tried to pick up his load and walk, but after a short time dropped down, stone dead. It was not in the least the kick which sent him to the next world, but the whole caravan hated that particular 'sahib', and perhaps rightly.

I employ two means, one entirely practical, the other entirely psychological, the first applied only according to circumstances, the second, on the other hand, at all times, every day, from the moment I appear at the door of my tent in the morning till the moment when I retire in the evening to my well-earned rest. By these two means I have been able to handle these men of mine as perfectly malleable material and to obtain from them every effort it has been necessary to demand for the perfect running of an expedition which was not easy to organize and certainly difficult to carry out, given the region in which it has taken place. Without these men, who are really wonderful, but also without these methods, success would have been impossible. But now, now that we have been living in common for two and a half months, now that they have ceased to feel that rather unfortunate diffidence which they have towards strangers even in spite of their ready smile that seems to be the same for everyone, and have come to regard me more or less as the big father of them all, who rewards them, takes care of them, welcomes and listens to them—now I feel that success will attend the last and perhaps most difficult trial, and that they will make all the efforts and sacrifices for me that are necessary.

What, in fact, are my actual circumstances? Not, indeed, very brilliant. For a month and a half I have been cut off from below, and have not been able to obtain anything, even ordinary news, from there. The way out towards the Saltoro Valley is open, but it would take me, with the whole caravan, into the middle of Baltistan, comparatively far away from Leh, and would therefore necessitate a completely new organization, a new provisioning which would perhaps be difficult, and the abandonment of all the preparations I have made in Nubra and Ladakh. I should also have to give up the further carrying out of my programme, which I have thought out with so much pleasure for such a long time. I shall not, of course, go by the Saltoro Valley, but shall, according to plan, attempt the unknown route of the 'new' way out, over the great Rimo Glacier.

The closing of the Nubra has left on my hands 17 men from Leh, whom I would otherwise have sent back. More men for transport—surely a great advantage, the inexperienced would think. On the contrary, it is a burden: the Leh men do not even suffice to carry their own provisions, considering the much longer way round from here to Panamik that they will now have to go. But an even more serious thing is that they will have to be provisioned for 21 days more than if they had been able to go straight down to Panamik by way of the Siachen. However, it might be worse. It is true that I was expecting still more supplies to come up from below, for ourselves and the men, but—though nobody knows it except myself—even the supplies which I have already brought up here will allow me a margin of about a fortnight beyond the stay I had intended to make on the Siachen. These were the 'reserves', which the head of an army does not waste in unimportant actions, but keeps aside, carefully protected; as it were hidden, and always intact, in case of serious and unforeseen eventualities of war. So also the head of an expedition: he must be inexorable in forbidding waste of provisions or of time on single excursions—as it were, on merely local actions in war—and must keep his reserves intact for unforeseen circumstances of real importance. So this margin of provisions will allow of my taking the 17 men from Leh with me, off the glaciers and then round to Panamik by the longer route across the Depsang Plateau.

All the same I risk not having enough provisions for my 40 permanent porters. I had actually planned for my friend Hashmatullah to come and meet me in the upper Yarkand Valley, at the north front of the great Rimo Glacier, with a relief caravan; I had even told him that I expected the 26th of this month to be the day of my leaving the glaciers, but added that more exact instructions would follow when it drew near the time of my leaving the Base Camp on the Siachen. The instructions, of course, like everything else, have been held up by the Nubra. And now, though relying upon the devotion and intelligence of my friend Hashmatullah, I have also to be prepared not to find him on my return journey. Therefore, in order to make the reserve supplies go further, there is nothing for it but to start sooner. I had thought of leaving the Base Camp on the 12th: now I shall start the day after to-morrow. I shall allow full rations all the time we are going over the glaciers; but directly we leave them, no more tobacco, no more tea, and only a third of a ration of flour. The men have already been told, and immediately understood that the future restrictions are due, not to improvidence on my part, but to the violence of the Nubra, which has completely cut us off from the world: whatever the 'bara sahib' does is right.

Such is my situation at present, and it looks as though it were depending on a thread. If it happens that a period of bad weather pursues us while we are crossing the glaciers and before leaving them, all the calculations for my commissariat will collapse and I shall have to start rationing the whole caravan, ourselves included, earlier and more strictly. But there is still time to think about this gloomy possibility; otherwise the few hours of sleep still left me by responsibilities and worries and continuous tormenting anxiety will be even further diminished.

When I appeared from my tent next morning, a long night of thinking had made my course quite clear to me, and as usual I had a smile for my men, at whose comic awakening it always gives me pleasure to be present. All the useless or superfluous baggage is already at Zingrul, and from Zingrul all the last remaining sacks of flour have arrived; as they came up the Siachen the men also brought a supply of 'shupa'—that is, juniper-wood—from my old 2nd Advance Camp on the glacier.

For some days I have been sending flour and *burtse* up the Teram Sher, to a point about eight hours from here where my 1st Camp will be on the way out of this great world of ice. This I have done because my transport problem will be extremely complicated and delicate, and from this moment I must start to solve it. Part of the baggage will go with me. Thus I shall start with a caravan of barely 30 porters, of whom six are sick, and more than a hundred loads—36 of *burtse* alone, that is, a whole ton of fuel. It is certainly essential that my head should remain firmly on my shoulders!

My poor Base Camp, which was so full of people and tents and sacks and boxes until a few days ago! It makes me feel sad to see it being emptied of everything so quickly. Even the ibex seem to be surprised, and come every morning in greater numbers to watch these changes: yesterday there were about 30 of them in one herd. The whole oasis seems anxious to pay me its last respects, clothing itself every day with new flowers. The primulas which greeted my arrival are over, but an immense and many-coloured variety of sweet-smelling flowers are coming out in the meadows on this last day before my departure. A slight melancholy comes over me when I think that in a short time I shall go away, and that the oasis of Teram Sher will remain a mere memory of this wandering existence of mine. A large smooth stone on which time has spread a dark, purplish glaze now bears a short inscription to commemorate this little handful of men, led by an Italian into the midst of this wonderful, immense ice-world of the Siachen.

Base Camp on the Siachen, August 5th, 1930.

Chapter XVIII

WE LEAVE THE SIACHEN IN A STORM

These last days have been extremely agitating for me. Not only were there the difficulties of commissariat, the surprises which the glaciers might spring upon me (and I knew beforehand, from the Workmans' description, that the glaciers were by no means easy, in fact very difficult, to cross), and the anxieties about the near future (when I shall have got off the glaciers with my 60 men, my very scanty supplies, and a long, difficult journey before arriving at a village)—but there was added to these bad weather. I do not think Miss Kalau notices it, and the men even less, but my anxiety is such that my hours of sleep get less and less. Being forced to stop contrary to plan may mean exhaustion of supplies and *burtse*; to press on at all costs, in spite of mist and snow, may mean losing ourselves in the flat immensities of these glacier-heads, which seem endless, or in some labyrinth of *séracs* and crevasses. Last night I only rested one hour: at 10 o'clock yesterday evening I had already begun putting my head out of the tent to examine the signs of the weather, and I did so again several times during my long sleepless night.

We left the Base Camp late in the afternoon of the 6th, not really intending to do a whole stage, but to shorten the first stage by a little, as the coolies who had been going up and down with baggage reported it to be long and difficult. But it did not really turn out to be so.

I felt an even greater sadness that day at leaving my Base Camp. I sent on all the men with the few remaining loads from the abandoned camp, and only my own tent was left, amongst the squalor of débris and rubbish scattered over the ground. The sky was overcast, grey, heavy, sad, and every now and then there was a passing shower of fine, cold rain which lashed one's face with a pricking sensation; even the colours of the flowers, usually so serene and brilliant, seemed to have become washed out to match the grey monotony of the sky. The lake, too, usually so calm and bright and full of movement, increased the impression of deserted, dreary abandonment at the Base Camp; during the two previous nights, after a period of standstill, its level had again sunk by about 3 feet, but this morning, when I awoke, I found it had gone down another 6½ feet, again reaching the line of shore which was visible when we arrived two months ago. It did not stop there, but continued to go down with increasing speed. The surface of the water, which for so long had attracted my attention owing not only to its vicissitudes but also to its constant changes of colour—now sparkling like the sun, now confused and opaque, calm and smooth like oil or slightly ruffled or broken by little waves which pursued each other from bank to bank—had been shrinking with even greater rapidity. Ridges of moraine and shapeless lumps of rock were now visible at the bottom, and great blocks of ice which up till now had been gently rocked, as they floated, by the slight lapping of the water had settled down, as though tired, on the banks. The ice-wall of the Siachen, which forms the bank on one side and which had been emerging to a greater and greater depth, now shows regular horizontal lines caused by melting, and curious overhanging vaults pierced with small, smooth niches, like a kind of Arab vaulting in which the architectural *motif* of the 'media naranja' has been repeated *ad infinitum*. Whole pieces of the wall, enormous blocks of ice, have given way, being no longer supported by the water, and have weakened and then collapsed, at first slowly, then finally falling with a quick and unexpected plunge into the water, bobbing up and down with a regular movement and then floating off, drifting gently until they also become stranded on the bank. And as the level of the water has gradually become lower and the wall of ice higher, all the mountains beyond the Siachen also seem to have become lower. I seem to have been present at one of those transformation-scenes which look so unreal in the theatre or the cinema, but here all was real—with a reality which made me melancholy. "The *bara sahib* is going away," a coolie said to me, "and the lake is going away too." It was true; but the 'bara sahib' seemed, that day, to have feet of lead; motionless at the door of the only remaining tent, he could

THE FIRST CAMP ON THE TERAM SHER

[face p. 185

not take his eyes off the water which went down and down, farther and farther, quicker and quicker, disappearing by unknown ways beneath the glacier. And the dream life that he had dreamt of so long, and had led for two months in the green and flowery oasis of Tarim Sher, seemed also to be vanishing.

Then a rapid awakening; the tent was soon dismantled, and we started. That day we went up the lateral branch of the Teram Sher which comes to an end near the lake, to the point where its ragged tongue flattens out into the great tongue of the Siachen's most important affluent. During the night it snowed.

Next day we went on up the Teram Sher. The weather was uncertain all day, the sky cloudy and grey and threatening snow, but just occasionally it cleared and there were gleams of sunshine which lit up this superb scene of mountains and ice. We went up a moraine, without difficulty. On our right, precipitous, overhanging, threatening, was one wall of the great frozen valley, rising into ridges of rock and snow-cliffs of amazing boldness; there were short valleys occupied by glaciers which came down in falls of *sérac*. Beyond the moraine was the immense tongue of the Teram Sher, white with ice and snow, and only on the opposite side striped with a multiple row of dark moraines. Beyond were the rugged spurs of mountain into which the Teram Kangri chain divides—the chain which marks the watershed of this vast mountain-range. Looking back, we could see the Tarim sloping gently down, getting wider and wider and more regular and flat towards its point of confluence with the Siachen, beyond and on the opposite side of which we could see the openings of the Lolofon and "Peak 36" Glaciers and of the other smaller ones which flow from every mountain and valley. Never, from any point of view, had the Siachen looked so superbly grand to me: its grandeur was fascinating, but almost unreal. The great beak-like top of the Hawk, the great saddle of the Ghent, and the mighty snow-covered shoulder of the Twins formed the background of the picture.

Our camp that day was placed at an altitude of almost 17,720 feet, at the point where the moraine originates at the foot of a great ridge of granite, the sides of which seemed to be crumbling away; during the night, in fact, there was a continual falling of lumps of rock and detritus, which added their dull prolonged rumblings to the sharp, sudden cracking of the ice beneath our tents. The weather was fine.

I have already explained to my readers the secrets of my organization and of the carrying out of my plans, and they know the mechanism of my advance up the Siachen. I applied more or less the same principles in going up the Teram Sher, but with this difference, that now the number of men at my disposal was reduced almost to a third, whereas that of the loads was relatively increased. In order to get everything transported, I had to allow one day for the moving of each camp and in each case two more days for bringing up all the other baggage—that is, provisions and fuel. At each camp, of course, the baggage diminished slightly, both because the men consumed three days' rations of flour and *burtse*, and because they left one day's ration, both of *burtse* and flour, for the use of those men who, after a few days, had to follow me. At each camp, therefore, there were eight loads less.

From the 1st Camp, therefore, I sent forward an advance caravan, with orders to dump their loads of flour, not near the opposite side of the glacier, but in the middle of the Teram, where I expected to find an easier road for our march. And the next day, the 9th, I advanced with the camp.

That day marked the beginning of my greatest troubles. It had snowed all night, but at 6 in the morning the signs of the weather seemed to be better; in the East, towards the top of the glacier, the sky was clear and pink and seemed to promise a fine day. But this was a complete deception, for half an hour afterwards the sky was entirely overcast again and snow was falling very heavily.

After three hours it stopped again; we pulled down the tents in haste and were off without a moment's delay. Any halt, as I have said, would be disastrous for me. Leaving the 1st Camp, we went straight off the moraine and entered upon the main part of the glacier, in order to keep in the central part of it as we went up. Though it had been even and very slightly inclined and entirely of living ice up to that point, from the 1st Camp onwards it became steeper, was covered in snow, and appeared to consist of great undulations, the surfaces of which were alternately concave and convex: the latter were streaked in every direction with long and complicated crevasses like scars. We moved fairly fast that day; the snow was not yet very deep on the glacier, and was firm, as the sun had not yet softened it. The mist and clouds had lifted enough to give us another amazing view of the whole of the gigantic tongue of the Teram and of the Siachen, receding ever farther into the distance and enclosed in its majestic circle of mountains, but not enough to prevent the sky from being still obscured, and the nearer peaks and ridges from being covered with a thick white veil. The long back of Teram Kangri and the sharp point of Apsarasas have never appeared; we just had to imagine them above the ravines full of fallen ice and débris which come down from them. But in front of us an entirely new sight was at moments visible, perhaps just as grand. The Teram, in the direction of the high basins which feed it, opened out into at least four immense valleys full of snow, separated by curtains of high mountains, sharp as thin wedges, in which the living rock was visible here and there. Four immense valleys, with tributary valleys each of which by itself would appear large in the Alps; and the bottoms of these valleys rose gradually as though in enormous steps, blending in the distance into the uniform grey of the sky. This was only visible at moments, however; then the grey curtain of mist descended from above, so thin that we were hardly aware of the vagueness which gradually obscured each line and contour of the mountains, until all at once we realized that the curtain had indeed fallen completely, and there was no view left.

After a five-hours' march up the glacier I deemed it advisable to stop and pitch the tents, at an altitude of about 18,370 feet; the opposite side was still a good three-quarters of an hour off, but separated from us by a belt of ice, part of which was full of crevasses, and part of it marshy. And those three-quarters of an hour would be saved when we started off again up the Teram. There were a few cracks in the ice, covered over with snow, even quite close to our tents, but we were safe if we took precautions when moving about. The thing which caused me anxiety was that there was a wide belt of crevasses beginning a little higher up, the farther end of which could not be seen; it was this which the Workmans had found impassable, even without a caravan and with well-known Alpine guides. My

attention was therefore mainly concentrated on the upper part
of the glacier, over which I should soon have to lead the whole
of my heavy caravan.

The moment they had pitched the tents, the men returned
in haste to the 1st Camp, for the weather was threatening.
The mists, in fact, came down again and soon after it started to
snow heavily. I felt more and more gloomy—like the vault of
mist which shut me in on all sides.

We stayed there a day to give the men time to finish bringing
up the baggage from the 1st Camp—a day of continuous mist
and snow. I went out every now and then, but only to shake
the roof of the tent. I consoled myself philosophically with the
thought that the bad weather would exhaust itself during that
day, and that it was all the more probable that the next day
would be better.

But it was no better. I had planned to start at 5 o'clock,
because I wished to go on as far up the glacier as possible, and
also to get over the initial area of crevasses before the sun had
softened the snow. After an almost sleepless night I went out
at 4 o'clock to examine the horizon, but the mist concealed it
in every direction. A thick, icy hail was falling. Why should
bad weather dog me so persistently, just when progress was
most difficult, responsibility heaviest, and the necessity of getting off the glaciers most urgent? Just when a forced delay
of even one day might ruin all my plans of commissariat, which,
necessarily, were calculated to a hair's-breadth? It was no use
hesitating; at half-past eight I put on my skis, struck camp and
started off at the head of my faithful and admirable porters.
The *jemadar* of Tia was invaluable in helping me, urging on
his comrades both by word and example, and on occasion with
witticisms and jokes.

The belt of crevasses which had held up the Workmans in
their attempt stretched its swelling convex ridge parallel to, and
close to, the right side of the glacier. There was no doubt that
the shortest way up the glacier would be across it. But the day
before, during the short moments when the mists, though they
did not clear off, thinned a little, I had observed, when examining the Teram, that, parallel to this raised belt of crevasses,
there ran along the central part of the glacier a gentle depression,
a kind of wide channel, in which crevasses, though visible, were

fairly rare. This was the road I took, following it, however, principally from the impression of the topographical conditions of the glacier which I had tried to fix in my memory the day before. Actually nothing was visible except in the immediate neighbourhood; there was mist and snow all the time, and it was very cold; it was heavy going, not for us two, but for the coolies, owing to the quantity of snow which had fallen the day before and during the night. There were few crevasses, however, and they were not dangerous provided one took proper precautions; but of one thing I wished to be absolutely sure, that even the slightest mishap should be avoided as far as it was possible, for I did not want to complicate a situation which was already quite difficult enough.

Soon the slight depression came to an end, and I had to cut across to the left to get near the side of the mountain. I had now left behind me the raised, convex belt where crevasses were most plentiful. There were still wide, deep cracks with lovely fringes of icicles at their rims, but these were easily skirted, or could be crossed by bridges of snow. There were also other cracks, thin and treacherous and just hidden by more recent snow, but we took continuous soundings of the glacier with ice-axes and were warned of them in time. Certain places were rather delicate, not for us two who wore skis all the time, but for the porters, whose loads made them heavier and clumsier, and then I would stop and help them over one by one according as was needed, to their great satisfaction and an accompaniment of many exclamations of "ju" and "mervani".

However, the moment arrived when we had to stop; the snow on the glacier became steadily worse, the mist thicker and the sleet more intense. Under these conditions it was impossible to go on. Towards noon, therefore, I had the tents pitched at about 19,020 feet, in a line on a narrow piece of ice between two parallel crevasses. The men, who are really wonderful, went straight back to the 2nd Camp.

The ill luck which dogged me began to be really dangerous. I was already behind my programme, and this had been too short a stage for me to be able to deceive myself into thinking that we should get off the glacier as soon as we ought to, if we continued at this rate. Without letting Miss Kalau and my men notice it, I was racking my brains night and day to

189

find a solution which would entail as little sacrifice as possible; but there was only one solution, not to stop but to press on, not to consume provisions but to be as sparing as possible with them.

During the afternoon the sky cleared and raised my hopes for the next day. We were already high up, near the rocky side of that valley which must be considered as the chief affluent of the Teram. Down below we could again see the Siachen, far away and quite small, no longer majestic as we had seen it from the 1st Camp. The grandest scenery now was near us, at the place where the Teram, above its zone of crevasses, flattened out into an immense expanse into which opened the four great basins which feed it: we could not manage to see the heads of these basins, partly because of the mist which was again invading the whole landscape, driven by frequent squalls, and also because of the great distance to which the snowy slopes of these basins extended. The mountains on that side were extremely beautiful. These were the mountains the other side of which encloses the Siachen on its left side, in the lower part of its course. We had seen them when we had made our first advance up the glacier, as rather small, almost insignificant mountains, rather commonplace and hardly deserving of our attention. From here, it was quite another matter; except where their sides displayed a uniformity of bare, black schists and their peaks were hidden by the twistings of narrow ravines, these mountains, separated by deep, ice-covered saddles, were so bold in form and so beautiful in outline that they compared favourably with the most celebrated mountains of the Alps. And yet one had only to turn one's eyes down the Teram towards the distant Siachen for the Ghent and the Hawk and the Twins to make one again realize that these nearer mountains, though majestic, were, in comparison, mere pigmies.

Beyond us, and where our road would lie, the glacier widened out and continued to slope slightly upwards; then it evidently became flatter again, since it disappeared from view. It was obvious that it was now definitely assuming the characteristics of a plateau glacier, characteristics which would continue until we passed over on to the immense, endless, flat stretches of the upper heads of the Rimo. Where was the point at which we should pass over? There was an apparently

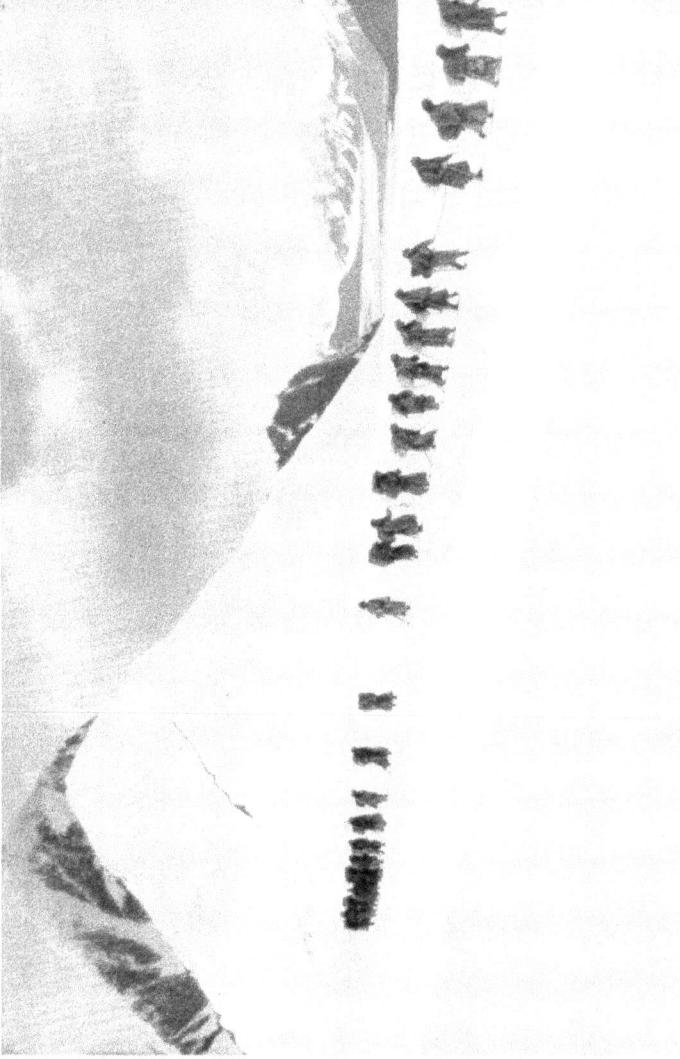

THE SIACHEN IN THE DISTANCE, DURING A FINE INTERVAL

[face p. 190

isolated conical mountain, rising from the line of ice which lay flat across the horizon, which I thought I recognized without any doubt as a mountain which, sixteen years before, I had seen from the other side near a wide, flat gap which I had judged to be the gateway from the Rimo towards the Siachen. My future path therefore must lie between the rocky flank, near which were my tents, and this isolated conical mountain. But it ought to be in clear weather, in bright sunshine, in a blaze of light, both to crown my labours and also to prevent me from missing my objective. Mist on these immense plains would mean that progress would be utterly impossible.

But meanwhile the mist, between the moments of clear sky, returned persistently—heavy, grey, gloomy, threatening.

Certainly I was pursued by bad luck, or perhaps the elements wished to test my powers of resistance to the utmost. During the whole of the night of the 12th violent squalls seemed to be trying to carry away the tents, which had been hurriedly pitched on the ice, and there was almost continuous snow. In the early morning a violent storm was still raging. At 10 o'clock the men, loyal and patient in spite of every kind of hardship, arrived from the 2nd Camp with all the remaining loads of flour. They put them down, making the characteristic whistling sounds that they utter when feeling most exhausted. But I was forced to disregard this, and the tents were immediately taken down; there was no time to be lost and we had to press on at all costs. We went on over easy flat surfaces and gentle snowy slopes with very few crevasses, but it was heavy going and there was still mist and snow. Things were getting worse and worse and the elements persecuted us more relentlessly, for the storm lashed us with redoubled fury as if it were only just beginning. Whenever we reached the top of a rise in the glacier, even a slight one, or a corner of its rocky flank, the violence of the wind seemed trying to resist our progress and push us back again. We had been going only an hour, but it was impossible to proceed farther. We pitched the tents at the foot of a rock, at an altitude of about 19,360 feet or little more, and that was my "upper" 3rd Camp on the Teram. The men, as usual, went back again on our tracks, to the 2nd Camp.

The storm of snow and wind persisted the entire day; it

was impossible even to show one's face outside the tents, and we remained shut up by candlelight, listening to the wild and ceaseless whistling of the wind. It continued thus the whole night. Only at 1 o'clock (I went out every hour to look at the weather and follow its hoped-for changes) the mist had disappeared and wide trailing masses of cloud allowed the moonlight to cast lights and shadows over the fantastic scene of ice and mountain. However, my hopes were short-lived; the wind started blowing again in such violent squalls that at moments I had to hang on to the tent-ropes with the whole weight of my body, as the tent threatened to fly away completely. At midday the men arrived from the 2nd Camp with the loads of *burtse*. I made them rest a little, then sent them down to the "lower" 3rd Camp, to bring up the loads of flour. Then they took up their position here, against the rocks, but with very little shelter from the violent squalls of wind.

And so it lasted the whole of yesterday. At 11 o'clock in the evening it calmed down a bit and began to snow instead— quiet, icy, thick, persistent snow which went on all night. It was useless to awake the men, for it would have been madness to start in such weather. Later on, so as not to lose the habit, and also to give myself a little distraction—a distraction, however, which to-day really moved one to pity—I went and looked on as my porters woke up of their own accord.

I must explain how Ladakhi porters usually sleep. They make a little raised place with stones and place upon it a few knapsacks or rags of their own; then they kneel down in front of it and take off everything they have got on, and then crouch down with their legs still doubled up and their stomachs naked to the ground, resting their bare heads on the little raised place they have prepared. All their clothes, their fur cloaks, empty sacks and anything else they may have managed to scrape up in the camp, is then thrown on top of them and covers them up completely. Thus they occupy a space of 16 by perhaps not more than $27\frac{1}{2}$ inches, and thus they remain without moving, as still as death, the entire night. They look as if they had been transformed into a heap of clothes and rags, from which issue half their heads, with the beginning of a pigtail just showing. If it is unusually cold the whole of the head disappears into the warmth of the coverings. It was in vain that I distributed tents; they have hardly ever put them up, and even then not properly or in the way I had taught them. They put them up (when they did so) so as to form a kind of wide shelter, large enough for an entire group of porters, open at the bottom all round, and at the top open in the middle so that the smoke of their cooking might escape. But generally the tent-cloths were used merely as a final common covering for two or three heaps of rags, that is for two or three sleepers, kneeling and crouching on the ground one almost on top of the other.

In the morning, the awakening of these men (who during the day are so amazingly and surprisingly energetic and active) is heavy and slow. For a long time after they are awake they remain completely motionless and one would think they were pretending to be dead. Then they attempt to move their heads slowly, then to raise them a little. And if one is there then, waiting to look at them, one sees the most comical faces in the world—still sleepy, astonished and stupefied, as though everything around were new to them. They look at one with an expression of amazement and struggle to raise a smile, but immediately fall back again into complete immobility. If by this time they are rather more awake, then the smile they give one is more open and complete, and their first instinctive movement is to get up and stand in front of one, as they always do in token of respect; but as they raise themselves on their knees they become aware of their own nakedness and in a moment have slipped on their clothes and burst out laughing; they are at last completely awake and the day begins.

This morning when I got up I had the impression that my men had all vanished. I looked in vain for them at the spot where I had seen them kneeling and crouching down the evening before. If they had not vanished, they were at all events invisible. But then I saw the snow, here and there, moving and cracking in a strange manner; then a tuft of black hair just appeared above the surface of the snow, and one or two heads stuck up and quickly disappeared again as though horrified. My men, half buried in the snow, were beginning to wake up. It was an extremely comic sight, as always, but this morning it moved one to pity. But there is no reason to be too much moved; these are their usual customs and habits, and they would always prefer to be half buried in snow rather than be shut up in the shelter of a tent, which they would consider almost suffocating.

This was a brief distraction, however. The mist soon brought me back to the actual realities of my struggle against the elements, my struggle to get away from the Siachen safe and sound, with all my men and all my baggage.

"Upper" 3rd Camp on the Teram Sher, August 14th, 1930.

CHAPTER XIX

THE NEW CROSSING OF THE "ITALIA" PASS (20,000 FEET), AND LEAVING THE GLACIERS

The heavy snowfall on the night of the 14th seemed to me a good omen—perhaps it would be the last outburst of the bad weather. One ought always to imagine and foresee the worst so as to be able to guard against it, but also to hope for the best, that is, to have faith, without which one would not have the moral courage to go on and persevere and come out victorious. It is always like this in human life. My hopes, that day, were realized.

Towards 11 o'clock the whole camp was dismantled for departure. The porters, though always obedient to my orders, had, however, raised objections. I was rather sorry for them; after a good week of continually marching up and down between one camp and another, always laden when coming up and always in mist and snow—and especially after the last two nights of raging storm—it was quite natural that they should want a day's rest and that they should be afraid of the continuance of bad weather. But they did no more than express their opinion; when I gave my orders, they were perfectly ready to carry them out with that energy of theirs which always seems to be upheld by real enthusiasm. We started in a thick mist. However, it was absolutely necessary that we should start.

There could be no doubt as to the way we ought to follow, even though one's eye had no possibility of choice; we had to keep near the rocks at the side, which, jutting out slightly but continuously, also marked the shortest way.

We made slow but regular progress, without any very great anxieties, for the surface of the glacier seemed to get more and more smooth and regular and the crevasses rarer, and there was firm snow immediately underneath the snow which had recently fallen, which was still cold and dry. Then the mist gradually cleared away and lifted; the curtain which I had seen descending from above so many times during the last few days, blotting out the view and dashing my hopes, now lifted and gradually displayed to view the immense snowy stretches of these gigantic glaciers, which now have the decided characteristics of plateau glaciers. Then we saw the lower sides, of ice and rock, of the enclosing mountains, then the sides, higher up, then the peaks— first of the nearer mountains, then of others farther off, finally also of those which, in one short piece of the horizon, could be easily recognized, though diminished by distance, as the giant mountains beyond the Siachen. Then the last, thinnest veil of mist lifted and dissolved into the air, and a blaze of brilliant light spread suddenly over the entire scene, and the ice glowed and the rocks shone golden. It was like a sign of victory for me— for my determination, my enthusiasm, my faith; difficulties had been faced and overcome in spite of the storm, and a clear sky and glorious sunlight surrounded me as I approached and reached my goal. Even the men looked victorious.

The slope of the glacier grew steadily slighter; in front of us it appeared to flatten out immediately right across the wide saddle between the rocky flank near which our path lay and the isolated cone-shaped mountain which looks like a huge sentinel planted between the Rimo and the Siachen. This, to a certain extent, was an illusion; even though the broad saddle was certainly now quite near, it was not actually visible; the line of ice on the horizon actually corresponded all the time with a change—that is, a diminution—in the snowy slope of the glacier. This illusion was repeated continuously. I realized that the pass was still too far off for it to be possible for us to reach and cross it and also to discover a suitable camping-place near one of the sides of the Rimo. And when I also realized that a short spur of bare rock which we had now reached was the last spur jutting out from the mountain-side nearest to us into the glacier before the pass, I decided to stop at its foot. Just at its foot, beyond a little lake which lay in a deep depression between ice and rock, where the latter jutted out farthest, stretched a small bank of moraine which seemed to have been put there on purpose for us to pitch our tents upon it. We were at an altitude of about 19,700 feet. This became my "Camp below the . . . Pass"—the pass being for the present unnamed.

It turned out a particularly interesting camp. To begin

196

with, the fact that it was the first camp to be brightened and warmed by a clear sky and a hot sun after such a long period of mist and storm made me regard it with the greatest sympathy, almost with gratitude. But it also had merits and qualities of its own. Its position, to begin with: it was in the midst of a region of ice unsurpassed in the breadth and grandeur of its forms, and at such an altitude that all the mountains near by looked like little insignificant hills—and naturally, since their relative height was to be measured merely in hundreds of feet, even though their real height places them amongst the giants that seem to reach the sky. Towards the pass the view was interrupted, quite a short distance off, by one of the changes or diminutions in the slope, of which I have spoken, and which gave one the illusion that the saddle at the end of the valley was quite close. But on the other side we still had a view—more impressive even than before, because wider in extent—of the higher tributary basins of the Teram, and of the steep, sharp-pointed mountains which surround them. Between two of them, looking as it were through a window formed by a low pass, we could see a mountain very far away and looking quite small because of its remoteness, though we could guess that in reality it was gigantic; this was the double peak of the Twins, sending us a last greeting from the Siachen.

My Camp on the (still nameless) Pass held another quite different surprise for me. On the short spur of rock, outlined against the sky, was a cairn made of stone, perfect in its construction as though it had been made only the day before; and there was another one, in ruins. No European caravan had ever passed this way, and there was therefore no doubt that these two cairns had been built, on the last rocks before the pass, by the Baltis who, as I have already suggested, used to cross this way from the Saltoro Valley—by the Bilafon-la, the Siachen, the oasis where our Base Camp was, the Teram, the still unnamed Pass, and the great Rimo Glacier, right to its northern extremity—going through the great ice-region on the way to Yarkand by the natural and probably the shortest, though by no means the easiest, way. When one finds a confirmation, or a further confirmation, of a theory of one's own, one has a right to a certain satisfaction.

The night was extremely cold, and I slept little, for my anxiety, though lessened, was not yet over. I slept little, but, odd though it may seem, I felt a great inward contentment at feeling myself numb with cold. Intense cold should mean a clear sky, that is, an easy and certain attainment of our goal. At 7 o'clock it was still 22 degrees below freezing point, but a brilliant sun was already giving warmth.

At midday all the porters arrived whom I had sent back at once the day before to bring up the baggage left at the previous camp; this necessity of the men going backwards and forwards in order to take all our baggage along with us still worried me and will do so till the end. But no matter; the greater part was now done. I allowed the men an hour's rest; then we all started off.

It was as easy as going for a walk. The glacier became steadily less sloping, flatter and flatter, wider and wider. The snow was excellent, the going safe. Nevertheless, the men became tired, almost all of them complained of headaches and stopped to rest every few steps. We two were all right; we, of course, had no loads and, as on all the preceding days, had put on our skis—which were indeed extremely useful. I enjoyed going over the great plateau of ice; behind us we still had the same magnificent view as we had had from the camp, though it was growing wider, and in front of us, as we went slowly up, the peaks of new mountains, so far unknown to us, gradually appeared and gradually grew larger over the line of ice which formed the horizon close to us; these were the mountains beyond the Rimo. At 5 o'clock in the afternoon the slight slope of snow finally flattened out into an immense expanse which started to descend again slightly on the opposite side towards the upper basin of the Central Rimo. We were on the pass at last, at about 20,000 feet. My own feelings were naturally much more intense than those of Miss Kalau or my faithful men. For me, above everything, it was the end of a period of anxiety, it was the victory which compensated me for it, and it also reminded me of another memorable journey which the ice and the rocks and the mountains of the Rimo brought back to me— of the time when I, with other companions but leading my own little independent caravan, had explored and brought to men's knowledge this boundless glacier which lies on the border

THE "ITALIA PASS" AND THE FIRST CAMP ON THE RIMO

[face p. 198

between the huge serrated chain of the Karakoram and the monotonous, endless stretches of the Tibetan plateaux. I saw again the smooth sides, black as coal and streaked with the whiteness of the snow, and the steep sides of strangely red dolomite upon which not even a flake of snow could rest; and, between them, the gentle windings of the gigantic Central Rimo Glacier, bending, down below, towards the right, and pressing against the sides of other mountains of relatively modest height, but all of them of wonderful, extremely brilliant colours—red and orange predominating—which look as though they had been thrown on hastily by an impressionist painter.

We stayed half an hour on the pass, in order to enjoy the superb view and to taste the pleasure of victory. Then we started down the other side, over the gentle snowy slopes of the Rimo, making straight for the distant rocks at the foot of which the glacier makes a bend between its upper basin and the lower part of its course. The men went along at a good pace; we, with our skis, were of course much quicker, but in order not to get too much ahead of them and arrive too early at our goal, where we should have been chilled by a long wait in the early evening, we went down the slopes with turns and evolutions in which Miss Kalau was able to display her elegance and prowess as an accomplished ski-er; I, on the other hand, could only display sufficient calm to avoid the falls which might have brought me down from the eminence upon which my men have placed me!

A little before 8 in the evening we reached the rocks, where there is a kind of ditch which has been hollowed out by the force of the wind between the side of the mountain and the edge of the glacier; restricted space, roughness of ground, and complete darkness made the pitching of the camp rather a difficult matter. But at last it was ready for us to take our well-earned rest—at about 18,870 feet.

Yesterday and to-day we remained here, in order to allow the men, as usual, time to bring up all the baggage which had been left behind.

My readers may perhaps imagine that this crossing from the Siachen to the Rimo does not represent anything very extraordinary. But I hope they will realize that, in telling it, I have not dramatized it. Actually I cannot say that I encountered any difficulties except the very great ones caused by the continuous, persistent, violent adversity of the elements. And yet . . . and yet it is a fact that other Europeans—or rather Americans—though experienced, without a heavy caravan, and with celebrated Alpine guides, attempted the pass from the side of the Siachen and failed. This is actually what the Workmans wrote about the Teram Glacier:

> Seen from the Siachen this glacier [the Teram Sher] appears to rise gradually for miles, but in reality its higher part was composed of three slopes broken by short snow-terraces, and its whole upper area was cleft by crevasses of a size and depth not met with on the Siachen or its other large affluents. A wide plateau was finally reached [my 2nd Camp on the Teram] lying at over 18,000 feet. This white sea is cut up by schrunds and chasms running in all directions. Leading the caravan cautiously in and out of this maze, we advanced slowly, until Savoye said the responsibility for him was too great, as the caravan might at any moment become engulfed in this vortex of, seemingly, bottomless chasms. We had wished to reach the end of the plateau, now quite visible [for they thought it to be the pass, which in reality it was not], and see if any possible passage existed leading towards Nubra and the Rimo glaciers, but this was no smooth, lustrous expanse, such as are some elevated plateaux in Himalaya, but a mountain-devil's snow-continent set with death-traps to entice unwary men into their pitiless jaws.

This, perhaps, is really being a little dramatic—even rather too much so. But the fact remains that my predecessors, without a heavy caravan, and with celebrated Alpine guides, made the attempt and failed. And so my satisfaction was justifiable when, safely established at the camp near the pass, and fine weather having at last arrived, I knew that I had achieved a victory which others had failed to achieve and had won my fight against the stubborn adversity of the elements.

Then, sitting in this lofty camp, I cut a piece of green cloth from my bed, and took a little white sack, used for collecting specimens of rock, and undid the red lining of my "topee", and got Miss Kalau to make me a little tricolour flag. And next day, apart from other sensations, I had the unspeakable joy—I, the only Italian, in the presence of the highest mountains on earth and in the midst of the grandest region of ice that exists—of shouting a "Viva l'Italia!" which went straight up to a sky of marvellous purity, while my little flag, tied to my ice-axe, floated triumphantly over a pass which had been crossed for the first time by an Italian caravan—the pass between one glacier, the Rimo, which had been explored by an Italian expedition, and another, the Siachen, which had been studied from end to end by another Italian expedition. I named it the "Italia Pass".

The only Italian, perhaps; but my thirty loyal Ladakhis were round me, and, raising their arms instinctively as in the Roman salute, they also intoned: "Har-ghialu, har-ghialu, har-ghialu; Itā-līa!"

1st Camp on the Rimo, August 12th, 1930.

This 1st Camp on the Rimo was by no means the best camp during the time we lived on the glaciers. We were in a very narrow, small valley shut in at both ends and squeezed between the rocky mountain-side, which consisted here of continually falling loose stones, and a wall of ice with a fantastic fringe of icicles at its upper edge. It was one of those narrow marginal depressions which are quite commonly found close to spurs of rock when they jut out even only a little, and which owe their existence—largely at any rate—to the force of the wind and to the melting of the ice by heat reflected from the rock. They are an interesting and picturesque sight when one comes upon them from the top of the glacier-edge, but seem much less interesting and picturesque and extremely inconvenient when one has to use them as a shelter for tents, or when one is manœuvring to get down to the bottom of them or to get out again. For two days, therefore, we remained in this sort of bear-pit—like the one at Berne, for instance; but it was quite impossible to move about at all in the immediate neighbourhood of the tents.

On the third day, the 18th, having collected all the baggage that had been left behind, we proceeded on our way down the Rimo. I trod again, so to speak, in the tracks I had followed myself 16 years before. We at first descended over a tract in which were a certain number of crevasses (at the place where the glacier rounds the little spur of rocks in whose shelter we had camped), but after that the great river of ice flattens out and at moments seems to be almost level, were it not for the streams of water from the melting ice which run all over its surface. It was almost level, but by no means smooth, for the running water cuts furrows in every direction, most of which twist continually, first one way and then the other, just like the beds of rivers or streams in the middle of a plain where the watercourses seem to hesitate as to which way to go, owing to the very slight slope of the ground. The surface of the Rimo is anything but smooth, owing also to its being pierced all over by the regular hollows of the so-called "baignoires", full of water, and obliging us to take great care where we placed our feet, and often, as their name implies, giving us an unexpected bath, if, as sometimes happened, the water was hidden by a coating of snow-covered ice.

I felt myself, in a way, to be the owner of this region; none of my companions had ever been there, whereas I was one of the few men who had ever been on the Rimo. I seemed to recognize the smallest details—the little moraine where I had camped, with its marginal lake into whose waters plunges a tributary glacier, breaking up into lovely "icebergs" which wander and drift about; the bank a little farther down, formed by the glacier against the rocky side as though it were compressed with immense force; the right flank, on the other side of the immense bed of the glacier, smooth in its shapes (which sometimes remind one of the shapes of certain slopes of the Apennines) and owing to its smoothness covered plentifully with snow, and very black between the snow slopes owing to the ancient schists of which it is formed; the left flank, near the foot of which we were walking, steep, jagged, broken up into great towers of rock and overhanging walls, pink and yellowish, with red streaks that look like open wounds; and in front of us, in the far distance, where the mountain ridges open out a little to make way for the glacier, in the direction of its monstrous, ragged extremity —there one could see, far away, a reddish-coloured slope culminating in a regular horizontal line, the beginning of the Depsang Plateau, the beginning of Great Tibet, with its endless, desolate plains nearly 16,500 feet high, which form the vast roof of the world.

I should have liked to go on down as far as the point of confluence of the two main branches of the Rimo where, 16 years ago, I encamped on the top of a moraine which was raised on both sides above the surface of the glacier. But the men had to go back again, and, besides, I had with me a man who had been ill for over three weeks, with an illness which I had not been able to diagnose nor, therefore, to cure, and he was necessarily extremely slow on the march and could not do too long a stage. I stopped at the side of the glacier, at a point where it was joined by a lateral affluent which came headlong down a deep, rugged ravine in the pink and blood-red wall of dolomite. It was a fine, picturesque position for the camp, planted on top of a chaos of moraine on which were vast lumps of rock from a landslip, between the wall of rock on one side and on the other side the glacier, which was here thrust up into a great ridge and broken into a forest of white pinnacles. We were still at a height of about 18,000 feet.

The next day's journey was a journey of disappointment. It was easy to reach my old moraine at the confluence of the two main branches of the Rimo, but if I had not known its position with such exactness I should certainly not have recognized it. Instead of being raised up above the glacier it was now a depression; instead of forming a straight and regular line, it was reduced to a wretched heap of rocks and loose stones. The glacier had evidently increased in size; a great flood-wave was in process of coming down its whole length and, arriving here, was submerging my old moraine. One had to climb down from the latter, 16 years ago, to get on to the glacier again, that is, on to its most northern branch; now, on the other hand, one has to climb up. And once we had climbed up, the way was not as easy as it had been before. The glacier was now all swollen, and its surface was broken into rugged banks, ridges and pinnacles, amongst which one had to find one's way by long zigzags and steep ascents and descents. But the greatest difficulty was caused by two rivers, two real rivers, tumultuous torrents in beds several yards wide and sunk even deeper than that into the solid glacier. We had to follow their windings till we could find a snow bridge by which to cross; and these crossings required considerable precautions and the use of ropes.

Beyond, the northern arm of the Rimo sloped gently upwards, uniform in surface and easy, broken only by an infinite number of "baignoires". Our progress was made rather exhausting only by the heat of the sun.

Since the work of exploration of the De Filippi Expedition it has been known that the watershed of the Karakoram runs across this northern arm of the Rimo Glacier—a watershed which, at the place itself, is almost imperceptible, though in one of the highest regions of the world. This is because here on the Rimo the chain of the Karakoram may be said to have already passed completely into the uniformity of the Tibetan plateaux, where the watersheds are often so flat and level that it is difficult, sometimes quite impossible, to see in which direction the water is running and at what point it begins to flow down the slopes of the opposite side. Here at this point the great Rimo Glacier stretches right over one of these doubtful watersheds, and the same uncertainty is also produced in its own surface.

Thus, when I started from my old moraine 16 years ago, I thought I was going up the gentle slope of an arm of the glacier; but after some hours I realized that it was becoming flat, and then descending, still gently, in the opposite direction, towards a portion of glacier which I took to be merely a lateral branch, but which I afterwards realized to be an independent tongue, no longer on the southern slope but on the northern, no longer flowing down to the Shyok, but the actual source of the Yarkand.

I went the same way as before, sure of my facts. I remembered that, once the lateral portion of glacier had been reached, its regular surface sloped gently down right to its extreme end, and that the latter merged almost insensibly into the flat, alluvion-filled bottom of the Yarkand Valley. I remembered having gone down at a good pace—almost the pace of a Bersagliere, with my axe "at the trail"—and having reached the alluvion just at the point of the extreme end of the glacier to which chance had brought me after my easy descent. This time, too, I descended at the same pace but with the increased sureness authorized by old experience.

As we descended, there suddenly appeared in front of us, beyond the front of the glacier, the Yarkand Valley with its wide, alluvion-covered bottom. It looked to me strangely far off, and above all, strangely far below us, but I did not pay much attention to that. However, after a little, our rapid descent over the even and gently inclined surface of the glacier brought us, quite unexpectedly, to the top of a veritable wall of ice which rose sheer above the valley to a height of about 330 feet. It was only then that I understood why the valley had looked to me so very far below us.

We retraced our steps, looking for another way down; then went farther and farther still. I sent out men in every direction to examine the wide curve of the whole of the glacier-end, but it ended everywhere in the same wall, with the same impassable precipice of ice. In short, after all these attempts, which lasted for almost three hours, we had to give up, and at half-past seven, when it was already nearly dark, I was compelled to pitch the tents·on the ice, just where we were, almost on the edge of the precipice. We had no dinner that evening, we lit no fires because the *burtse* was already finished, and the outer roofs of the tents were given to the servants and the porters to make themselves a shelter. The Yarkand could be heard murmuring immediately below us, as though mocking us. It was indeed a day of disappointment.

One thing, however, was certain; we must get past somehow. Next day we went back at least half-way up that northern branch of the Rimo which had deceived us; then we left it, passing by a thin junction of ice on to a lateral glacier which went down from its right side; we crossed this, finally coming out on to the rocks which bordered the glacier-end that had so unexpectedly and undeservedly betrayed us. We made a brief halt, during which the porters whom I had sent back the day before to bring up the baggage left at the 1st Camp appeared on the Rimo, like so many little black dots in the distance. We shouted loudly to them to make them come round in our direction; then we all went on together.

Our way was neither short nor direct nor altogether easy. First we had to go across the side of the mountain; then steeply down over a long slope of detritus to the bank of a small lake shut in between the glacier and the rocks; then round, along the bank; and thence, from the other side, up very steep, sometimes overhanging cliffs, parts of which were rather risky, especially for the coolies with their loads. Finally we went down again, over detritus and rocks and smooth surfaces, but this time we did actually come out in front of the extremity of the glacier. I pitched our tents there, so as not to make too long a march for my invalids who had remained behind, but it had, in fact, taken us a whole day—and an exhausting one—to get off the Rimo. We were at a distance of perhaps 650 or 1,000 feet from our improvised camp of the evening before—a whole day to go this miserable distance. There was, however, also between us the precipitous wall of the glacier.

But a careful inspection of the extremity of the Rimo from below showed us one weak spot, by which, taking great precautions and cutting a certain number of steps, a caravan of men was able to climb up again on to the glacier in order to return to the 2nd Camp and bring back the last of the baggage. They returned to-day.

Yesterday morning I moved my tents a few hundred yards, to get a little farther away from the threatening extremity of the glacier, and put them against a rock, out of the wind. I was rather moved when I saw, close to the rock and right in the middle of the coarse sand which fills the whole of the bottom of the valley, a little tuft of dried *burtse*, reduced by time almost to ashes. It was *burtse* left behind by me 16 years before, when I left my camp which had been planted on the same identical spot, because then too I had needed a shelter against the wind. It is well known that high mountain air sometimes has extraordinary preserving properties.

We had now left the glaciers for good and all, after two and a half months. The whole of my programme had been accomplished. The most acute of my anxieties and cares were over. This was the beginning of our return—indeed, the beginning of the end. But still I could not breathe freely, nor had I yet that complete sense of relief which comes after one has been through a period of trials and anxieties. What had my friend Hashmatullah been doing in the meantime? Would he have remembered my programme and my intentions, or would he have been in doubt about them, not having received any more news from me nor the instructions I had told him to expect? I should have liked to stop here for a little while in order to carry out some researches. During these two days of waiting I have collected some fossils, and have also found a human jaw-bone which confirms the theory that the Baltis used to use this route. But it is impossible to stop. The men have already been told that from now onwards they will have no tea or tobacco, and that their flour will be reduced to a third of the normal ration, and that they will have to march at a good pace. The day before yesterday I sent on two coolies with orders to hurry on and to turn back and tell me if by any chance they met the *wazir*. I have also sent on the sick man (who, I think, is rather seriously ill), so that, accompanied by one of his fellow-villagers, he may do the stages slower and with less fatigue.

The vengeance of the Nubra is going to make itself felt to the very end. But in the end we shall arrive, and the Siachen has been conquered, even in spite of the defences that the Nubra has tried to put in my way.

Camp at the Northern Front of the Rimo, August 22nd, 1930.

CHAPTER XX

THE CARAVAN-ROAD OF DEATH

There are times when we experience certain impressions
about which we would have to think and reason at length if we
really wished to explain them; we would have to attain real
subtleties of psychological self-examination. When, towards
the end of July, I began to make my plans for leaving the
Siachen, I had a continuous and complete feeling that my
journey was already ended; yet it was not half over, and the
worst was yet to come—that is, the hitherto unexplored passage
from the Siachen to the Rimo, which one could foresee would
be difficult in itself and would also have to be accomplished
under great difficulties as regards commissariat.

If I had this feeling then, it may be imagined what I
felt later—the long way that I travelled seemed at moments
as if it must be leading straight to my own home, and my
arrival at Panamik gave me the sensation that it was definitely
the end of my journey, whereas there are still three months
of it in front of me, of which almost two will be caravan-
travelling. For most of my fellow-Florentines, who appear
to be so attached to their homes, even the journey which
I still have in front of me would be enough to cause them
to make their wills before starting. It is a question of nature,
and human nature varies in every man. Some, when far away,
feel a nostalgia for their own country, and some, when in
their own country, feel a nostalgia for distant lands. I belong
to the latter class. Leaving the Siachen meant, to a certain
extent, starting on the return journey, and since then each
stage seemed to take me nearer instead of farther—nearer
to that future encampment which would be the last of this
wonderful journey of mine. All my orders and arrangements which did not actually refer to our march and our life
from day to day, but looked a little further into the future,
were no longer made with a view to organization but to

demobilization. It was true that four months, three months, and many hundreds of miles, still separated me from my return home; but it already had to be thought of. I felt a subtle melancholy. I thought of the free, healthy, vigorous life, of the satisfaction of feeling that everything, both for oneself and for others who trust in one, depends on oneself alone, of the infinite pleasure of eye and mind in the midst of untouched and marvellously beautiful nature; and I compared it with the life which again awaits me, shut up in a city, in a house, in a room, glued to a desk, writing like a machine from morning till night, with the feeling of not being able to breathe. Here and like this only does one breathe fully. As for one's own country, one perhaps loves it all the more when one is far away from it, and even far away from it one can serve and honour it. Even my Ladakhis have learned to honour it, and acclaimed it when they shouted "Har-ghialu Itā-lïa!" on the top of "my" Pass.

Our return journey has begun, but not even when, on the morning of the 23rd, we left the camp beside the swollen end of the Rimo, was I free from anxieties. I was of course counting on the intelligence and loyalty of my friend Hash-matullah, but I had also to admit the possibility that, not having heard of my exact arrangements which were prevented by the Nubra from reaching him, he might not remember my plans, which I had explained to him only summarily, in order to forewarn him. In the event of this being so there was no time to lose; there was a long and difficult journey in front of us before we could again reach human habitations; and our baggage was heavy, our men tired, and our provisions decidedly short.

Early on the morning of the 23rd we were all on the march down the Yarkand Valley—which was discovered, 16 years ago, by the De Filippi Expedition, that is, by Marinelli and myself, and also, independently of us, by two other members of the Expedition.

It would be difficult to find, or even to imagine, a more sudden and radical alteration in the characteristics of an entire landscape. Up to now it had been a world of ice of an immensity, a grandeur and a completeness such as is to be found in no other part of the world; henceforward it was all parched

and naked rocks and only a few small glaciers here and there,
looking like mere slabs of ice stuck on to the most sheltered
of the slopes, and becoming rarer and rarer till they disappeared
almost completely.   At first—and, one may say, including the
whole Siachen basin—there were deep-cut valleys like great
channels or gigantic ditches, the sides of the mountains were
rugged, the peaks and ridges precipitous, the mountains of
really remarkable height; later, on the other hand, the valleys
were less deeply cut, quite shallow, with wide, flat stretches
of alluvial soil, and, consequently, the mountains were only of
moderate height, with sides sometimes absolutely tapering and
smooth except where the natural character of the rock gave
a certain ruggedness of surface.   At first the structure of the
mountains was almost entirely of crystalline rocks such as
granites and schists, in which dark colourings, sometimes
quite black, were predominant; later, the rock was almost
entirely calcareous, of a very different and much later geological period, and of every tone between red and orange.
At first we were right in the Karakoram range; now we are
already on the plateaux, and the Rimo basin, which is on the
border between the two, has, like its situation, the characteristics
of both.

 I set a fairly lively pace as we went down the Yarkand
Valley that morning of the 23rd, as though it had been my
first day's march.   I was with Miss Kalau and the faithful
jemadar: the coolies followed more slowly, being heavily laden,
and were soon outdistanced.   I went quickly because it was
important for me to meet the *wazir* soon, if he had come to
meet me with a caravan of extra provisions, and it was even
more important for me to be as quick as possible in case I
had to reach the Nubra Valley with only the supplies I carried
with me.   It was easy to walk fast along the flat, alluvial valley-
bottom, but often we were forced to stop and admire the
brilliance and variety of the colours of the rocks—which people
might think quite improbable if they saw them reproduced
in a picture—or to observe the graceful and elegant forms of
a herd of "heran", the Tibetan antelopes, whose movements
were at first calm, then shy and circumspect, and who then
made off at a swift gallop, in single file, over the flat ground
and up the slopes.   We had to ford the Yarkand several times,

and when we could not do this by jumping from stone to stone, the strong shoulders of the *jemadar* were ready to carry us across.

We had been on the march for three good hours when, having arrived at a point of confluence, we sighted, in the lateral valley, the small, distant figure of a man who seemed to be running towards us and desperately waving his arms. What a sense of relief I felt at that moment! In that upper Yarkand Valley, which we had discovered and which had afterwards been traversed only by Mason, in 1926, in his journey towards the Shaksgam, this little man running towards us in the distance could only belong to Hashmatullah's caravan or be one of the two coolies whom I had sent on to reconnoitre two days before. Then, from behind a small fold in the ground appeared a second little man, then a horse, then another, and then two more. There was no doubt now; we stopped, and after a wait which seemed much longer than it really was, the men and horses came up to us. They were my two coolies who, having met the *wazir*, were bringing us back four horses, and, after more than two months of being completely cut off from the world, a big bag of correspondence.

I heaved a great sigh of relief, for this was the end of all anxiety. And the broad pack-saddle on to which each of us had to clamber seemed to me like the most comfortable English saddle in the world, though we had to sit with legs rather wider apart than we were accustomed, and to continue thus the whole way to Panamik. I had already had experience—and also cause for gratitude—in connection with the pack-saddles of caravan-animals; this time both the experience and the gratitude were increased, and by the time I reached Panamik it almost seemed to me that my real saddle was much less comfortable than a pack-saddle, on which one sits with one's legs dangling free on both sides, as far forward or backward as one likes, one's feet unencumbered by stirrups and one's hands unencumbered by reins, feeling as if one were on a lofty throne.

This return journey on a pack-saddle in the direction of the Depsang Plains reminded me of another very similar one. On that occasion, having come out at the northern front of the Rimo and guessed that it was actually the source of the

Yarkand, Marinelli and I—who had started with only the provisions necessary to return straight to the Base Camp on the Depsang Plains—decided there and then to follow the newly discovered valley. We went down it for three days' journey, as far as the lake in which the Yarkand had been supposed, ever since the time of Hayward, to have its source. Then we looked for a pass towards the east, and having crossed it, found ourselves again on the great Karakoram caravan-route, but to the north of its pass. There bad weather overtook us—a ceaseless snowstorm. How slowly we progressed, and how stiff seemed the brief climb up to the pass! We had been on the move for months and months, working with our customary zeal, and then, just at the moment of our final return to the base, our new discovery compelled us to lengthen our last marches—and to tighten our belts to an excessive degree, for our provisions were exhausted. We saw the trade-caravans passing with a feeling of envy we had never experienced, until one passed with two extra horses, which they gave us; and so we were able to get back to our Base Camp on the Depsang Plains, still in the middle of storm, snow and mist, but reposing on two wide, throne-like pack-saddles.

How many memories of the past this road holds! Even at the front of the Rimo, when I moved the tents into the shelter of a rock, I had found near by a dried-up bunch of *burtse*, left there by me 16 years before. And as we went down the Yarkand I seemed to see, in the outlines of the mountains we passed, the friendly faces of old acquaintances.

About 1 o'clock we were at the point of confluence of a lateral valley, where we found the *wazir*. What rejoicings we had! He had brought with him sheep and chickens and eggs, and flour and tea and tobacco for the men of my caravan. We seemed to be almost wallowing in abundance.

We had one day of rest, in order to arrange the order of march and divide the loads in such a way that nothing should be left behind: with the new supplies, however, there was much more than we could carry. So the next day 10 heavy loads of flour had to be left dumped near the Yarkand. We all started off, the men divided into three groups with different tasks assigned them.

We went up a small tributary valley of the Yarkand which

has its beginning in a low saddle right at the foot of the Kara-koram Pass; at first it seemed to me very interesting, then rather monotonous, and in fact it took us more than a whole morning to get right to the top of it. At its head we reached a saddle which is on the watershed of this vast mountain-range. But it is an almost unnoticeable watershed; if not actually flat it is at any rate quite indistinguishable, and there must be watercourses which at times flow towards India and at times towards Turkistan. Near by there is a moderate-sized gap in the mountains which is the Karakoram Pass; there is the trace of a path which comes winding down, and then, like a long and regular inclined plane, reaches the bottom of the valley, which falls gently in the opposite direction to that from which we came up. This is the Karakoram caravan-road—the caravan-road of death.

We had scarcely reached the low saddle and were scarcely in sight of the tracks left by caravans on the mountain-side, when we noticed that the ground was spotted with little patches of almost every colour, some white—these were the skeletons, whitened by time, of animals sacrificed tens, perhaps even hundreds of years ago, on this road of death—others grey, or maroon, or black, or yellowish—the carcases that time had not yet turned into skeletons and whitened, and which still kept the fur, the hides and the manes of horses, yak, asses and camels. For nine days it was like this all the way. The caravan-road is marked by these victims of high altitude and of wind, storms and snow—chiefly of high altitude—far more clearly than by the tracks left on the ground by long processions of trade-caravans. It seems a fate which pack-animals, going backwards and forwards every year between Chinese Turkistan and Ladakh, cannot in the end escape. The men of the caravans know this by long experience, and for this reason every caravan starts always with a few animals carrying nothing more than the big pack-saddles, to take the place of those who will inevitably fall by the way. But some-times if the caravan is overtaken by the fury of a storm, no animal can escape; there is a hecatomb; and then the loads are piled one on top of another on one side of the road, and remain there until another caravan comes to rescue them. Sometimes they remain there for years.

For nine days it was like this all the way. The whole of the ground was scattered with whitened skeletons and carcases: it is indeed the caravan-road of death. But where the ground was rougher and the upward or downward slope steeper, or where there was a precipice immediately below the road, then the skeletons and carcases were not merely scattered over the flat valley-bottoms and plains, but were thick on the ground, sometimes actually in heaps, as though it were a charnel-house.

Between the Karakoram Pass and the Shyok Valley it is certainly the high altitude which kills animals; the ground is often flat and even, or only slightly undulating, and even outside the areas of typical plateau the valley-bottoms are wide and very gently sloping; a gorge is more or less exceptional, but there the caravan-path is generally well marked, in such a way that it goes up and down over the rough, rocky cliffs of the valley with endless twistings, longer or shorter. Anywhere else this would be an excellent path for caravans; there are worse in the Sind Valley. But here it is the high altitude which kills the animals. When going down, or even on the flat, it is difficult to realize it, but the moment the ground rises even slightly, the animals immediately begin to pant violently, and stop every few steps, placing themselves across the path so that their whole organism may be in the normal position and that they may breathe better, then struggling to start again. But where the climb is steeper and more continuous, as between the Shyok and the Saser Pass (where, over a short distance, there is a change of level of almost 2,600 feet), then the hecatomb, the real hecatomb, begins. They no longer fall occasionally, here and there, but thick and fast, in whole groups, all along the caravan-road of death. Beyond the Saser Pass it is even worse, for there the path, steeply sloping, goes for hours and hours over glaciers, or—even worse—over shapeless banks and mounds of active moraine. There is no trace of a path, and one has to find one's own way among these shapeless, dangerous masses of rock and ice: so that, as well as the high altitude and the steep slope, there is the extreme roughness of the ground to contend with. The poor beasts, here more than anywhere, bleed from mouth and nose, and already weakened by the long way they have come under such abnormal conditions, cannot withstand the greater effort required by the roughness of the ground and by the continual knocking of their loads against the lumps in the moraines and the rocks which stick up from the ground. They stumble and fall and their legs also begin to bleed. Often their loads have to be taken off, so that, relieved of the weight, they may be helped up again and then re-loaded. But often they can endure no more, and are left there to their fate. Other animals are loaded up instead, and the caravan starts on its relentless way, strewing victims all along the road.

Going up to the Saser Pass we came across some which had been abandoned the day before—three poor little donkeys, which had made a supreme effort to get up again, and stood still, almost skeletons already, on trembling legs, their big fleshy lips trying to reach some little grass-like plants among the rocks near by. The next day, certainly, they would be unable to do this: their end was near. We saw others already stretched on the ground as though resigned; threads of blood ran from their nostrils and mouths and streaked the ground with thin patterns and complicated zigzags of dark red; vultures and crows circled in the air near by, sure of their future prey. We saw others already dead, a horrible sight; the great birds of prey, which have a certain majesty when they wheel slowly and solemnly, almost without moving their wings, were gathered in a bunch on the still warm carcase and the ground was covered with entrails and blood. In other places their work was completed: the animal was picked dry, and near by were crows and vultures, satiated and heavy-looking, almost incapable of taking flight.

But they are the salvation of the road, and of the caravans. They fly continually above the track of the caravan-route, like a flight of observation aeroplanes, examining the road. They scent their prey, then settle on the neighbouring rocks till their predestined victim is at the point of death. The victim falls, for the last time, and they hurl themselves upon it with limitless greed. They do not stop till nothing remains but skin and bone, and in this way they superintend and look after the cleanliness and hygiene of the caravan-route. But all along the road there remain skeletons and carcases in attitudes of contortion and despair.

THE CARAVAN-ROAD OF DEATH

Yet on this caravan-road of death there is for three months
on end an intense life moving backwards and forwards between
India and Ladakh on the one side and Chinese Turkistan on
the other. Bales of *namdah* come down from Turkistan, silk
from Kashgar, boxes of opium, rugs from Khotan; and silks
and cottons and manufactured goods of every kind come up
from India. This—though it seems almost ridiculous—is a
great international trade-route. Every year, the moment the
first sun of summer begins effectively to melt the snow on the
Saser Pass, the long processions of caravans start from each
side—horses, donkeys and yak from the direction of Ladakh,
and camels also from the deserts and oases of Chinese Turkistan. They start off at their slow, regular pace on their long
journey of nearly a month, through valleys, mountains and
plateaux, through hazardous fords, over dangerous passes,
knowing well that they will strew their path all the time with
new victims and that possibly a storm may even compel them
to abandon their precious cargoes.

As for the men, they have a greater power of resistance.
They are men who are naturally robust, and who are hardened
to every discomfort by the life they lead, and their physical
strength is supported by moral strength and will-power. But
the great road sees not only the trade-caravans and their men.
It sees also little groups of pilgrims journeying to distant
Mecca. They start from Turkistan often alone, or in families.
They are not always young and strong and hardened, like the
men of the caravans: some are old or sick, and there are women
and children among them, and I have even seen babes at the
breast in their mothers' arms. The majority, in fact, are feeble,
and among them the Karakoram caravan-road reaps a continual
harvest of victims. What does it matter to them? Paradise
is opened for him who dies on the way to Mecca. Along
the road there are little walls against the rocks which mark
the numerous graves of those who have fallen by the way.
But every year again the pilgrims start on the caravan-road of
death, trusting, not in their strength, but in their faith.

This, for nine days, was our road.

The day we left the Yarkand Valley (it was August 25th)
we did a long stage—as far as Chojos Jilga, a usual place of
encampment, but marked by neither a blade of grass nor a

bush of *burtse*, merely by a greater number of skeletons and carcases. It was an exhausting day. We arrived before 5 o'clock, but the caravan not before 10, and it was a weary wait. Next morning, profiting by experience, I deemed it necessary to make radical alterations in the distribution of the loads: the few horses which had arrived with Hashmatullah were to transport the camp, the coolies everything else; I gave them the task of fetching the flour which had been left on the bank of the Yarkand, and they were to have a certain freedom of march.

All the stages had to be long ones, as this region requires. This is certainly not a part where one can find any amusement along the road. In two successive days we crossed the Depsang Plateau, desolate in its bare vastness. I looked with some emotion at the place where the Base Camp of the De Filippi Expedition had been, 16 years ago. But why not have chosen instead the unusually green and flowery oasis of Yapchan which is not very far off, near the front of that very Rimo glacier that the Expedition was to explore?

From the Depsang Plateau we went down the narrow, reddish gorge—as its name implies—of Qizil Langar; then beyond again to the district of Burtse—but there was no grass, no *burtse*, in spite of the name, only skeletons and carcases.

From Burtse to Murgo was a way I already knew. But the mountains of dolomite, steep and as though bleeding from a thousand scars, and sprinkled high up with the snow which had fallen during the night, were still marvellously beautiful. At Murgo was the first grass, but even among the grass were the skeletons and carcases which seemed to pursue us all the way.

Beyond Murgo—where it began to be new ground for me also—opens out a wide, flat depression, enlivened by a small lake in which the mountains of dolomite are reflected, looking almost iridescent. But afterwards, in contrast to this, there is a sudden descent and a wild, narrow, tortuous gorge; one goes along the stony bed of a torrent, with no view, shut in, almost imprisoned between rocks black as coal. Then all at once one comes out into a gigantic channel, an immense ditch, the Shyok Valley. Up above us I could see the Aktash glaciers, which I studied 16 years ago. How they are transformed! At that time the Chong—or Great—Aktash de-

217

scended from its own valley right down to the Shyok, and went right across it, expanding into a wide fan-shape so that the river ran under the ice in a tunnel. Now the Aktash has retreated to the edge of the valley, some way from the river.

We forded the river with ease, and encamped on the other side near the mouth of the Saser Valley. There were piles of goods abandoned by caravans, skeletons and carcases heaped together by hundreds, and a great many tombs of *haji*, or pilgrims, for here begins the worst part of the caravan-road of death. Here we stopped one day, August 30th, to allow the animals a breathing-space.

At the Saser Camp we had come down to about 15,100 feet. But when we started again, a steep rise soon brought us up to the pass, at 17,720 feet again. The pass is occupied by a glacier, but the valley which leads down on the other side, towards the Nubra (it is less steep, because much longer), is, in its upper portion, invaded everywhere by the ends of glaciers which flow down from lateral valleys, and by shapeless banks and hillocks of moraine. It is a truly terrifying road, of which there is no trace on the ice and among the rocks except the blood which has been shed at every step by struggling animals and victims claimed by the unparalleled harshness of the mountains. There was a sharp, strongly blowing north wind, and icy sleet. I could well imagine what a storm on the Saser Pass must be like, and how disastrous for caravans.

We went farther down, leaving the head of the valley where it is invaded by glaciers and moraines, leaving the fatal road, and encamped in the locality of Gongmo-lung. Here it was a typically Alpine landscape—the valley was wider, with gentle undulations of green pasture, and a wealth of flowers of every colour and scent, and a splendid view of mountains, pinnacles, ridges and ice-filled ravines. However, the weather was terrible and there was a violent snowstorm during the night.

Yesterday we went on down the valley, which again changed completely. Wide at the top, it narrows below into a gorge, at the bottom of which runs a torrent, tumultuous and with one waterfall after another. We pitched the tents at Umkang, where the passage between the rocks was slightly less narrow. And to-day, at last, we are in the midst of green, inhabited country, back in the world again. However, we have had to work hard for it.

From Umkang onwards the bottom of the valley becomes wilder and wilder, and it is impossible to follow it. It is necessary to climb up the rocks to the point, up above, where the sides of the valley recede from each other and where one no longer has the feeling of oppression which weighed upon us at the bottom, close to the tumult of the torrent. As the landscape widens one can breathe more freely, and the eye can again wander over a wider horizon. We were now at the ancient high level where the valley which comes down from the Saser had once opened into the Nubra Valley; below us the ground fell away in a sudden precipice, above the Nubra Valley, gigantic between its granite bastions. In front of us, far below, was a green oasis, Aranu; and amongst the green of cultivated fields and trees were the little greyish cubes of houses and the tiny white cubes of *chorten*. It was like a dream. After our rough life, left to our own devices, all the time amongst ice, to see a village again, fields, trees, houses!

It was a long but swift descent down the twisting caravan-path cut in the precipitous granite wall; then over the flat alluvion of the Nubra Valley. One hour over stretches of gravel, and we were at Panamik. We have left the caravan-road of death and have returned again to life.

Panamik, September 3rd, 1930.

CHAPTER XXI

FROM THE NUBRA VALLEY TO LEH BY THE KHARDUNG-LA

The Nubra Valley seemed transformed; it was greener and full of flowers. It was three months since we had gone over its beds of gravel and burning sands and (when crossing its oases) through fields indeed, but between high hedges of dry, purplish thorn; the trees had scarcely put forth their leaves, which were still very small though of a bright, fresh green; the pasture-lands near the villages were mere yellowish-brown expanses, and the fields were nothing but earth, with the first shoots of the crops barely beginning to sprout in their regular furrows.

But now the Nubra Valley seemed transformed. Even the gravel-beds and sands and shapeless accumulations of stones that had fallen from the sheer granite sides of the mountains had their own crop of vegetation and flowers; it was poor and patchy, certainly, but nevertheless there it was, in full bloom. The pasture-lands on the fan-shaped deposits on which the villages are situated were all of a beautiful dark green and looked like carpets, so thick and close was the grass; but in contrast to this there were here and there gigantic tufts of grass, higher than a man. In the fields the crops—wheat and barley—swayed rhythmically in the wind, which seems to be a permanent feature of the Nubra Valley, and on certain pieces of ground, sheltered by low walls, there were vegetables and flowers. The foliage of the trees was thick and shady. And the hedges were no longer dry and purplish; the dry thorn-bushes, tied closely together by the *zemindars* in order to make the hedges thicker, had almost disappeared beneath a multitude of growing thorny plants which were clothed with masses of tiny leaves and laden with red, black and orange berries; the hedges were crowned with an intricate tangle of bryony and fringed with its light, cotton-like tassels, among which could be seen the pale, sky-blue bells of the convolvulus.

ON THE ROOFS OF THE *GOMPA* OF TEGUR

[*face p.* 220

There was great activity at Panamik—also along the road and at the oasis of Tegur. The harvesting of the crops had begun, and every family, both men and women, was at work. Some were reaping in the fields; others carried the great bundles of barley and wheat towards their houses, keeping a regular rhythmical step and singing short, endlessly repeated phrases, answering each other by turns; most of these phrases were monotonous and long drawn out, but some were charmingly rhythmical and melodious. Near the houses the bundles were divided, tied up in sheaves, and placed upright in order to dry further. If the work was more advanced, one saw the crops spread out on the wide circular threshing-floor, and a row of donkeys tied together with some wretched calf going round and round like the hand of a clock, urged continually by a long whip and the strident—or occasionally, silvery—voice of a woman. Farther on, at another threshing-floor, other men and women with primitive forks would be lifting the corn, after it had been thrashed, and throwing it into the air, in order to separate the grain from the straw.

This was the real native life, the real life of the place. But beyond Panamik there was another form of activity and life which I should never have imagined. As we came down over the caravan-road of death there was one thing which had surprised me—the scarcity of trade-caravans. I remembered how, last time I was here, during the few days I passed at the Base Camp on the Depsang Plains, there had been a continual passing, in one or the other direction, of long processions of horses, donkeys, and camels, accompanied for the most part by characteristic and typical caravan-drivers from Yarkand— tall, strong fellows with faces exactly like the faces of our own people and generally with great beards, wearing little skull-caps with projecting pads of fur all round them, voluminous, many-coloured robes, often with thin vertical stripes of different colours, enormous fur cloaks with the fur inside and the rough, natural skin outside, and on their feet high, wide boots of soft leather, generally bright red.

This time, however, we had met very few of these caravans. There was one perfectly equipped one which had stopped near Chojos Jilga and was all assembled round a large tent with the bales of merchandise forming a wall all round it. On the

Depsang Plains there were only two, one going in each direction —two little caravans of camels, making a clear and picturesque outline against the pink sky of dawn as they passed over the flat surface of the plateau. In front was a small donkey with a gigantic caravan-driver on its back, and then, each one tied to the tail of the one in front, the camels laden with great bales of *namdah*, ambling along with their long shaggy paws and big feet which look as if they were made of rubber when they put them on the ground, rather melancholy, rather timid, and always contemptuous-looking when they move their heads slowly this way and that and gaze out of eyes which always seem to look at everything with the perfect indifference of a superior being.

It is true that when we stopped at the Saser Camp, and afterwards, while we were crossing the pass and until we came out into the Nubra Valley, we had met with various caravans and had overtaken others, for the roughness of the ground there compels them to go slower and to stop frequently. They were caravans of horses and donkeys, for camels do not usually go beyond the Shyok. But on the whole there were not many of them, and I had begun to think that, in comparison with what I remembered of former times, the traffic over the fatal road must have diminished, to a certain extent at least.

But my doubts were set at rest when I arrived at Panamik. Whole troops of beasts—asses and horses—were at pasture in the great thorn-hedged enclosures of the oasis, and the large pack-saddles which they carried even while they were feeding showed at once that they were animals belonging to passing caravans. On many of the threshing-floors and on uncultivated pieces of ground here and there in the oasis were the great tents of the caravan-men, surrounded by bales of merchandise and guarded by dogs which snarled ferociously. The caravan-tents were generally placed by preference at the two opposite edges of the oasis, and the long, narrow, winding main alley of the village, which goes through it from one end to the other, hemmed in by low walls and hedges, was frequently traversed by long files of laden animals belonging to arriving or departing caravans. The whole alley would be filled with them, and often in complete confusion, for Yarkandi horses are accustomed to almost unlimited space and not to the narrow, winding paths through the oases of Ladakh; if a pack knocked against the wall or a calf came along in the opposite direction, there was always some troublesome or nervous horse which would try to bolt. It would not, of course, get its way, but the whole of the caravan would be thrown into a kind of revolt—other horses being violently pushed and giving back energetic, resounding kicks, packs falling off or in danger of falling, drivers running up, hoarse shouts, the thud of a kick in the belly of some troublesome beast, neighings, the whole caravan stopped, the road blocked up on either side. Then, with packs made fast again and order re-established, they would move on again at their slow, regular pace, accompanied by the silvery jingling of all their little bells . . . until the next mishap and the next obstacle on the narrow road.

All along the road, and especially in the neighbourhood of the *serai*, there was always a little crowd of spectators. It was odd: the majority of the inhabitants of the oasis were obviously attending to the work of the harvest, but there must be people who have come from other villages off the caravan-route, brought there by the possibility of earning some small amount by doing a little job of work for the passing caravans. Others, perhaps, had come to make some modest purchase from the men of the caravans—top-boots from Yarkand, saddle-bags, furs, or cotton stuffs.

We also were among the buyers drawn up in a little crowd round the men of the passing caravans at Panamik. The majority of the little crowd consisted, so to speak, of friends, because most of them were our porters. They had arrived separately, on successive days, as I expected, according to the three different groups (Leh, Timosgam, and Tia) and according to the different tasks I had assigned to each. To the Leh group, who were the first to arrive, I immediately gave orders to go up to Zingrul, at the front of the Siachen, and bring down the loads sent there from the Base Camp. They returned the same day, after a fruitless attempt to ford the Nubra, so I at once organized a horse-caravan and gave them peremptory orders, because I did not wish to be held up in Ladakh waiting for twenty loads or so, even though they were precious. In the meantime the porters, although free to proceed immediately towards Leh, also stopped at Panamik in order to play the gentleman and spend their money. They were the best clients

223

of the passing caravans; many of them even bought donkeys, and I had to be their banker!

Three days soon passed, in the lively oasis of Panamik. I found time to take the measurements of a first series of inhabitants of the Nubra Valley; the rest (to make up about fifty in all) I measured later at the next stopping-places, Tegur and Deskit. I wished to keep them distinct from the Ladakhis, because I thought I had discerned signs in them of slightly different characteristics. Perhaps, in the case of the inhabitants of the Nubra Valley, my *flair* may be as successful as it was in the case of the Purighis, whom I thought to be a separate people, as my measurements later proved. In the case of the people of Nubra reason tends to confirm my impression. Separated from Ladakh proper by the often unfordable Shyok and on the road to Kashgar, they must have been less intensely affected by invasion from Tibet—which means by Mongol invasion—and, on the other hand, more intensely by invasion from Yarkand. My impression may therefore be justified: the series of measurements will finally decide.

On the 6th of September we went down from Panamik as far as Tegur, a flourishing village situated on the same fan-shaped formation as Samur. My readers will remember Samur. At Tegur we stayed in a house which, for this region, is quite a palace. My room was up above, on the terrace at the end of the roof, and a wide *rabsal* opened from it, overlooking all the fields of the oasis and the whole gigantic channel of the valley; on one side a pretty wooden trellis formed a slight screen in the direction of the roof, on another side a small window commanded a neighbouring house and the life that went on there, and while I was working I could rest my eye every now and then on the harmony of design and colour in the pictures painted on the walls. I took measurements of men and also made plans of houses at Tegur, as I had already done at Panamik. I also walked about in the oasis, always in search of something beautiful—which is never lacking, since a feeling for beauty is so truly innate in these people. There is an old palace, perched against the first rocks behind the village, which is a marvel of picturesque art with the many *rabsal* which relieve the massiveness of its construction. Below it, on the rocky top of the cone, is a forest of *chorten*, and then

THE CONFLUENCE OF THE NUBRA AND THE SHYOK, FROM THE *GOMPA* OF DESKIT

[*face p.* 224

a temple which is a perfect jewel. It is a little temple of a kind of which I have seen many in the Nubra Valley but never elsewhere; it contains no altars or great statues of Chamba or Sanghiès or any of the numberless other divinities, good or bad, in the Olympus of the lamas, but, inside a very typical construction which is always repeated with the same identical architectural characteristics, there is an immense revolving *mani*, moved by running water. It is a 'mani-kang'.

We spent two days at Tegur, then started off again, but again left the caravan-route. We reached Lukjum, and remembered the tremendous storm of wind and sand which overtook us there when we were coming up the valley. From Lukjum we entered immediately upon the vast, wide alluvial valley-bottom at the point where the Nubra joins the Shyok. We forded the Shyok without anxiety, for the waters seem to have subsided considerably. This gives me hopes for my baggage at Zingrul!

My object in fording the river at a point off the normal caravan-route was to go by Deskit, the largest oasis in the Nubra region and the only one in that region which has an ancient *gompa*. After this my knowledge of the monasteries of Ladakh may be said to be complete.

We had a triumphal entry into Deskit, with music from the *mon* and music from the lamas and rejoicings on the part of the women and offerings of flowers and fruit and vegetables. Incidentally, fresh vegetables are the greatest and most pleasant surprise of our return to cultivated and inhabited country.

At Deskit we lived in an old house, half in ruins but of really supreme architectural beauty, which belonged to the *gompa*. Aged lamas and children appeared every now and then, cautiously and silently, at the door of my room—which is a marvel of columns and architraves, painted with dragons and flowers and scrolls—in order to superintend my work. It was amusing to watch their surprise and wonder as they followed the quick clicking of the typewriter, when Miss Kalau, the rapid and accurate interpreter and copyist of my writings and correspondence, was acting as my secretary. And every now and then, one of them, bolder than the others—and not only lamas, but women and even children—would come in on tiptoe, come up to the table and put down (still without a word) a little bunch of many-coloured flowers. I would raise my eyes, but the bringer of the flowers would already be disappearing, swiftly and silently, with nothing more than a tap of the hand against the forehead in sign of humble respect.

In the evening there was a grand *tamasha* in our honour on an open space in the midst of the grove of trees in front of the house. It was a truly fantastic sight. In the middle of the space, on a kind of central altar, a great bonfire was burning, which was continually fed and stirred up by a few men. At the sides were the public, with the men and women in separate groups. It was not an ordinary *tamasha*. It is true that the men danced those dances of theirs which end in swift gyrations, to a rhythm which becomes more and more accentuated and rapid all the time on the drums and trumpets of the *mon*; the women moved in a circle with little steps against the beat of the music, accompanying their dance with little sharp movements of the arms and hands and fingers; and the women also sang certain songs which appeared to have a refrain. But the dances were not the only thing in the entertainment; they alternated with imitations of the dances of different countries —the dances of Baltistan and Turkomania—and with a few comic scenes in which all the quickness, all the light and ever-smiling humour of the Ladakhis bubbles forth, spontaneously, surprisingly, unexpectedly. Next morning I recognized among our muleteers almost all the men who had taken part as actors the evening before. To see the seriousness with which they loaded up the yak and horses and led them over the alluvial bed of the Shyok, and, later, helped them over a really difficult, if not dangerous, part of the road, one could hardly have believed that they were actually the same men who, with faces whitened with flour—exactly like our circus-clowns— had entertained their audience with jokes which produced a general laugh, in which even we were forced to join by their comic attitudes and the expressions of their faces—the same men who had imitated every kind of animal from the cock and the snow-leopard to the camel and the horse, with a primitive simplicity of external aids, but an extraordinary power to reproduce gait and movements, displaying an extremely fine sense of observation and also a brilliant imitative power.

Many times have I made a mental comparison between the Ladakhis and our own mountain people, with whom they certainly have an enormous number of qualities in common; but I have been forced to recognize that, while our own mountain people are rather taciturn, rather heavy, and also rather rough and hard, the Ladakhis have an extraordinary fineness and gaiety of character, seasoned with an ever-ready humour. There can be no people on earth with so many and such varied qualities. And I must add that I have never succeeded in discovering any defect in them.

Deskit is the most extensive and the most flourishing oasis in the whole Nubra region. Towards the highest point of the alluvial fan on which it originated and developed (like almost all the other oases) the cultivated area is obviously of more ancient origin: it is divided up into smaller fields, with a greater variety of crops, and there is a great deal of shade from the fine leafy trees, willows, poplars and apricots. But lower down, especially at the extreme outer edge of the fan where it merges gradually into the flat, even alluvion of the Shyok, there are fewer trees or no trees at all, the fields are more extensive, and only corn is grown. This is the more recently cultivated area.

Nevertheless the oasis of Deskit forms a great patch of green, stretching along, and coming right up to, the foot of the steep and rugged mountain-side, in which the naked rock shows occasional traces here and there of mounds of moraine left by an ancient Nubra glacier; the aridity of these adds to the naked appearance of the rocky structure of the mountain where it shows through. Right behind the village the mountain-side is cleft by a wild, extremely narrow, deep gorge with perpendicular walls, piled up with huge rocks which make a bridge from one wall to the other, and echoing with the sound of the water which rushes down it, foaming as it falls from rock to rock. This gorge opens out at a sharp angle from the mountain-side, in such a way that between it and the outer face of the side juts out a ridge of rock—narrow, extremely steep, rugged and wild. At the top, upon a marked spur of this ridge, is perched the ancient *gompa* of Deskit, hanging right over the village and the oasis and commanding the whole width of the landscape of the Nubra region in every

227

direction. It has perhaps the boldest situation of all the monasteries in Ladakh.

It is a long climb up to it through woods and whitish hedges of *chorten* of every shape and size, and the lamas, collected at the edge of a terrace with all their instruments, gave us a loud welcome. Our visit was short, for the monastery contains only two little chapels which are not particularly rich, and we came rapidly down again past the *mani* and *chorten* till we re-entered the thick shade of the trees and reached my airy *rabsal*, which, with all its paintings, looked peaceful and almost smiling.

Our stay at Deskit was easy and pleasant, but our departure was attended with difficulties and was not at all agreeable. The *wazir* had employed a second caravan to come and re-furnish him with provisions at the front of the Rimo, and had had to pay for it almost entirely in advance, so as to be sure that it would not fail to carry out its task. The necessity which had compelled me to leave the glacier-end hastily owing to the un-certainties of my position (that is, whether relief reached me or not) had rendered this second caravan superfluous, and they were notified accordingly, by special courier, when they had only just left Panamik. It was perfectly right that the owners of the horses should receive some compensation, but it was also right that I should recover part of the many hundreds of rupees in ready money which had been paid them in advance. The contractor of the caravan belonged to Deskit. It was a long and very laborious business to settle how much compensation I ought to pay for each horse, and therefore what amount ought to be given back to me; but the negotiations which the caravan-contractor had to complete in order to recover in his turn the money from the separate owners of the horses, on the morning on which we finally left the village, seemed to me perfectly endless. It was a financial affair on a grand scale, for this district; messages were sent to all parts of the village, there were long waits, tiresome enquiries, discussions which were repeated again and again with each separate man, calculations of an extreme complication because other personal interests interfered in each case, and scrupulous and repeated calculations of money. It was like an affair of State, and as if it had been a question of high financial politics and of milliards of money.

THE *GOMPA* OF DESKIT

It took a good three hours before everyone was agreed and I recovered my money in accordance with our agreement.

Then we started. The Nubra Valley seemed anxious to show itself as it often is—that is, not to show itself at all: the sand raised by the wind formed an even, thick, grey curtain, so that we could not even see the opposite side. It was not a long stage, but extremely uncomfortable. We were still off the caravan-road, which runs close to the other bank of the Shyok, and on this side the river washes right against the rocky foot of a steep and rugged mountain-side. The path has to clamber up above, then runs across, then comes down again, steep, difficult and exposed all the time, on the top of a precipitous cliff above the river. The animals had to be unloaded and helped over the long difficult passage, the loads being carried on the men's shoulders, and then, the danger past, the loads were put on the pack-saddles again.

The rest of our march was as easy as going for a walk, even though we had to go a few hundred yards up again over the side of the valley and again across the mountain-side, and then down again to the level of the Shyok, for the wild, rugged grandeur of this Himalayan country necessitates this.

We encamped in the little oasis of Kalzar under the thick shade of some nut-trees. There were certain difficulties as to whether we had sufficient means of transport to continue our march and take all our baggage with us, so some twenty or thirty loads were dumped with one of my men to watch over them. Then off we went again, still up the Shyok, still following the side which was washed by the swirling waters of the river, going up across the mountain-side and coming down farther on, to the flat, sandy, alluvial bottom.

Finally we entered the lateral valley of Khardung, which is rather narrow and full of the clay deposit of a former lake, of coarse alluvion and of ancient moraines worn into shapes like ruined walls. Along the bottom there is a long thin line of trees—mostly willows—which accompanied us until the rise became steeper and the caravan-road, which we had now re-joined, clambered rather laboriously up the side, passing the ruins of ancient fortifications built by the Ladakhi kings as a defence against invasions from Yarkand; the road finally reached a high plain which was green with crops—but only barley, for the village of Khardung is at a height of over 13,450 feet.

It was a stormy night at Khardung, with violent rain—for the first time in my fairly long experience of the district. It left off to a certain extent in the morning, but the sky was completely overcast in every direction with great, heavy dark-grey clouds, as on a rainy autumn day at home. Our departure was a little delayed by the weather, but this was lucky, as we saw arriving all the baggage which we had had to leave at Kalzar and which had travelled by night, through the storm. Khardung has plenty of transport—shaggy yak of a dull black colour—and so everything was able to leave with us. The only thing which remained uncertain and unknown was the fate of the baggage left at Zingrul.

That day's march was anything but pleasant; no sooner were we in the saddle than a violent and persistent rain began to beat down upon us. Higher up this changed into snow. No view was possible, for the valley was completely filled with a thick mist. All I saw was the thick, fresh footprints of snow-leopards on the white blanket which covered the earth.

The climb became steadily steeper, the caravan-road worse, the ground more encumbered with a uniform litter of rocks and loose stones. The horses, panting at every step, toiled on, but frequent rests were necessary in order to take breath; then they would hop quickly along for a short space up the steep, rocky slope, as though to shorten the climb. There was icy hail and mist all the time. Only higher up the mist cleared a little and a few pieces of blue appeared through the rents in the clouds. Then, in front of us, the moderate-sized gap of the pass, the Khardung-la, became visible, with a small glacier coming down from it over the steep, almost precipitous side; on the glacier, here and there, were dark patches made by the carcases of horses, the last victims of the caravan-road before its goal, and near by were vultures satiated with their recent prey.

It was nearly half-past two when we reached the pass, which is at a height of about 18,000 feet; a slight but cold wind greeted us. It would have been unwise to stop there, so, in order to have lunch, we went down a few hundred feet farther till we found a little shelter where the air was slightly less sharp. From up on the pass—in contrast to the complete lack of visibility while we were climbing up to it—an extremely beautiful view opened out suddenly in front of us: the mountain-side sloped steeply down, curving like a great amphitheatre, and ended at the bottom in a narrow valley. At the sides there was a succession of buttresses and spurs of rock, falling away towards the wide, flat bottom of a great valley—the valley of the Indus—and breaking up and coming to an end in a hundred little spurs of rock round the edge of a great green oasis—Leh. Beyond the Indus a lofty chain of mountains formed a background to the scene—the mountains which make a barrier to the rugged region of the Zanskar. There were two supremely beautiful elements in this marvellous view of valleys, mountains, buttresses and spurs—the great number of level spaces and the variety of colour. Each separate level space had its own special colour. The nearer sides of the valley were yellowish, falling away gradually, as the plain receded in the distance, to tones of darker and darker brown, till the chain of the Zanskar merged into shades of colour between violet and black. The oasis of Leh was of an almost sparkling green; the sandy plain of the Indus yellow, with a luminosity, in places, almost of gold; and the sky bright blue with big puffs of white cloud.

We went quickly down the valley. But the shades of twilight were already descending over the whole landscape when we came out of the valley on to the wide fan at its mouth. Here were the terraced fields of an oasis—Ganglès. I knew that the caravan would arrive very late; on the other hand, I did not wish to arrive too late at Leh, where we wished to establish ourselves in a leisurely fashion; so I had our tents pitched for the night at Ganglès.

Yesterday morning a walk of just over an hour, in calm, brilliant weather, brought me back again into the capital, escorted by a few Ladakhi friends who had come to meet me. Leh also is more full of grass and flowers than when I left it— and, if possible, even more beautiful.

Leh, September 15th, 1930.

CHAPTER XXII

A HALT AT LEH, THE CAPITAL

We halted for 10 days at Leh. I had planned to stay
longer, and should have liked to do so; but it was already becoming late in the season, the autumn is notoriously short in the
Himalaya, and it was necessary as far as possible to avoid the
first snows having blocked the passes of the Rupshu before we
had got safely across. It is a question of three or four very
high passes which are not very much used. For this reason,
therefore, I am intending to start a few days earlier, and am
giving up the idea which I had of making a short détour on the
Rupshu plateau in order to see the blue surface of Morari Tso,
which I once crossed in winter on the great sheet of ice which
covered it.

It is a great pity to have to start earlier, for these days at
Leh are passing in a flash. I had allowed them to myself—
and had intended to allow myself even longer—as a sort of
reward: my journey is now at an end, I am no longer worried
by all the anxieties which pursued me during the difficult part
of my expedition, and I had been looking forward with pleasure
to the idea of being able to enjoy myself at leisure in Leh.
There was still a great deal of work, of course, but it was not
work which could prevent or lessen my enjoyment. As things
are, however, my enjoyment has been lessened because I have
had, so to speak, to condense the work into a shorter time.

It was mainly a question of the partial demobilization of the
caravan, and of reorganizing the whole of the baggage before
our final departure on our return journey. The baggage was
naturally in complete disorder: apart from the much-reduced
loads which had travelled with us from the Rimo to Leh, I
had left a small depôt at Leh before starting for the glaciers,
and another at Panamik; I had sent other baggage to Panamik
from our various camps on the Siachen; about twenty loads
were at Zingrul, waiting for the violent spate of the Nubra to

232

subside; also the great quantity of baggage which had left the Rimo with us had undergone two successive eliminations. Except for the boxes containing instruments, it may be said that there was not a single one whose contents were homogeneous. It was necessary to rearrange them all and, if possible, eliminate everything that was really useless to us. However, there was very little that I could eliminate: having replenished five cases of provisions which were necessary for the return journey, I sold all that I had left of eatables in the bazaar. There were about 4,000 lire's worth—a sign of the ample scale on which the provisioning had been planned. I also eliminated the medicine-chest, keeping only a few medicines and distributing all the rest between two small and extremely poor dispensaries here. But the biggest job—though it was despatched with the utmost speed—was that of making the contents of the various cases rather more uniform. If one opened a case at random, there might come out of it, quite promiscuously, a pair of heavy shoes, tins of milk or potted meat, bags of personal linen, ski-straps or tubes of "skyolina", samples of fossils or rock, boxes of negatives, bundles of plants we had gathered and which were already dried. The rearrangement was very rapidly made.

And yet the preparation of the baggage seemed endless. During our first stay I had already found means of increasing —and of effectually enriching—the collection of Tibetan objects, consisting largely of articles connected with religion and with the life of the lamas, which formed a permanent and vivid record, in my house in Florence, of my peregrinations on Tibetan soil during the De Filippi Expedition. But now the collection has been further enriched: rapid excursions to the bazaar and to the houses of the principal merchants who have direct connections with Lhasa, also to the houses of my Ladakhi friends and to one or two *gompa*, have led to a daily influx into my room at the bungalow of new objects, charmingly painted or ornamented or modelled. And every day there has been a concourse of people at the bungalow, and of intermediaries of others who did not wish to reveal themselves, laden sometimes with simple, innocent baubles, but generally with garments, musical instruments, rugs, tea-pots and jars and cups, reliquaries and pendants, little painted, lacquered or carved tables, and small religious statues or paintings—all of which they declared to have come from Lhasa (for the people here have discovered the attraction and the feeling of mystery which the very name of the sacred, forbidden city has for us Europeans) but which actually, in most cases, were of local make. One does not know whether to admire more in them the delicacy of taste which is innate in these people, or the fineness of their execution. In this way my Tibetan ethnographical collection has been steadily growing day by day, and every day it was necessary to order and arrange new cases. This went on almost till the moment of starting. For the nearer we get to the day of our departure, the greater the number of would-be sellers, and the greater, also, my frenzy to increase and enrich the collection of Tibetan objects to take back to Florence. And the rivalry of Miss Kalau makes our haul even more abundant.

Then there was the demobilization of the caravan, with the calculations of all the 'fees' of each porter, consisting of wages, of compensation for tobacco which was not distributed, and of a final present. These calculations were made with the utmost care and the utmost latitude, but this did not prevent the men from asking me for 21 days' extra pay, on I know not what basis of calculation according to the Tibetan calendar. The Ladakhis ask frequently and without hesitation, because even they know quite well that 'nothing venture, nothing win', but after that they are perfectly content with little, or even nothing: with great generosity I distributed another two rupees to each, and they were perfectly content. But what gave me much more cause for regret was the departure of the *jemadar*, my faithful Zewang Tashi. I would willingly have taken him with me to India as confidential servant in my new caravan; he hesitated a long time and a considerable struggle went on in his mind, but finally he confessed to me shyly that he did not want to come quite alone. The Ladakhis have these odd forms of shyness: though brave and inured to every kind of hardship, and full of curiosity for everything that is new and even for a spice of adventure, they are terrified of finding themselves completely alone among people not of their own kind; they feel themselves lost and out of their element. So the faithful Zewang Tashi has gone back to Tia, his own village. He was very much distressed at leaving me; his voice trembled when he said good-

LEH AND THE GREAT STREET OF THE BAZAAR

[face p. 234

bye, his eyes were red and he blinked quickly to keep back the
tears. I remember that last time, when Sonam Kontchok had
to leave me at Kashgar to go back over the Karakoram Pass
to his own wonderful Ladakh, he too wept and stood still looking at me till a bend in the road took me out of his sight amongst
the thick green of the oasis. I do not deny that it gives me
great inward satisfaction to see that these men, from whom I
have asked so much, from whom I have claimed so much in
effort and fatigue during long months of really hard life, should
be distressed at leaving me. It certainly means something.
Zewang Tashi was moved; but so was I also. Undoubtedly,
without Zewang Tashi, I do not know how I should have succeeded in managing the men when we were on the glaciers, or
in procuring the intensity of effort that was necessary for the
complete success of my plans in face of so many difficulties.

I also demobilized Rasul. Rasul is a man with excellent
qualities, but he is also a sick man. On the Siachen he may
be said to have had a temperature the whole time, often with
very high fever, and was laid up all the time, shut up in his
tent; I had to look after and wait upon him—much more than
he did upon me. I think he also suffers from high altitudes—
and we shall have to cross more than one pass of over 16,400
feet. He belongs to Shushot, which is quite close to Leh
on the opposite bank of the Indus, so I am leaving him at his
own village. In his place I have engaged a Ladakhi, Sonam
Wanghel, whom I call 'The Duke' because he has a title that
has come down to him from the ancient 'gyalpo' régime; but this
nobility that he has inherited through a branch of his family
has made him extravagant and reduced him to poverty, and
now 'The Duke' has asked to be my servant on the journey
between Leh and India. I have also demobilized a few men,
such as the 'couriers', whose special functions were now fulfilled;
among them was Musa, who was so faithful to his orders that
once, when held up by the flooded Nubra on the way to Zingrul,
he came on his own initiative and quite alone over the caravan-
road of death and reached the front of the Rimo, where he
had never been before, in order to deliver a bag of letters to
me—which, of course, he was not able to deliver, because the
time had not yet come for me to leave the glaciers. So, still
all alone, he went back over that terrible road, in order to

attempt again, and again in vain, the impetuous Nubra fords. Such are the men to be found in Ladakh.

Alas! I am now changing caravans, and, except for 'The Duke' and one other Ladakhi who also wished to go to Lahul and whom I have engaged as fatigue-man, I shall have a caravan of Punjabis—about 45 mules, led by queer little men, small and lean, with little thin, dried-up legs which look even more thin and dried-up in narrow, tight trousers of white cloth, which make one feel cold even to look at them; they wear enormous white turbans which frame little thin faces the colour of bronze. They chatter in sharp, quarrelsome voices, and I know they will give me no help on the road. It makes me all the more sorry at having to leave my Ladakhis.

But I have by no means deserted them during these last days. The Haji, the Kalon, and Kalzan seem to be always completely at my service; either I go to them to ask their help again and again, or they come to me, so ready and anxious to assist me that they seem really desirous of foreseeing and fore-stalling all my wishes. I go more often to see Kalzan than the others. This humorous friend of mine had an old house, which had belonged to his fathers, perched on the steep slope of the rock on which rises the majestic palace of the 'gyalpo' kings. It was not easy to get to it through the maze of little streets, of mysterious archways and little disconnected flights of steps, and I remember that one also had to face—or rather to avoid—two or three fierce, snarling dogs which were always ready to hurl themselves at any passer-by who had not a really and truly Ladakhi face. But once one had reached the house and had clambered up to the upper floor, where all the rooms were encumbered with the most varied merchandise but whose final terrace commanded a view of the entire city—then one was really rewarded for the short fatigue of the climb. From there one enjoyed an immense view over Leh, the oasis, and the valley, and also felt oneself in intimate relationship with the fas-cinating life of Ladakh. I also remember a dinner which I had up there on the fine *rabsal* of Kalzan's old house: it was a gala-dinner, at which I was the only non-Ladakhi among all the notables of the capital, and when I looked round ecstatically, fearing to miss some detail of this supremely picturesque scene, the moment my eye fell on one or other of my fellow-guests (who were all seated on the floor on beautiful Chinese carpets, each in front of his little Ladakhi table) I noticed that one closed hand would start tapping with quick little blows against his forehead, and his tongue would be thrust right out of his mouth, denoting the depth of respect to which this sahib was entitled. Kalzan, who is a man of wide outlook, has now left the old house of his fathers that stood under the shelter of the palace of the 'gyalpo' kings, and has built himself another near this bungalow. This one is not a typical Ladakhi house, but is slightly fantastic—with verandahs, little covered galleries, and a great central hall wide open at the front; its walls and ceiling are all painted with frescoes, and it has two rough wooden pillars supporting great beams which are painted all over in bright colours with dragons and curling vine-branches and lotus-flowers, and a great piece of furniture with eight regular square panels, in each of which is one of the eight Buddhist symbols surrounded with a charming ornamental pattern of old gold on a brown background; all round are low cushions upon which are stretched soft Chinese rugs, with as many little lacquered tables in front of them. This is, as it were, a trap laid for the few travellers who pass this way—a few English, at most, who fly from the scorching Indian summer to hunt some game or other in the hidden valleys of the Karakoram. As they pass through Leh, Kalzan is there at his post with his beautiful trap ready laid and a cup of Ladakhi or Chinese tea as a bait. For me it does not really constitute a trap, for in Kalzan's house I feel almost as I do in my own. Whenever I leave the bungalow or return there after an excursion to the bazaar or elsewhere, a little visit to Kalzan is almost a matter of course. I sit down, more or less comfortably, with my legs crossed—for 'when in Rome, do as the Romans do' is an ancient precept which should always be observed—and ask my friend if he really has nothing more to show me. With a mischievous smile he joins the palms of his hands and assures me that he really has nothing more. But then, little by little, as I go on insisting, from the beautiful painted cupboard, from some hiding-place in the wall, from one or other of the innumerable boxes standing in rows in other rooms, come forth tea-pots, cups, jars, reliquaries, masses of turquoise and jade and coral, spices and perfumes, carpets and stuffs, skins and silver—

237

which gradually fill all the empty space in the room and cover the little lacquered tables. Of course I end by myself falling —quite consciously, however—into the snares of Kalzan's trap.

And I fall into the trap not only consciously, but with enthusiasm; for it means the acquisition of another of these exquisite objects which seem to have been made by almost miraculous hands. I often wonder how it is that this race has such a fine sense of beauty and such exquisite taste, combined with such ability to execute (using only very elementary and primitive methods) works which are chiselled, engraved— as it were embroidered—with the most surprising delicacy. And all in the twinkling of an eye. There are tea-pots here of two main types, apart from a number in which the inventive imagination of the artist who created them—for he deserves to be so named—seems to have become capricious. The most admirable quality of all, apart from their shapes, is the way in which the various metals are combined—brass and copper, with ornaments of silver and sometimes of gold. My favourite is the perhaps simpler type known as the 'lotus' because of the flower with closely folded petals on the top of the little lid. I remember, last time I was here, that we came to a wretched village in the Zanskar basin, in which lived one of these artists who make 'lotus' tea-pots—who are naturally rare in the country. Professor Marinelli wanted one: the man asked for an instalment of only a few rupees and undertook to have the tea-pot ready in two days, when we should be passing through his village again. Marinelli, who had only just arrived from Europe, did not want to trust him. I, on the other hand, had unbounded confidence, and left the small deposit; two days later the tea-pot was ready—lovely, shining, perfect, with its closed lotus-flower on the top of the lid and two great worked silver dragons forming the handle and the wide spout, into the eyes of which were set little turquoises which made them look as if they were alive. It was a miracle of quick work—and would have been so for anyone, not only for these people. In my more recent experience there was the case of the trumpet belonging to the *mon* of Basgo. I had never seen such an exceptionally lovely trumpet: the wood of the instrument was all coated in silver. It was not, of course, smooth, but all ornamented with dragons, peacocks, strange, grotesque, stylized animals, scrolls of vine-branches and flowers, with lapis lazuli and turquoise and coral beautifully inlaid. I thought it really wonderful, and had tried to get possession of it by means of every sort of flattery—which had been pure waste of time. But the trumpet of the *mon* of Basgo remained regretfully in my memory. At Leh I entrusted the Kalon, perhaps the most authoritative person in the whole of Ladakh, with the task of making another attack himself and getting possession of it. But it was waste of time for him too: this particular trumpet had been in the family of the *mon* of Basgo for who knows how many generations; his father, his grandfather, his great-grandfather, all his ancestors had played it; on every solemn occasion, on every feast-day, at every *tamasha* in the countryside, its complicated flourishes had been heard. He said he could never part with it. But what the Kalon had been able to obtain was to have the trumpet in his own hands for a few days. And now, on my table, I have a faithful copy of it, with the same dragons and peacocks and scrolls, the same lapis lazuli and turquoise and coral, and I look at it every now and then with infinite pleasure. It may not be the actual one belonging to the *mon* of Basgo, but what does that matter? Its artistic value is the same, and it is an eloquent proof of the extraordinary ability of these craftsmen, who really seem to have something miraculous about them.

I dined again with the Kalon. And again also—this too being in the complete Ladakhi style—in the house of Nasrullah, one of my faithful friends from last time I was here. Hardly a day has passed that Nasrullah has not come to the bungalow to offer me either a charming tea-pot, or a few *tanka* (votive paintings), or some little statue of Sanghiès or of some Buddhist divinity or specially venerated lama. I also gave a large dinner for my Ladakhi friends, a dinner which will certainly mark an epoch in the annals of their simple, monotonous life. At the end, when the 'champagne' was foaming in the glasses, I made Hashmatullah tell them how much I love this fantastically beautiful and picturesque country of theirs, and how much I appreciate their good qualities, and how grateful I am for their welcome, and how sincerely I hope that they will remain true Ladakhis, as they are, with all their fine qualities.

I hope nobody will be shocked, but in wishing that the Ladakhis should remain as they are it must be understood, essentially, that I wished them to remain Buddhist and polyandrous.

It is necessary to know—and not superficially, as most travellers do—both the Baltis and the Ladakhis, and to compare them. The Baltis, although their country is relatively rich and has oases of surprising fertility, are a poor and wretched people; the Ladakhis, in a country which is decidedly poorer and which has a harsher climate (which often means that only barley can be grown), have everywhere a high standard of comfort. But this is unimportant: the essential thing is that this difference in the general conditions of material life is reflected in the whole moral and social life and in the cast of mind of the two different peoples. The Baltis—the very sight of whom shows their wretchedness, covered as they are with a few rags in which there is no note of colour to gladden the eye—are suspicious, rather gloomy, taciturn, not at all gay or expansive; the Ladakhis are picturesque in appearance, with their characteristic, sometimes rich, costume, and are, on the other hand, jovial, happy, sociable, communicative, always ready to smile, always inclined to a gaiety and humour which bubbles forth spontaneously, genuinely, subtle rather than commonplace, on the slightest opportunity even in their ordinary daily life.

They are peoples of different origin, someone will say. But their origins are not so very different; in fact, in the main they are derived from a single common stock. I can also record, from the results of my researches, how the present population of the entire region, along the great valley of the Indus between the mountains from Ladakh to Baltistan, has been formed. There must originally have been a different people from the present, who came from we know not where: their surviving descendants can be recognized in the inhabitants of Purig, that is, in the intermediate zone between Ladakh and Baltistan, and I alluded to this when passing through Kargil, which is the chief centre of the region. It is also quite easy to see why in Purig the present population should have preserved the characteristics of the race which originally, as is probable, inhabited the whole region. Over this original race there actually spread another race, coming from the West: these were the Dards (the only Himalayan people, it seems, which was known to classical antiquity), who, in ancient times which are

AN ORCHESTRA OF LAMAS

[face p. 240

not definable in our present state of knowledge, certainly spread over this whole region, as is proved by surviving traditions and by ornamental parts of the feminine dress which have also survived, and by the original form of many place-names even in Ladakh; their migratory movement from the West also continued later, even until quite recent times. There is, in the Indus Valley, exactly between Purig, Ladakh and Baltistan, an island of Dards who arrived later and who have remained completely pure owing to the topographical isolation of their settlement; there are also other Dards—the so-called Brokpa—who have immigrated quite recently and are even doing so at the present day, in the high valleys of Baltistan which lead down to the Indus. This has been a really important racial phenomenon, since, at a certain moment, the entire region from Baltistan to Ladakh has had its original population overspread by a Dard population, with a consequent superimposition of language, traditions and costume. However, the immixture of Dard blood is naturally less marked the farther one goes away from the West, whence the immigration came.

Let us take our argument a step further. Later on, from the opposite direction, that is, from the East, came the Tibetan invasion, of Mongol races, who arrived not as a real migratory phenomenon, as people who were seeking a new place in which to settle, but as a politico-military phenomenon, a movement of armed men in search of places to conquer. They did not constitute a complete new population in bulk, which would have been able to make radical and profound modifications in the racial constitution of the region they had reached; they were merely a number of conquering invaders, relatively small in comparison with the existing population and therefore incapable of making racial modifications in it, except to a quite superficial extent. All travellers have always affirmed that the present peoples, from Ladakh to Baltistan, were Mongol. This is a mistake, as my very large number of measurements has quite clearly proved. Mongol characteristics have been infused, and are therefore recognizable, but only partially, and to a steadily decreasing extent the farther one goes from the point at which the Mongol invaders entered; that is, they are recognizable sporadically among the Ladakhis, but may be said to be entirely lacking among the Baltis. The people of

Purig have thus undergone the greatest degree of infusion neither of Dard, nor of Mongol blood, and for this reason have better preserved the characteristics of the ancient and original population. But, though the small number of Tibetan invaders was incapable of making any profound modification in the racial constitution of the region, it had nevertheless the power to impose its own rule, a dynasty of its own, its own language, and its own civilization, so that the whole region remained fundamentally Dardic as regards race, but became Tibetan in the whole of its cultural, religious and political life. I think that the Baltis and the Ladakhis were not, at that time, so very different from each other.

At a certain moment, however, there arrived from the North, from Kashgar, a kind of great Musulman saint and prophet. Actually—but I do not feel that this in any way lessens the satisfaction I had in the conquest of my 'Italia Pass'—it is not at all improbable that this prophet came by way of the Yarkand Valley, up the Rimo Glacier, over 'my' pass, and then by the Tarim Sher and the Bilafon-la, coming out into the middle of Baltistan in the neighbourhood of Khapalu. He stopped there, and initiated and developed his proselytizing with such effect that the whole of Baltistan became Musulman in a short time. That is the reason of the profound difference at the present day between the Baltis and the Ladakhis. The Baltis have remained Tibetan only in language; otherwise they have lost the civilization which they had, without knowing how, or being able, to acquire another. They have destroyed the beautiful temples and picturesque monasteries so that no trace of them remains, and have substituted small, plain mosques; they have destroyed the great statues and the other sacred figures carved in the rocks (there remain only a very few in the most hidden recesses, which I went patiently to find), thus removing, together with the *chorten* also, and the *mani* and the *lato*, so many picturesque elements placed by man in a landscape which is already in itself so beautiful; they have given up monasticism and also polyandry—that is, two customs which contribute to limiting the population, which, now that they are Musulmans and polygamy is permitted, must tend to increase to a very marked degree; they have also given up, together with polyandry, all the hereditary customs which contributed to the preservation of inherited family property. Thus they have become what they now are—a people living in a relatively rich country but poor in goods, badly clothed, miserable in appearance, colourless, gloomy, reserved, taciturn in character. The Ladakhis, on the other hand, owe their present condition and character, with all its fine qualities, essentially to the fact that they still preserve their Tibetan civilization, their Buddhism and their polyandry.

But I will further describe the condition and character of the Ladakhis to-morrow.

Leh, September 20th, 1930.

CHAPTER XXIII

LADAKHI LIFE

I do not intend to give an exact account of what Tibetan
Buddhism is, and in what it consists: all I wish to do is to dispel
an illusion some people may have that the original moral
teaching of Buddha has been preserved here intact, among these
people. There is nothing but the name of Buddhism in common. I remember the faint smile of contempt and disdain on
the face of a Cingalese Buddhist monk when I asked him about
the religion of the people of Tibet. It is, in fact, a form of
fantastic and imaginative polytheism.

What exactly it is, it is really not necessary to examine here;
volumes have been written upon it, but I would be prepared to
say that the last and final volume has yet to be written.
The chief interest for me—and, no doubt, for the majority
of people—is to study the influences and social consequences
of this religion.

Tibetan Buddhism shows itself outwardly—and with direct
results on the people—in the enormous number of its monks.
If one goes round the Ladakhi villages one sees, in almost every
house, a little boy wearing a lama's cap or a little girl with the
cap of a 'chomo', which is the equivalent of a nun: they are the
children destined from birth for the monasteries, that is, they
are an extremely numerous element of the population which is
practically excluded from contributing to its increase. The
population, as a result, increases little—or rather, it does not
increase at all but remains stationary.

We cannot judge, in this matter, from what happens
in our own countries. We also have monks and monasteries,
but the monasteries, however numerous they may appear, are
nothing in comparison with the frequency and extent of the
houses, hamlets, villages, small towns and cities in which the
civil population throngs; in comparison with the latter, the
monasteries contain a minute and absolutely negligible pro-

244

portion of the inhabitants of a whole region. Here, on the other hand, it can be said that the monasteries are actually larger than the villages; each contains hundreds of lamas; there are convents of *chomo* dependent on the principal monasteries; every village, even if only of a few houses, has its temples and chapels, presided over, naturally, by lamas, who are more or less numerous according to the importance of the chapel or temple; and every house belonging to a notable or a rich landowner has its own private chapel, to which also a lama is attached. In fact, the individuals who form the monastic orders certainly represent a considerable proportion of the total population of the region. In actual fact, marriage is apparently not forbidden to the monks; but in practice it is as if the prohibition did exist. I only know of one case, of a *kushok* who got married; but his lamas chased him out of his monastery and he was reduced to living in a beautiful house in the Nubra Valley near Samur, where we paid a visit to his no longer young but still extremely elegant companion. Certainly they do not all observe the austere rule of life of the 'pure' monks of Rigzon, but there is actually an enormous number of men and women who are practically excluded from contributing to the normal increase of the population. The population, therefore, increases very little, or not at all.

There is also polyandry. My readers must not be too much shocked, for every race has its own standard of morals: the important thing is not to err from the standard of morals which one has, or ought to have. We have all only to look round in order to see cases of polyandry which our own standard of morals would certainly not permit; yet they are tolerated, pardoned, often even justified. We should, therefore, not be shocked too much if a standard of morals different from our own allows it officially and builds an entire social system upon it. Among the Tibetans (my own personal experience, however, is mainly in regard to the Ladakhis) there is a form of fraternal polyandry. If the eldest son gets married, his wife also becomes the legitimate wife of any younger brother or brothers of his who have not been destined from birth by the family to be monks. It cannot be said that the bonds of family feeling can possibly be, in this way, as intensely alive and profound as it is possible for them to be with us. The children have a 'big

245

father', and, as well, one or more 'little fathers', and they can hardly be expected to possess such wealth of feeling that they can distribute it very liberally among so many fathers. The same applies to the woman, since she has so many husbands at her disposal. But since this has gone on for centuries and the whole mind and sentiment of the people is unable to conceive of any other family system, the only result is that real excesses of feeling are avoided, though there is at the same time a calm, diffused affection and all live peacefully together without jealousies or passions.

It may be thought that in a family in which there is only one wife and more than one husband the woman may perhaps acquire a position of supremacy. But this is not so: though Tibetan polyandry undoubtedly gives the woman a greater freedom of movement, it does not imply matriarchy as a natural consequence. The eldest son alone is the sole heir of his own family; younger brothers and sisters possess nothing and can dispose of nothing. There is one lord and master, and all the others, including the wife, have nothing to do but obey him. It is a matter of simple obedience, not of subjection, on their side, since I believe that on the side of the head of the family there is never any abuse of power, or at any rate no real tyranny. It makes for a peaceful life, *par excellence*, for everybody; but there is certainly no question of matriarchy. In order to remove all doubts on the subject, I also succeeded, last time I was here, in getting information about the order in which rights of succession descend: it is the eldest son; then the eldest surviving son, each in turn; in default of male offspring, the eldest daughter, or the eldest surviving daughter, each in turn; in default of direct descendants, the eldest brother, and so on. Then follows the eldest sister—provided, however, that she is not yet married—and then each sister in turn according to age, but only provided she is not married. Then, in turn, the younger uncles, according to age—that is, those who have not inherited from their own family. And then—a good last—the mother, then the widow, and finally the widow of the eldest son.

The result of all this, as can be seen, is that the women in the Ladakhi family system have very infrequent and limited rights in the inheritance of family property. This is a rather interesting fact in the Tibetan social system, but there are others which

LADAKHI WOMEN

[face p. 246

are even more interesting in their economic and, indirectly, their social results. The patrimony is never, in any circumstances, divided. There is never more than one heir. Thus family property tends to be kept perpetually intact; it can be diminished or increased only by extravagance or by personal enterprise on the part of the head of the family, and these are two qualities which have very little opportunity of showing themselves in a country like Ladakh which is not rich in natural conditions and is almost completely cut off from the outside world. I do certainly know instances of decadence and of economic development in Ladakhi families—the commercial enterprise of Kalzan, who has large and active businesses in every direction, has made him a rich man, rich even according to our ideas of wealth, seeing that his property can be counted in millions of lire. And, on the other side, the excessive lordliness of Sonam Wanghel has reduced 'The Duke' to ask for a position as servant in my caravan. These are certainly exceptions. The rule is that family property tends to be kept perpetually intact.

I expect one objection to be made, but will forestall it and dispose of it at once. It may, in fact, be objected that an increase of property will occur when an eldest daughter, who has no brothers and is therefore heiress of the property of her own family, marries and forms a new family. However, there is no increase of family property, for an heiress can only marry a younger son, that is, a young man who himself inherits nothing from his own family. Thus not only is the perpetual preservation of family property assured, but any fusion of two properties resulting in a single excessively large property is prevented.

But let us return to the subject of polyandry, in order to show how it exercises a function in the family system which limits the number of births and, as a natural result, the increase of population. I am far from wishing to start propaganda for the introduction into our own countries of polyandry and its natural consequences. Ladakh, which neither has, nor ever can have, aspirations towards a power of its own or any expansion into the outside world, would gain nothing but certain misery from a high birth-rate—like Baltistan, though the latter is by nature so much richer. On the other hand, as it is, owing to monasticism and polyandry, owing to the whole family system and all the hereditary customs, there is in Ladakh—

though it is naturally poor, has a poor soil, a severe climate, lies at a high altitude, and is not very productive—a relatively high standard of comfort throughout the whole of the population, a general well-being, and an equality of economic conditions which excludes envy and also arrogance, and diffuses a sort of satisfaction and a measure of happiness over individual lives. All this naturally has an influence upon the serenity of character of my friends the Ladakhis. Perhaps, once upon a time, the Baltis were also like this, but they are certainly so no longer; now they are wretched and gloomy, colourless and taciturn, since they adopted, together with Islam, social conditions which are so different that they may be said to be quite the opposite of those in Ladakh. It was for this reason that, at the end of the dinner which I gave to my Ladakhi friends, I expressed the really sincere wish that they would remain always as they are, that is, Buddhist and polyandrous. But it was only to them that I was speaking: that must be understood!

The very appearance of the Ladakhis is pleasing, because their very appearance is picturesque. They wear a great robe of fine white wool (in the case of the notables it is of a dark wine-colour) which comes right down to their ankles, has a wide cross-over in front, and is held close to the body by means of a long blue scarf wound several times round the waist. On their heads is a large cap of the same blue, with a fur lining which is turned up at the edges but can be turned down all round the head in very cold weather. Their legs are wrapped in a sort of white felt, soft and warm, which is kept in place by a kind of thick ribbon of black wool wound closely round. On their feet they wear picturesque shoes made of bands of yak-hide sewn together, with narrow, turned-up points, and round the ankle a fold of cloth which may be of any colour, but is generally bright. This characteristic costume of the men varies slightly in different parts of Ladakh. It is completed by large silver rings with little bits of coral in them, for ear-rings, heavy brace-lets of silver or white metal or brass on the wrists, little 'kau', or reliquaries, generally of copper or brass but sometimes also of silver, and always of very fine, elegant shape and workmanship, which are hung round the neck together with necklaces in which strings of coral are generally interspersed with the brilliant blue of a few turquoises. This I consider a picturesque costume—

not like the wretched, unadorned, colourless costume of the Baltis. To make it even more picturesque, imagine that the cap, which the Ladakhis usually only take off when they go to sleep, is removed for a moment: you will see a head the front half of which is completely shaved, while the hair is allowed to grow as long as nature wills on the back half, and gathered into a fine pigtail, artificially lengthened in such a way that it falls down the back to below the waist; and so that it shall not dangle too freely, it is tucked behind the scarf which is tied round the waist.

As for the women, they wear a heavy woollen garment of dark wine-colour, rather narrow at the waist, with a full petticoat which is wider at the bottom and ends at the ankles, but shows their beautiful shoes which are like those worn by the men, but generally richer both in workmanship and in colour. A woman when she is working—that is to say, working in the fields or in the house—always has on her shoulders a goatskin, with the long hair turned inwards, the hide outwards. But at Leh, the capital, this usual custom has been improved upon and embellished: at Leh the most elegant of the women (who, even here, dictate the fashion to the rest of the country) have substituted for the plain, natural skin a big, square piece of flame-red cloth bordered all round with a stripe of vivid green and lined with thick, rich fur, which is worn on the shoulders and closed in front with two knots: the more voluminous it is, the greater the wealth and elegance of its wearer. This was the fashion 16 years ago. But fashion changes even in Ladakh, radiating outwards from Leh and then gradually penetrating into the villages farthest from the capital. Just as the wine-coloured garment had taken the place of another much more picturesque one, in which the petticoat was made of so many thin vertical strips of every colour and alternating irregularly (this can now be found only in the most remote and lonely villages in the direction of the Tibetan plateaux), in the same way I have now seen the big square red and green cloth lined with fur only outside the capital; the women here—at any rate the most elegant ones—now wear on their shoulders a large square piece of fine Chinese silk of the most varied colours, adorned all over with the most charming embroidery. But the half-tones of the stuff and of the embroideries show that this is merely a return to a former fashion, and that they have been re-exhumed from the family 'bsot' or store-house, in which a collection of garments and stuffs and wools is kept.

The clothes, however, only form as it were the background of the Ladakhi feminine costume, the essential character of which lies in the immense number of its ornaments. The hair is divided into so many little plaits, artificially lengthened and tied together at the bottom, and ending in a long tuft of thin tassels reaching to the ankles. One sees very little of it, however, as the piece of cloth worn on the shoulders covers the plaits to a great extent, and the head is covered in its turn with what are perhaps the most picturesque and showy ornaments of the Ladakhi woman. A great stiff lozenge covered with bright red stuff starts from the forehead and, passing right over the head, hangs down behind the shoulders to the waist, but the red of the stuff bristles thickly all over with the bright blue of innumerable turquoises and beautiful *kau* (of filigreed or embossed silver or gold set with stones of every colour) which would make the most charming lids for little *bonbonnières*. On the left shoulder a long narrow rectangle made of several close rows of coral is attached to this great flame-coloured lozenge, which is called the 'perak'. But there is more still; at the sides, immediately behind the ears, two large, stiff fans made of black lamb's skin are attached tightly to the hair and stick right out beyond the head. Then there are silver pendants behind these fans; more pendants, also of silver, hanging from the left shoulder in front; necklaces of silver and coral and turquoise, of every shape and every length; and on one side of the waist is placed a great round plaque of brass or silver perforated in such a way as to represent one of the usual Buddhist symbols, and hanging from it are a number of long strings of little pieces of glass and white cowrie-shells, often with tiny little bells at the end. Thus, when a woman walks in the lanes of her village, on her soft, silent shoes, her coming is announced by the silvery tinkling of all her pendants. One looks round and sees her, supremely picturesque in her varied, ornamented, richly-coloured clothes, and cannot help following her with one's eyes as she goes away, showing the projecting turquoise-studded *perak* and the great square of silk with its lovely embroideries; below it, the great tuft of tassels in which the plaits of hair are gathered swings rhythmically.

These women, who are so picturesque and full of colour in

FAMILY LIFE IN LADAKH

[*face p.* 250

their manner of dressing, do not fly from the traveller: they are even willing to stop, and smile or laugh openly in face of the curiosity, the wonder, the enthusiasm of anyone who, new to the country, examines and admires all the little jewels that adorn them. This is part of their open, jovial, gay, happy character—which, naturally, shows itself even more freely in the Ladakhi men.

This will already have been understood from the account, disordered and hasty as it is, which I have given of my journey. These men, who are capable of long, exhausting, uncomfortable marches, carrying a burden that would frighten the strongest of our mountaineers, do not stop the moment they have arrived at the end of the journey; they put down their loads and at once begin to help the traveller, their *sahib*, in pitching his camp, in looking for water and fuel, in arranging the baggage in good order. And all this without any air of long-suffering or of doing something beyond what is necessary simply in order to please, and also without showing the fatigue they must be feeling; they do it quickly and skilfully, willingly and energetically, and accompany each act and each new task with a ready smile, with witticisms and a quick humour. Only when absolutely everything has been arranged for the *sahib* do they sit down on the ground round their own fire and round the pots which one of them, specially told off for the job, has already prepared for their interminable meal. Even then one can see them smiling and joking, for these seem to be essential attributes of the happy character of the Ladakhis.

If they are like this during the hard life of an Expedition, it may be imagined what they are like in their normal village life. Both men and women are quick and industrious at their work in the house, in the fields, and with the livestock, but they are always ready to be gay, to make jokes, to laugh, to have a *tamasha*. Any occasion is good enough. I have already given some rough idea of what these Ladakhi *tamashas* are: they consist not only of the characteristic dances of the country, but of jests, farces, comic preludes, imitative turns, which display a quick and lively intelligence, full of fun and humour which is both surprising and winning. I confess that, even though all these qualities were not altogether a revelation to me, the whole character of the entertainment was new to me, if not quite unexpected. I have seen an immense number of these country dances. This time, too, I had no sooner entered Ladakh than, almost on the very threshold of the country, at Bot Karbu, I saw my first dances, both of men and women, to the accompaniment of drums and trumpets. It was the same in every village, whenever I pronounced, as an invitation or an encouragement, the fatal word 'tamasha'. Even the caravan-porters asked no more: the sharp twittering of a little flute drawn forth from the bottomless depths of some porter's garments was enough to make two, three, four of them jump up and move round with little rhythmical steps. The weariness of a long march was immediately forgotten.

I also knew the official *tamashas*: I had seen them last time, and saw them again here this time. The country dances are generally performed by men and women in turns, but they also perform the more traditional dances and figures, such as some, for instance, which are very similar to the present ones but in which the dancers put on ancient Chinese clothes, others of a warlike nature accompanied with a vigorous flourishing of swords, and also a sort of miming dance. They carry on these traditions faithfully, as though to show their guests the developments and changes in the local dances. But the best of all is when the organizing initiative of a *tamasha* is left to someone of the people who has special talents in that direction—a kind of "metteur en scène", who assumes the responsibility of planning, preparing and directing it. Not very long is required for all this; a few hours is enough, for their inventive imagination is quick, their methods are extremely elementary, and the performers have no need of rehearsals. My readers will remember the *tamasha* at Deskit. I wanted also to have one here, also by night, in the open space in front of the bungalow which is enclosed all round by a tall curtain of transparent poplars. I shall never forget the lively, fresh comic spirit which bubbled forth at each new entry of the performers. The turns were, for the most part, imitations of animals—either a great monstrous dragon which might have come down out of some mural painting in an old *gompa*, but was really alive as it advanced with frightful contortions, belching fire from nostrils, eyes and mouth; or it was the attack of a snow-leopard, gliding cat-like or motionless and vigilant, upon an unfortunate camel, which let forth kicks to defend itself and elongated and twisted its long neck in attitudes of despair; or, again, it was a cock-fight, with the preliminary coming on guard and the spiteful thrusts. Naturally it was only simple peasants who performed all this, and with the simplest of means—a few rags fished out of the family *bsot* or scraped up in some little shop in the bazaar —but they did it with a feeling for imitation and a sense of fun which were really amazing.

For this, in fact, is one of the essential qualities of my friends the Ladakhis: they have a quick, lively intelligence (please let no one be offended, but it is an intelligence that, without the slightest doubt, I consider to be superior to the average intelligence of our own people); a degree of culture that is by no means inferior (many European countries might learn from it: Hashmatullah, who was Governor here for so many years, assures me that more than 90 per cent. of the Ladakhi men are literate); a serenity and a sort of contentment with life which makes them always satisfied, ready for anything, always happy and laughing; but, added to all this, a spontaneous subtle humour, which bursts forth as though by a natural instinct in every circumstance of their daily life.

My readers should have seen the comic appearance of the head of the *heran* found dead on the Tibetan plateau when my men, suppressing their laughter, presented it to me carefully dressed up in rags which gave it a face which was quite different but ridiculously expressive. They should also have seen how one of the men that I took with me this time—almost a boy, who was quite exceptional in that he almost always wore an expression of seriousness and composure—whenever he could get hold of a little piece of paper, took a stump of pencil out of a fold in his cap and quickly scribbled, with a few lines, a caricature of a European hunter, while a sardonic little smile just touched the corner of his mouth.

I remember I have already explained that it is unwise to be too familiar with these men, that is, with a familiarity of the kind that lowers a traveller in the esteem and the high opinion that the men should always have of him; the abundance of intelligence and humour which they have at their disposal gives them an easy way of getting their revenge. The unwise traveller is given nicknames which are apparently very exhilarating, to judge from the succession of laughs to be heard among his followers, and they can discover his weak or comic side with infallible sureness, imitating and exaggerating it with little discreet motions.

Be careful, therefore, future travellers, if by any chance you think that you will come to Ladakh and find there a simple, ingenuous people, whom you will be able to smile at behind their backs because they wear pigtails, or because there are so many husbands in one family with only one wife, or because they remain for hours at a time repeating their eternal prayers. Nothing and nobody can escape the ever-ready humour of the Ladakhis.

Not even can their very religion escape it. There is sometimes to be seen on the brilliant white fronts of their houses a great 'swastika' painted in red. I remember one swastika in which the four arms were distorted and misshapen in such a way that the whole thing represented a grotesque puppet. And I shall never forget the feeling—of uneasiness, almost (because I was unable to explain to myself what I saw: I had not then really understood the spirit, the character, the soul of the Ladakhis)—when, during a great religious ceremony that was being performed in the *gompa* of Piang, I saw with astonishment that, while all the lamas, in their rich vestments of silk embroidered with gold, were officiating in the ceremonial and solemnly chanting amid the perfumed smoke of benzoin and the music of full orchestras, there were, even at that moment, two lamas, with masks on their faces and dressed in dirty flowered garments like street-clowns, performing a counter-scene based upon jokes and drolleries of an extremely comic kind and actually aping the priests who were engaged in the ceremonial.

A superficial observer might think that the Ladakhis, by doing this, were making fun of their own religion. But this is not so: it is merely a form—carried rather far, certainly—of their spontaneous, fresh, healthy sense of humour, which, owing to these very qualities, never wounds or destroys, but touches lightly upon things and as lightly dissolves.

Sonam Wanghel, 'The Duke', enters my room. What does he want? He announces a peasant with a large bundle who wishes to show me, in strict secrecy, certain of his treasures. I understand: I shall have to provide yet another box for my caravan on the return journey.

Leh, September 21*st,* 1930.

CHAPTER XXIV

HOUSES, PALACES, MONASTERIES

Whenever I have a moment's respite from my endless occupations, I cannot resist temptation. I come, almost instinctively, out of my room on to the verandah of the bungalow and stand looking through the trembling curtain of poplar-trees at the little lake that glitters just beyond, at the fields planted with trees, at the great frowning rock surmounted by the palace of the 'Gyalpo' with the little ancient chapels as the end, at the blue, clear sky and at the dark background of the Zanskar Mountains. I have the same longing to gaze, the same passion as when I arrived here more than four months ago. Then, still instinctively, almost unconsciously, I descend the few steps of the verandah, go out through the fence which surrounds the little shady enclosure belonging to the bungalow, and go off at a venture, leaving my way to chance. I feel as if it were a dream. Suddenly, as though I had just woken up, I find myself standing in some remote corner of the city, whence, through the narrow opening of a lane or framed in a small archway under a dark, mysterious portico, can be seen the majestic beauty of the royal palace, or the succession of the roofs of the whole city stretching away into the distance, or a crowded mass of *chorten* lined up like so many soldiers. The nearer I get to the moment of my departure, the more frequent become these almost unconscious walks of mine— without any definite goal or exact aim but just with the instinctive object of seeing and enjoying myself.

I have already initiated my readers into the unsuspected comforts of the village houses—either *à propos* of Prandas or of Lotsum, I do not remember which. I know that my first conquests and invasions of these houses occurred at Prandas and Lotsum. But they were afterwards repeated several times along the road—at Timosgam, already in Ladakh proper, and later in almost the whole of the Nubra Valley. Profiting by old experience, I applied one elementary principle of war—to make use of local resources as far as possible. And, in spite of the little grimace of disdain which may wrinkle the noses of inexperienced and over-timorous travellers, I shall always proclaim the advantages of a native house over a tent. There is, perhaps, a risk of finding it . . . over-inhabited? I can only say that anyone who is too fastidious had better stay at home. All travellers, even if they do not dare to adopt my plan, know very well that it is not in the least necessary to adopt it in order to discover that Ladakh—this is perfectly true—is often quite excessively over-populated. A little fatalism is needed, to begin with, and then, a little long-suffering. But I still proclaim the advantages and merits of native houses.

Perhaps I run the risk of repeating myself, but the discussion demands it. In the whole region between Ladakh and Baltistan, there is a uniform design in the main structure of the houses; it varies only in degree of development, and consequently in details of construction and in external appearance. The latter seem to reveal both the economic and spiritual poverty of the Baltis, just as they also reveal the widespread well-being and the fine artistic taste of the Ladakhis. But more of this later. The essential part of a house is its structure, for this interprets and reveals the kind of life of the people who inhabit it; the rest is a mere frame, which may interpret and reveal, instead, the essential type of mind of its inhabitant. Take the case of the Alpine house: the internal arrangement is almost always identical or at least very similar, for it corresponds to identities or similarities in natural conditions and in manner of life; but some are content to keep it simple and unadorned and rough, while some seek to embellish it, at least outside, with even a certain coquettish feeling. Passing from the Western Alps, whether in Italy or France, to the Upper Adige and many of the Swiss valleys, one notices the difference at once. The same applies here, where the structure may be said to be perfect.

In the whole of Ladakh, which I have now traversed from end to end, in all its valleys, I know only a few little villages, right on the edge of the Great Tibet of Lhasa, which have houses confined to a ground floor only—and generally wretched into the bargain. But these villages are in quite special circumstances. In that part, at the edge of the plateaux, where the valleys become immense channels, extremely wide and only slightly inclined, and the mountain-ridges look like small, low rows of hills (there are places, however, where the bottoms of the valleys reach a height of 16,400 feet), the people are not true Ladakhis, but Changpa, that is, inhabitants of the plateaux. They are shepherds, dedicated to a nomadic pastoral life, and going eternally backwards and forwards with their flocks and herds between winter and summer pastures. I shall certainly meet some of them on my return journey, and I hope I shall be able to observe their interesting form of pastoral life. But at the edge of Ladakh these Changpa, as all nomadic shepherds eventually do, have begun to settle and lead a stationary life. They have abandoned their tents and taken to living in houses.

The transition has not, of course, been sudden. There comes a moment when one family, instead of still following its own tribe in its eternal wanderings back and forth, stays at the place to which the last move has brought it. The time has not yet come to build a house; all they do, to begin with, is not to take down the tent any more, and to begin to cultivate a few little fields near by. I have noticed one interesting fact, which, up to a point, seems to contradict accepted theory. I have not actually noticed it among the Changpa, but among the Kirghiz; but probably it also holds good in the case of the Changpa. It is usually said that agriculture represents a more advanced, more developed form of human activity than the pastoral life. But the curious thing is that among the Kirghiz the people who settle and become agricultural are the most wretched of all. It seems almost a contradiction, but it would not be difficult to explain it.

Observe then our family of Changpa, who one fine day decide not to take down their tent, but to leave it at that point in their endless wanderings which fate has ordained. Large stones are arranged all round the tent as a shelter against the wind, which otherwise would penetrate into the inside beneath its loose, fluttering flaps. Then, as these flaps become more and more worn out with age and use and gradually fall to bits, a little wall takes the place of the simple outside circle of stones. Years pass, perhaps: the more the tent decays at the bottom, the higher the little outside wall grows, till the moment comes when the last remains of the tent are removed; beams are put across to form the framework of the roof, with faggots, straw and earth to make a new covering. Thus the house originates. It is therefore a house of one single room, in which the internal structure of their tents remains unchanged: I will speak of this again later, when I get to the Rupshu region and have reached an encampment of nomad Changpa.

The important step has been taken. Needs increase in time—for instance that of shutting up the livestock in winter, of putting the harvest in shelter, of having a safe place in which to keep such wealth as the family possesses, clothes, stuffs, wool, provisions of tea and salt. Gradually the house becomes larger, a new room is added, a second, a third, all adjacent to the original room, which still retains its characteristic structure and unites in itself the whole life of the little family. And so the house is complete, but it is poor in appearance and limited to one single floor. It is in Ladakh, but is not for that reason a typical Ladakhi house.

I do not really know what the origin of the Ladakhi house may be. The architecture and all the ornamental part is typically Tibetan; as to whether the internal structure is also Tibetan this can only be known when someone gives an account of what the houses of Lhasa and the surrounding country are like. It is a hypothesis by no means to be rejected, that in Ladakh Tibetan civilization may have merely superimposed external forms of its own upon a pre-existent internal structure. There is no Ladakhi house that has not at any rate two floors—a ground floor and an upper floor. On the ground floor there is an abundance of stables and store-rooms and—well protected against the cold because a long way from the entrance-door and without windows—the winter quarters. It is stuffy there, and one has a slightly unpleasant feeling of suffocation, and there is a smell of stables and smoke and lack of ventilation; but there is always more air and space than in the 'étables' of the upper Val d'Aosta, and at any rate the object is completely achieved, for the outside rigours of winter do not reach the living-room. When the first warmth comes with the spring, the family moves up on to the first floor, as if they were going to their country house. On the

THE MAJESTIC PALACE OF THE ANCIENT LADAKHI KINGS

[face p. 258

first ·floor there is no need for the natural heating-system provided by the livestock, and so there are no stables and therefore much more free space for the family, and the rooms have windows and balconies, and sometimes open wide on to large terraces. Air enters and circulates freely in every direction; one is high up, and therefore not directly smitten by the heat of the summer sun reflected off the hot ground, but fanned by the wind and the breezes of the valley. Such is the house of the poorest peasant in Ladakh.

However, though there are not, on the whole, very great economic differences between one family and another, there are some families which are relatively rich. This can be seen at once even from their houses. The house that I lived in at Tegur in the Nubra Valley, for example, was the house of a rich man—and more than that, of a notable, a gentleman. However, the structure was just the same, except that his greater wealth and importance was displayed in an additional floor. On the ground floor were the stables and store-rooms, on the first floor the winter quarters, and the summer quarters on the second. I am still speaking merely of the structure, for achitecturally it was quite a palace. But there are houses —peasants' houses, I mean—which have even more spacious quarters, since between the winter and the summer quarters are interposed yet other quarters for the seasons between. Anyone who may have imagined that I have been travelling among people who are less than civilized should by now be entirely convinced, for what more could one desire? Every Ladakhi house also has a room on each floor (not cut down to the smallest possible extent, as with us, but spacious like all the other rooms) specially for purposes of—shall we say? —hygiene; and almost every house also has a chapel (forgive their being mentioned, by chance, in the same breath), but this is placed on the top floor, high up. It is almost as if the prayers, repeated there several times every day by the lama who has charge of it, might thus ascend the more easily to heaven and be heard by the numberless divinities of the Tibetan Olympus.

The structure, therefore, is perfectly adapted. But in the interior of a Ladakhi house, when one has noticed and admired the structure, there is very little else either to notice or admire.

The rooms, almost without exception, are simple in the extreme; the four walls are not always even plastered, and there is some sort of central post to support the ceiling. But it must be remembered that almost all the rooms are stables, passages, or store-rooms. There are really only two which deserve more attention—the one in which the whole material life of the little family is concentrated, the living-room, which serves for kitchen and everything else, and the one which serves for its spiritual life, the chapel. Generally even the living-room has very little in the way of decoration: there is a space in the middle in which is the fire, a few stones are used to put the pots on when they are actually being used, and a few recesses in the walls contain the pots which for the moment are not being used; all round, the family sleep the sleep of the just, right on the floor—but the simplicity of their sleeping-place is not to be wondered at when one knows how the Ladakhis are accustomed to sleep when travelling. But in a few houses belonging to rich men I have seen kitchens which were really worth looking at, and which reminded me of the pantries and kitchens in the villagers' houses of the district which comes down from the mountains of Friuli and Cadore to Bassa and even to the gates of Venice; one can get an idea of them by going no farther than Torcello. The fireplace is in the middle of the room: it is square, about 3 feet high and the same in width, massive and made all in one piece out of a compact substance formed of a kind of black clay, with mouldings and ornamentations in relief which remind one of the Baroque, with great iron fire-dogs and supports, also of iron, for the pots, which are always of amazing size. Along one or more than one wall there are several rows of shelves, perfectly simple and without ornament or pretence, upon which are arranged, very tidily, long rows of pots of shining copper, of every size, teapots of brass or copper with silver patterns, great jars for *chang*, teacups (which are used both as cups and as bowls and as plates), some quite simple and ordinary, made from the wood of a root, but quite often lined with silver, others, more luxurious, of Chinese porcelain, standing on high saucers and covered by lids, both of these being made of silver finely worked with ornamental designs and Buddhist symbols. There is often also a beautiful *kau*, or reliquary, so that the divinity may protect even the ordinary daily life of the family, and in front of the *kau* a little brass cup in which burns a wick, which generally gives very little light and burns very badly. But these kitchens in rich men's houses really look very beautiful.

They are rather dark, certainly; but if one wants light and air one can go up into the little chapel on the top floor, where the front wall is usually formed of a partition which can be removed bodily. There large and small statues of Buddha, of divinities, of venerated lamas, stand on the altar against the opposite wall; on every wall are hung beautiful *tanka*, and one sees all the varied and endless artistic religious trappings, musical instruments, cups for lighted wicks, trays and vases and jars for sacrifices and offerings, revolving *mani*, miniature *chorten*, in all of which is revealed—if one has not seen it before—the exquisite taste which seems to be as innate in the Ladakhis as the blood in their veins. And, the moment the master of the house opens the door of the little family sanctuary, one is surrounded with a subtle perfume of benzoin.

However, it is not the internal form of the Ladakhi house, but its outside appearance, that travellers generally know, more or less. There are, of course, some very poor houses which make very little attempt at decoration, but the majority show an obvious desire for it, and with complete success. One should look not so much at the houses in villages where there is scanty soil for cultivation; here the houses are crowded together, for economy of soil, at the edges of the oasis, at the foot of the rocks, which they even climb up in steps. The more the houses are crowded close to each other, the more each of them loses its own individuality: it seems to disappear in the thick mass of habitations, to merge into the houses near it, both on the same and on different levels, and so loses its character. Not even Leh, though there is no lack of space there, is the best place to give a clear idea of the Ladakhi house, unless one is by nature observant enough to distinguish the constructive and architectural elements of each. Leh has the characteristics of a real capital city, with houses joined laterally so as to form blocks, among which circulates an irregular network of narrow lanes. Down on the flat ground there are a few houses which rise independently in the midst of a vegetable-plot and a garden, but I am quite certain that no traveller has ever gone to look for them among the mass of habitations, nor has passed by their outside enclosing walls. There are others as it were hanging on the steep slope of the great rock from which the mighty mass of the palace of the 'Gyalpo' dominates the city, but I doubt if the ordinary—in any case rare—summer visitors to Leh either desire or are able to distinguish them in their minds from all the others near them. But not far away, on the wide alluvial bottom of the Indus Valley, there is abundance of soil, and of a soil more fertile than usual; here the country-people had no need to crowd their houses together in villages, but have scattered them here and there among the fields and, for their greater comfort, have made them almost perfect.

On the plain of Shè and the plain of Shushot, in fact, every peasants' habitation, rising isolated in the midst of a thick green patch of willows and poplars, is a regular country house. It is perfect in shape, rectangular, and perfect in symmetry also. The walls are built accurately, plastered and whitewashed, and get narrower as they rise towards the top, in such a way as to give grace to the building. The entrance-door is usually in the middle of the front of the house, facing south. There are no windows on the ground floor, but there are high, narrow windows like loop-holes on the first floor; on the second floor they are wider, and one or two, or even three, balconies project from the front of the house, with little roofs above them; on the top floor there is generally a large gallery running round three sides of the house, enclosing a great terrace which is open in front.

This typical Tibetan house is beautiful in appearance, and picturesque in its few ornamental details. The edge of the roof is always surmounted with a band of branches tied closely and tidily together and placed at right angles to the walls and dyed a dark wine-red; above the little windows, as also above the balconies—the characteristic *rabsal*—are little projecting roofs formed of rows of small beams one above the other and differently arranged so as to form an ornamental pattern, and often, on top of them, is a little layer of boughs coloured dark red. The means used are extraordinarily simple, but the effect is supremely picturesque. Then there are also small posts set upright on the roof, generally at the corners, from which hang little strips and pieces of cloth of every colour; cords stretched between them with festoons of little flags fluttering in the wind add to the effect of festive gaiety.

There are also the palaces. It was a palace in which we stayed at Tegur in the Nubra Valley, as I have already said. It was no larger than the farmers' houses in the Indus Valley at Shè and Shushot, nor yet was it fundamentally different in external appearance. Its superiority of structure and decoration was perhaps more visible inside. The stairs leading to the upper floors were not narrow, with high steps between two walls, and therefore dark, but had banisters all the way up and conveniently low steps, and wound round a wide central well which opened directly on to the great terrace on the top floor. Here the rooms which had *rabsal*—from which one looked out over the whole village and oasis and the immense channel of the Nubra Valley with its rocks and sands and thickets—also had their walls frescoed in bright colours with the most commonly seen of the Buddhist symbols, the eight 'glorious emblems'. Elsewhere I have seen large paintings representing the 'guardian Kings' of the different cardinal points, especially the 'Guardian of the East' with his pale face (the rest of them have green or red or yellow faces), his fixed smile and arrogant little moustache, the tiny 'mouche' in the middle of his chin, and the great lyre which he touches lightly with his long tapering fingers: these were obviously of Chinese influence.

But the most perfect modern palace—for others, such as the wonderful Castle of Chiktan, in the Bot Karbu Valley, form a natural part of the history of Tibetan architecture—is the one that the deposed 'Gyalpo' of Leh has built himself at the mouth of the Stok Valley, opposite Leh, which, from the top of a rock, dominates the whole of the oasis which the Dogra conquerors left to them as a perpetual fief. It is a perfect cube, its surface relieved by innumerable *rabsal*, and is inexpressibly picturesque in spite of its obvious richness.

In short, the architectural elements are always the same: they vary only in their distribution and in the number of times they are repeated. I am never tired of going back again and again to admire the palace of the ancient kings, standing high on its great rock above the dwellings of Leh which cluster at the feet of the abode of its one-time lord. It is a truly gigantic mass (there are at least ten successive rows of windows and balconies), its walls are solid and compact and extremely high; and yet it gives an impression of extraordinary elegance and grace, which would seem impossible for such a vast mass of masonry. There are two special means by which this effect is achieved—the progressive narrowing of the walls towards the top and the progressive increase in size of the apertures for giving light to the rooms. At the bottom, and for some way up, the walls are quite continuous, like those of a fortress; then, for several storeys, there are little windows so narrow that they look like loop-holes; then, on the storeys above, the windows become gradually bigger and wider, and on the topmost storeys are no longer windows but balconies, *rabsal*, and these also gradually become wider from one storey to another, till they end in terraces. At the bottom the walls are solid and uninterrupted: at the top, on the other hand, they are like open-work lace, giving grace and lightness to the strength and massiveness of the building.

Real palaces, however, are rare, as a natural result of the even and uniform distribution of wealth, which depends in its turn on the Tibetan social system. There are, however, the *gompa*, the monasteries.

The *gompa*, like all monasteries of every country and every religion, are generally situated in remote and solitary places. A traveller who, anxious to taste the pleasures of caravan-life, comes from Kashmir even only as far as Leh, at once comes upon the fantastically theatrical *gompa* of Lamayuru, almost the moment he has crossed the threshold of Ladakh. But after that he sees no more *gompa*. He passes close to Spituk, skirting the foot of the great ridge of rock on which the monastery is perched; but the monastery turns its back, so to speak, on the traveller, and he does not see it. If he has a fancy to look at some of them, he must go aside from the caravan-road to Rigzon, Likir, Piang, or Spituk, or make special excursions from Leh, if he wishes to find Tikse, or Himis, or even Chimre. I mention the larger ones, omitting those of Deskit and Samur in the Nubra Valley, which are less easily accessible. I think that I myself have seen almost all the *gompa* in Ladakh, great

IN THE *GOMPA* OF LAMAYURU

[*face p.* 264

and small, rich and poor, right up to the distant borders of the Great Tibet of Lhasa, so I can speak of them with some knowledge.

Their situation is always supremely picturesque—whether spread out, like an amphitheatre, down the rocky slope of a valley, like Rigzon, or clustered upon an isolated summit, like Piang and Likir and the little monastery of Stakna right in the middle of the Indus Valley near here; whether laid out in steps down the steep side of a ridge, like Tikse and Chimre and Spituk, or crowning a lofty, precipitous terrace, like Lamayuru, or crammed into the narrow windings of a valley, like Himis—they always—or almost always—have the special and intriguing quality of concealing themselves from travellers until the very last moment, when they suddenly spring into full view at a bend in the valley which encloses them and a turn in the path which leads to them. They are not formed of one single building, but of a whole crowd of buildings which look as if they were on top of each other and almost as if they rose out of each other. The larger buildings are the chapels and temples, in which are kept the sacred images of the innumerable Buddhist divinities, good or evil, calm and serene or grotesque and monstrous, with the whole store of furnishings required by the religion of an extremely imaginative race, and with all the paintings which entirely cover the walls, repeating endlessly the image of Buddha in his various attitudes of meditation or prayer, or representing in a succession of pictures the whole story of the founder or of the reformer of the faith. The smaller, more modest buildings look like miniature reproductions of the peasants' houses, and each one is the habitation of two or three lamas.

Even in the *gompa* the architectural and ornamental features are always the same as in the houses of the *zemindar* or in the palaces of the notables and the rich men, but are used in an unexpected variety of combinations and amalgamations. There are windows and *rabsal*, porches and galleries, narrow loopholes and wide terraces, balustrades which are connected from floor to floor, outside walls formed of a veritable lace-work of pierced wood, small projecting roofs made of beam-ends arranged in various ways, bands of boughs tied together and coloured, used not only on the top of the roofs but as though

to divide up the mass of the buildings. And if one's curiosity
urges one to penetrate inside the enclosure of one of these
gompa, which from outside gives the impression of being a
compact whole, one finds, between one building and another,
a complete labyrinth of courtyards, of open spaces, dark cor-
ridors, vaults, blind alleys, a regular village, a small city, an
entire world almost, in which—praying and singing psalms,
but also smiling—perhaps hundreds of lamas pass their
lives. And if one's arrival has been announced beforehand
as that of a great *sahib* worthy to be received with honour,
no sooner has one turned the last bend in the valley or the
path which brings one face to face with the sudden, fantastic
sight of the *gompa* than they are all drawn up on the roof of
the highest building, outlined clearly against the sky in their
flaming monks' robes, ready to welcome one with the sound
of all their instruments—quavering trumpets patterned with
silver, drums held by a long handle and beaten with a long
curved stick, trombones of inordinate length which have to
be held up by boy-lamas at the opposite end to the one into
which the musicians are blowing with all the power of their
lungs. Then one starts up the winding path that climbs up
the rocks and leads to the entrance of the *gompa*, one penetrates into the internal maze of little streets, and in the first
open space the orchestra renews its noisy welcome from closer
than before, the Superior of the *gompa* receives and greets
one surrounded by his lamas, and invites one to a hospitable
tea in the mystic twilight of a temple or in his own private
apartment, in fascinating, enchanted surroundings; then he
puts one in charge of the administrator of the monastery, for
one is allowed to go all over it without any limits being imposed
upon a curiosity which may well be endless.

Endless, indeed, if one is capable of appreciating the sense
of beauty that breathes from everything one sees, from the little
silver cups used in the ceremonies, from the hundred little
statues of divinities in rows upon the altars, the innumerable
tanka hanging from walls and cross-beams and pillars, the
great vessels in which tea and a compound of *satu* are taken
to the lamas as they pray in the chapels, the little pierced and
lacquered tables, the very long, narrow, soft Chinese carpets,
and even the external ornamentations which make the *gompa*

266

look gay as well as the houses—such as the poles with banners and frills and festoons fluttering from them, the monstrous masks, the great points of worked iron from which hang coal-black tails of yak.　One comes out with a strange mixture of memories and images, which, however, resolve themselves into one single image, one single memory—that of an art which is truly consummate.

Leh, September 22nd, 1930.

CHAPTER XXV

FAREWELL TO LADAKH

I am now on the eve of my departure from Leh, and when
I think of it I feel even sadder than I did when I came down
from the Rimo Glacier into the Yarkand Valley. To-morrow
is really the beginning of the end.

In the agitation of this approaching departure, memory
brings to my mind valleys and mountains and glaciers, villages,
houses, palaces, *gompa*, chapels and temples, all the men who
have served me with such loyalty, and the inhabitants of the
villages who seemed to have no other object than that of
fulfilling my never-ending desires. I see my men during long,
exhausting marches, struggling with adversities of weather,
but always ready to comply with my wishes and to make any
effort required of them, smiling and patient under every trial
that circumstances placed upon them. I also see the others, the
whole population of the peasants, always so gay and serene,
so contented and happy, yet always pervaded with profound
religious feeling.

Religion can certainly be said to form an essential part in
the character, not only of the inhabitants, but actually of the
country. It would be impossible to imagine that a people
should not be religious which dedicates not less than a quarter
of its children to the monasteries, and, if only for that reason,
lives in continual intimacy and community of life with all its
innumerable lamas. Just as the lamas have to mingle in the
life of the rest of the people, not only through ties of affection
with their families and friends but also for the more earthly
and practical reasons of the economic interests of their own
gompa, so the country-people can be said to live always within
the orbit of a monastery—generally the nearest one, but sometimes one which is rather more distant but more specially
venerated.

It may be that, with the exception of a few old men, one no longer sees the peasants, as they walk in their village lanes or field-paths or even as they attend to their little affairs, turning with their right hand the pretty little 'prayer-wheels' which were so convenient because every turn meant a prayer for the faithful. But this is no reason for thinking that religious feeling has grown less. The day that it grows less or ceases to exist, or that the Ladakhis (may all their innumerable Buddhas protect them!) are converted, not only the people, but actually the country, will completely lose its character—a character which, in the case of both people and country, is one of happy, picturesque, perpetual gaiety in the beautiful, impressive setting provided by Nature.

One must have traversed the great valleys of Western Tibet, and have traversed them, not as an inattentive tourist, but with one's eye and mind ready and anxious and on the alert all the time to notice and criticize and appreciate everything: then one cannot fail to realize that this country, impressive and beautiful as it is, would be very much more desolate, and, above all, very much more dumb, were it not for the innumerable *mani* and *chorten* and *lato* and the innumerable chapels with which the piety of the inhabitants has sprinkled it. And every one of these traces left, or rather imposed, upon the country by the piety of its inhabitants has something gay and festive about it. Not so much the *mani*, perhaps, which are long walls (sometimes many hundreds of yards long and as much as 33 feet wide) covered with innumerable stones on which is carved the eternal prayer of the Buddhists; but certainly the *chorten*, which are of every shape and size and always rise in a graceful pyramid with irregular steps and terminate in a slight gable; also, certainly, the *lato*, from which many-coloured banners gaily flutter, so that the wind, as it shakes them, may repeat the prayers written upon them. For everything in this country —not merely everybody—has to pray, for the glory of the numberless divinities. Thus one will see huge *mani*, made like great reels and revolving on their own axes, driven by water diverted from a neighbouring stream: these are praying for the people of the neighbouring village. One will see other revolving *mani* placed on a wind-swept ridge, so that the wind may make them turn perpetually: they also are praying for the inhabitants of the nearest village. There are sometimes long festoons of flags right across a valley, but much more often they are on the top of the outside rim of the roofs of houses, chapels, small temples, and also of *gompa*: branches with the same prayer-inscribed banners rise above the roofs at corners of buildings; and great high poles are planted in front of the houses also carrying a long strip of cloth which one might almost think is really murmuring prayers when it vibrates in the wind.

All this bears witness to the religious feeling of the Ladakhis, but it also gives a character of extreme gaiety and joyousness to the country itself.

The colours, also, add to this. The houses are white, brilliant white, as are also the temples and the *gompa*, but they often have their corners and the upper edge of their walls tinted with red. The larger monastery buildings have broad stripes also of red or brown just under the roof, above the windows, and above the fine balconies; some chapels, dedicated to Chamba, are bright red all over outside, and sometimes one will see even rocks or tree-trunks painted red.

Such is the mentality, the character, the picturesque and artistic feeling of my friends the Ladakhis. And apart from the exquisite taste with which they design, decorate, paint, or carve their scanty domestic furnishings and their extremely rich religious furnishings (both of which are only to be found in the sanctuaries, either in their houses or their temples), they also give proof of this delicate sensibility of theirs in the way in which they scent the air with sticks of benzoin and little juniper branches burning at every corner of the streets, at every entrance to a house, and in the way in which they make little beds of grass on the terraces at the tops of the houses, so that the green of the grass may refresh and comfort them in the heat of summer, and in the way, too, in which both men and women wear, in their caps or their *perak*, behind the ear or on the shoulder, a flower which they have grown with goodness knows how much care and difficulty.

I am sure that my readers, for whom I am writing these hasty observations and impressions, will not be able to help loving—at any rate a little—and also really appreciating, these people who have so many qualities and give one so much pleasure. In moments of leisure during these last days I have tried to mix with the people again, with the humbler people, going about the narrow, tortuous streets where none of the ordinary travellers go, entering the passages into the houses, revisiting the palace of the ancient kings, going again into the temples and in among the *chorten* and the *mani*, running off to the neighbouring *gompa* of Sankar, where my old friend the *kushok* Bacula has made such a rich and beautiful collection of Tibetan religious objects: I wanted, in fact, to take a last plunge into the joys of the life here, into the gaiety and perpetual serenity which breathes in everything one sees, in every face one meets which immediately breaks into a smile.

I wanted also to see one aspect of Leh which I did not yet know—the comings and goings of the trade-caravans. These comings and goings are certainly full of life. Now I understand why the State keeps the immense *serai* which I had always seen shut up and which had seemed to me to be completely useless, and why there are all those other large private stabling establishments, which had looked to me as if they were deserted. Now the courts of the *serai*, surrounded with sheds, are swarming with horses and donkeys, and the end courtyard is swarming with the men of the caravans, while the great open space in the middle is encumbered with big bales of merchandise; in the tiny huts all round (each hut consists of one room with a small verandah in front) are lodged Punjabis, Yarkandis and Kirghiz. Even the private stables are full, and if one goes out of Leh only as far as Sankar one sees herds and herds of beasts, with their pack-saddles always on, feeding in the fields where the harvest has already been gathered. And in the city itself, in the broad avenues of the bazaar as well as in the little narrow streets where the houses are close together, there is an unaccustomed coming and going of people of almost every race and costume, in which my poor Ladakhis seem to be almost submerged.

I have seen very few caravans arriving, at the moment, but many more starting. Their preparations take a long time: the day before they start there appears an interminable file of beasts of burden coming from the pastures outside the city, which stops in the bazaar or near the *serai* or at the house of some important merchant; the loads are all ready in some courtyard

near-by. Then early next morning begins the lengthy work of
fitting them to the pack-saddles, for each animal's two loads
must be fairly similar both in shape and in weight, and they
have to have a third load added to them if it happens that the
weight of the first two is not up to standard. There is much
shouting on the part of the caravan-leader, who runs hither and
thither, gives a helping hand here in a case where loading is
complicated and a blow there if he thinks a man's work is slow
or badly done. The raucous voices of Yarkandis and the sharp,
quarrelsome voices of Punjabis mingle with the stampings and
neighings of horses, while the Ladakhi spectators smile slightly
maliciously. This goes on till the afternoon. Then the caravan moves off, with loud shouts from the caravan-men and the
tinkling of the beads and bells on all the animals. But, as they
only start in the afternoon, they go only a short way the first
day: they stop at Ganglès, but this short march is long enough
for them to make sure that the loads are well packed and
well distributed, and they can be changed if necessary before
they set out towards the caravan-road of death.

Other caravans take different directions. There are few
and small ones going towards Baltistan; more frequent ones
towards Kashmir; fewer perhaps, but more numerous in animals,
directly towards the Punjab by way of the Rupshu plateau: it
is a more difficult route and it is just as well to be in larger
numbers when going by it, so as to help each other better. It
is also to be my return route.

As for the merchandise which goes with them, it is impossible to see it; it is packed and tied up in bales which all look
the same from outside, in large, uniform loads. Something
may be seen in the bazaar or in the *serai*—enormous loads of
namdah, the white felt from Kashgar to which the marvellous
embroiderers of Kashmir will later add the loveliness of their
designs and colours; beautiful carpets from Khotan, their dark
blue backgrounds scattered with stylized red flowers and with
a charming velvety sheen on them; silks from Yarkand and
from Kashgar, red or yellow or green or blue, but in which the
colour is distributed as it were in great irregular flames on a
white background, and others in which the background is of
one colour and has scattered upon it little roses with four petals
only, of different colours—both are so fine and light that they

look transparent—and dresses and furs and Yarkandi top-boots such as are sold locally. But among all the other kinds of merchandise there are certain small, perfectly-packed loads of regular shape which are not scattered about between the bazaar and the *serai* but which, the moment they arrive, always take the same road and end up in the same house, a solid house which is almost always shut up and has strong bars at its windows: these are loads of opium, the importation of which is limited and therefore has to be rigorously controlled.

Among all the departing caravans I have waited in vain for one which I should have followed with the greatest longing—Kalzan's caravan for Lhasa. It was to have started during these last days but has delayed from one day to another, and now I shall not see it, as to-morrow I start myself. Every now and then I see the loads being moved from different places to be collected at his house. It is easy to recognize Kalzan's animals which are going to Lhasa: they are vigorous mules, smooth and glossy, with great bells hung round their necks and long, thick tassels of flaming red which swing rhythmically at each step, and they are all of them adorned with frills and ornaments made of little pieces of red cloth. They are animals belonging to a Tibetan caravan—which is tantamount to saying that they are picturesque. And they are led by Tibetans from Lhasa, pure Mongols, physically strong and with a gait that shows the self-confidence and decisiveness which are the result of being long accustomed to caravan life in places that are inhospitable and harsh. They are well dressed, in the manner of Lhasa, naturally, with great dark blue robes which bulge out in ample folds above the band which holds them in at the waist; Chinese shoes, and caps, also of Chinese type, an abundance of coral and turquoise necklaces, heavy bracelets on their wrists, and a long pendant in one ear. Above all, they are always ready to smile and to give one a welcome. They are Tibetans—which is saying enough. What a difference from the hardness and obstinacy of the caravan-men from Yarkand, and from the chattering petulance of the Punjabis! But even making this momentary mental comparison immediately revives the subtle sadness of leaving. I shall certainly be sorry to leave my beloved Ladakh and my Ladakhi men.

For this reason it only gave me a passing and unsatisfactory distraction each time I went back to the bazaar, into the little shops, even into the *serai*, crowded with merchandise and with the men and animals of the caravans. Certainly it was all interesting. But even in the *serai* it often happened that I took my eyes off the beautiful carpets of Khotan which the merchants were spreading in front of me and raised them to admire, again and again till the very last moment, the ancient palace of the 'Gyalpo' kings, as it appeared, through the poplar-grove already yellow with autumn, dominating the city from the height of its great rust-coloured rock.

Leh, September 23rd, 1930.

We left on the morning of the 24th. Starting was such a laborious business, with the new caravan of chattering, quarrelsome Punjabis, that at half-past ten I decided to go on, leaving Hashmatullah at the bungalow to be sure that none of the baggage should be left behind at Leh. It was impossible to wait any longer if I wanted to see the beauties of Shè and Tikse again on my way.

What a blessing it is to leave punctually by train and cut short the farewells of one's relations and friends! The bungalow was filled with all my Ladakhi friends, and as there was no train and no time-table to be respected, there would have been a danger of prolonging the farewells *ad infinitum* if I had not made up my mind to cut short the delays and start.

It was rather a wrench, nevertheless. Not that there was any exaggerated or affected sentimentalism. It has happened to everybody, at least once in their lives, to feel sorrow at tearing themselves away from some great work of art that they have admired in the room of a museum; in the same way I feel sorrow at having to leave a country and natural surroundings which in themselves constitute a much grander work of art than any that can be contained within the narrow limits of a frame or placed upon a pedestal. There are few natural landscapes grander and more beautiful than those which Western Tibet offers to our admiration.

An unspeakable melancholy came over me as I went through the little streets of Leh and the wide avenue of the bazaar at

MILKING THE GOATS

[face p. 274

a quick trot on my mule—my new mount—and at every corner and from every shop someone looked out to greet me with a 'salaam' or a 'ju' full of sincere devotion. Even when I had come out beyond the close-packed houses and had passed through the forest of *chorten* that almost looks like a continuation of the city towards the cultivated fields and the nakedness of the first rocky spurs, I could not control the spontaneous desire I felt to turn round and look again—once again, before they disappeared from view—at the beautiful palace of the Ladakhi kings, the little ancient *gompa*, perched on the top of the ridge of rock, and the whole of Leh, looking so gay with the innumerable banners fluttering on the roofs of the houses.

Down, past immense *mani* that seemed endless; down through a gap between rocks in a short spur which runs out towards the Indus. I turned round, but Leh had disappeared; between the rocks there was nothing to be seen but a little piece of the green of its lovely wooded oasis. Farewell to Leh—this time, a real farewell.

I looked absent-mindedly at villages and fields, palaces and chapels and *gompa* which I already knew. Shè, with its fine old royal palace, honeycombed with *rabsal*, but inside all desolate and abandoned: the private chapel, like all chapels, was interesting, and the pious descendants of the 'Gyalpo' kings have placed two poor lamas there to keep it up, and they live more or less banished among the ruins. The neighbouring village, with its little temples, is of primitive antiquity, like the villages of Alchi, Chiktan, and Basgo. They are very different from the more modern villages. Here we are again in the 'age of wood', not yet in the 'age of metals'; the statues of the divinities in the little chapels are all carved roughly in wood, and the wreaths of leaves and vine-branches and flowers above the altar and forming the statues of the divinities are also in wood. This is art in its primitive stage. Near Shè the rocks at the bottom of the mountain-slope are carved to represent gigantic figures from the Olympus of the lamas, stylized like those of the numerous steles scattered all along the road. The fields are well cultivated and among them are sprinkled those perfectly constructed houses I have mentioned. Then there is Tikse, wonderful Tikse, with its *gompa*, perhaps the most picturesque and beautiful in all Ladakh, whose hundred buildings descend

in steps from the top of a great ridge of rock right down to
the plain below, which bristles with a forest of *chorten*. We
had a noisy and festive welcome from the lamas; and I acquired
a new object for my collection. Then, beyond the Indus—
which is an easy river to ford, here and at this season—are the
fertile fields of Shushot, sprinkled with the fine, rich, roomy,
well-built houses of the *zemindars*, and the rather wild and
primeval forest in the midst of which our tents were pitched—
our last encampment in Ladakh.

The following day we reached Himis, the largest and richest
gompa of the region. On the way, however, I revisited the
gompa of Stakna, which is perhaps the smallest and also the
poorest. But it is picturesque nevertheless, on the hump of
a great rock isolated in the midst of the alluvion of the valley.
There were only two lamas there, but shut up and barricaded
into his own private room, with no company but that of two
minute Lhasa dogs, there was also the *kushok*, a poor little boy
who looked ill from being always shut up, and also almost
humiliated from being forced to stay there and be a superman,
while the village boys made as much noise as they pleased down
below without being oppressed by the semi-sanctity which fate
had imposed upon him.

Himis is certainly the largest and wealthiest *gompa* in the
whole of Ladakh: it is the wealthiest because, by agreeing to
pay a large tax to the Dogra conquerors, it avoided being
sacked and thus saved its treasures. But it is not the most
beautiful or picturesque or interesting. Instead of being
placed in a commanding position on top of a rock or spreading
up and down a steep slope, Himis looks as if it were trying to
hide in a little valley and is enclosed between two ridges of rock
which come down from each of the opposite sides. There are
thick, very carefully cultivated trees, irregular poplar-groves,
the lovely autumnal colouring of whose foliage reminded me
of the indescribable splendour of the beech-groves in the
Apennines, and a crowd of buildings and temples and well-kept
houses. But the antiquity of the *gompa* and, actually, its
wealth (which was preserved even during the storm of the
Dogra conquest) have caused a lack of homogeneity, of organization in the structure of the whole, owing to alterations, additions, and superstructures of every period, left by all the

276

kushok who have governed the *gompa* in turn; even inside, next door to really precious objects are to be found baubles of European origin, tasteless and unnecessary. This is what happens inevitably when the large endowment of a *gompa* has to be administered by an unintelligent *kushok* such as the present one, Stakchen Ralpa, who spends largely but without taste, consulting mainly the illustrated catalogues of the big shops in India and elsewhere. I am forced to make the comparison again with the intelligence and exquisite taste and noble manners of my old friend the *kushok* Bacula, and with the beautiful treasures of Tibetan art which he has collected at the two *gompa* of Spituk and Sankar.

At Himis I said my last farewell to Ladakh. Ladakh, strictly speaking, is the name given by the inhabitants to that particular tract of the Indus Valley which opens out into a basin of imposing proportions: the capital is there, and the ancient seat of the local dynasty, the cultural, commercial and political centre, the finest of the *gompa*, the most majestic of the palaces, and the most fertile country. Outside this basin, as far as the inhabitants are concerned, it is not Ladakh proper, but other districts each of which has a special name, unless it is considered unworthy of possessing a name at all. Immediately beyond the little valley in which Himis hides itself, and the valley opposite it in which is the marvellously beautiful *gompa* that stands above the village of Chimre, the great basin of Leh narrows down and then closes in, and that is the end of Ladakh proper. Above this point the Indus flows through a narrow, very rocky valley which gives a foretaste of the rugged, wild desolation of the Rong near by, with tiny villages which get more and more scarce and more and more poverty-stricken. We reached Upshi, at the mouth of a valley coming in from the left.

Then we started to climb, roughly towards the south— which is the main direction of the return journey that will take me over the high passes of the Rupshu, back again into India.

We went up the Upshi Valley, which is very very long and seems endless, but which has no grandeur of form because it cuts across the line of the rocky strata of a secondary chain; but the strata of rock are remarkable because of their alternating colours—the very dark green of the conglomerates, the light

277

green of the sandstone, the wine-red of the marly schists and because of the varying hardness of the rocks, owing to which the most resistent project upwards like high, straight walls, furrowing the opposing sides of the valley. Yesterday we stopped at Miru, a wretched village with very few houses and poor-looking fields.

To-day we severed our last link with Ladakh, though not yet with the region of Tibet. We arrived about noon at Ghia, the highest village in the valley and actually the last in the country of Ladakh; but, as if for the benefit of new visitors arriving from the direction by which we are going out of the country, as if to give them immediate proof of how beautiful and picturesque Ladakh is, Ghia has not the miserable appearance of Miru. On the other hand, its fertile fields (of barley only, because of the altitude) stretch over the wide space of a flat basin, the only one which interrupts the narrow ruggedness of the valley; in the fields are scattered the houses, well built, well plastered, with fine *rabsal* and little windows adorned with the architraves characteristic of the country, and with festoons of flags crowning the roofs; and, all round the village, innumerable *mani*, innumerable *chorten*, of extraordinary size, perfect in construction, as though to prove and to assert that the character of the country does not change, but preserves itself unaltered right up to its very borders.

We went on beyond Ghia for about four hours up the valley, the outlines and sides of which are no longer rugged, but smoother and more tapering. It seemed as if both the valley and our journey would go on for ever. We stopped a short time ago at a small tributary valley, at the considerable height of about 15,420 feet, with night already falling and an intense cold. This has been the first of the long stages which are necessary when crossing the inhospitable zone of the Rupshu plateau, without losing too much time on the way. It is, in fact, absolutely essential that the first snows should not catch us on the road: it is we who must arrive first.

Camp at the foot of the Stakalung-la, September 28th, 1930.

CHAPTER XXVI

THE LIFE OF THE NOMADS

Last night it was intensely cold at our camp in the little valley at the northern foot of the Stakalung-la, but the cold was welcome if it was a sign of good weather to come. It was still intensely cold this morning when I appeared early at my tent door to hasten on the men. The sky was completely clear.

Getting up early was absolutely essential. The caravan, unfortunately, no longer consists of Ladakhis. I do not say that the Ladakhis do not like to dawdle round their smoking pots over their morning tea, and to enjoy the warmth from their great blazing fires; but their *sahib*, if he has acquired a certain influence over his men, has only to tell them that it is time to start, and they swallow down the last cup of tea, fill their mouths with the *satu* compound the very sight of which makes one choke, and spring up to get ready to start. But as for these Punjabis, one needs a windlass to make them budge: they have their own programme of the march, and it is very difficult to get them to alter it in accordance with the ideas of the caravan-leader (which is myself) as to what is best or most opportune, or what he thinks most suitable for reasons of his own. Then there is another thing which makes it worse. In a caravan of porters each man has his own load; he finds it without hesitation, places it on his shoulders, and is ready to start. But in a caravan of mules each animal has three loads, and it takes two men to fix them on the pack-saddle, and there is naturally a much smaller number of men than of animals. So that the business of loading is not short, speedy, and almost exactly synchronized, but is slow, lengthy, often difficult, and the mules have to be loaded one after another. Over and above this—seeing that I have to do with Punjabi muleteers—there are quarrels, discussions, interminable chatter, and then objections on the part of the mules, who are extremely clever at withdrawing themselves just as the loads are about to be placed on each side of the pack-saddle: two little steps forward, and the loads find themselves *ipso facto* on the ground, and the work has to begin all over again. I assure you it needs a good deal of patience: before, we took even as little as half an hour to move camp, now it takes two hours at the quickest. And the marches are long; I do not wish to shorten them, in order not to multiply them, and also so as not to lessen the probability of my being able to get over all the passes before the snow comes. This is the explanation of the reason why I appear early, just after dawn, at my tent door—to act as an absolutely necessary stimulus.

The Stakalung-la, at a height of about 17,700 feet, was the pass which I feared perhaps most, not only because it was the highest, but because the slopes approaching it on both sides were the steepest and it was also perhaps the least practicable of all, so that a heavy fall of snow, obliterating such traces of the road as there are, would make it difficult to cross. Yesterday evening, however, I had no more fears.

The weather was fine this morning. But an icy breeze was blowing down the little valley which goes up to the pass, making us all stiff with cold. But fortunately, shortly after we had begun the climb, we came into the full sunshine and also to a certain extent out of the wind, which sufficed to melt our numbness a little.

The climb is certainly steep, but the ground is not in the least rough. In fact, after one leaves Ghia, the more one rises, the gentler the formations of the country become. The sides of the little valleys here do not rise into ridges at the top, but into smooth, gently rounded humps—though at this altitude! The fact is that beyond Ghia one comes into a different kind of country, no longer a mountain- but a plateau-country. And with the Stakalung-la one comes right on to the Rupshu plateau.

We were on the wide, rounded summit of the pass—which is marked by a *lato* with little flags flying—when the wind suddenly struck us again. It went with us the whole day, blowing full in our faces. It was not very strong, but persistent, continuous, without a moment's respite, and, for this reason, extremely trying. A steep but not rugged descent from the pass led out into a strange valley, a wide, long valley with a bottom so flat that it was difficult to tell at a glance from which direction its waters were flowing. Streams were few and rare, however, for no torrent-bed cut its way through the level valley-bottom. Little hills of meagre height—relative height, of course—and of meagre shape, extended along the sides of the valley. It was the beginning of the Rupshu plateau-country.

Here, indeed, the Himalaya has not yet assumed the character of a mountain-range; here the erosion of torrents and rivers has not yet completely destroyed the primeval landscape; a portion of the primeval plateau is still preserved in the Rupshu, and is connected with the immense, limitless plateau of the Great Tibet of Lhasa. What may appear, as one comes up from India, to be the summit or high ridge of a mountain-range, is simply the edge of an enormous high plateau which declines on that side towards the sun-scorched plains of the Punjab. This typical plateau-country is interesting to one who does not already know it, but it becomes rather monotonous in the end: I already knew it, having traversed its length and breadth sixteen years ago, in the winter—that is, when the snow made an already monotonous landscape even more monotonous.

It consists, in fact, of a succession of wide, flat valleys like the one which opened out in front of us this morning at the foot of the Stakalung-la; these are enclosed at the sides by extremely smooth, gently sloping flanks, which are not high and end in gently rounded summits. These valleys, unusually wide and flat as they are, are not normal in the sense that they mark a regular system of watercourses or form part of a regular network of valleys. On the contrary, if one looks closely one can very often see that the valley-bottom, though, as a whole, flat, is actually made up of slightly inverse slopes, and very often—and this is more easily visible—these great flattened channels do not open out into each other, but are closed like basins. The Rupshu, in fact, consist of a series of these closed basins, which have no normal drainage for their waters. In consequence there are innumerable lakes, large and small and always salt. The largest of all—and it is really very large—is the Morari-tso, two days' march from here, which I crossed last time I was here on the great sheet of ice which covered it.

I should have liked to see it again with its dark blue surface free of ice—as some traveller has described it—and reflecting the smooth hills which surround it on every side. But this necessity of hurrying on—I might almost say, of escaping— until my caravan has crossed all the passes, compels me to give up the short détour which would be necessary. So we have not come across Morari-tso or any other lakes on our way; but more than once the gentle counter-slopes of these wide depressions showed clearly, by the traces of yellow clay that marked their edges in an even line, that in past times, when rains were more abundant and evaporation, perhaps, less, there had actually been lakes there.

It is certainly interesting country, but monotonous and desolate. But less naked than elsewhere, perhaps. We are now getting near the southern slopes of the Himalaya whence come the rain-bringing monsoons, so that a little humidity must reach even as far as this; a proof of this is the grass which grows here—much more plentifully than we were accustomed to see it in the valleys of the Karakoram. But it is a grass which is scarcely green, and gives no feeling of freshness; it is a curious yellowish colour. In the distance, when all the blades of grass growing on the flat valley-bottom are one behind the other on the same level, one seems to be looking at real meadows— yellowish in colour, but meadows all the same. This is a complete illusion, for the stalks are isolated and far apart, and curiously stiff and dried-up, and as one goes on, the thing which looked like a meadow of grass vanishes and dissolves into the uniform expanse of shingle, sand and clay. The wind blows perpetually, not strong, but persistent and trying, never ceasing or dying down. We had lunch in the very meagre shelter afforded by a wretched, half-ruined *chorten*.

And on we went, not stopping too long for lunch, and never at all for any other reasons, for the distances here are great— even when some object sticking up from the ground, such as a bush, a rock, a sand-dune, would appear to be quite near. After a bit one realizes how continually deceptive these great flat expanses are, and one goes on and on as though one had lost one's bearings, no longer believing what one sees—or, more often, imagines that one sees. One also sees certain mirage phenomena which, in a strange manner, multiply the number of the 'heran', or Tibetan antelope, or the 'kyang', the wild asses, which one has seen quite clearly not very far off but which look as if they were multiplied into a regular herd as they gallop off into the distance; they also make the man and boy who have just passed, driving one little wretched donkey in front of them, look like a large caravan; and, most of all, one always seems to be seeing shining expanses of water, which are unattainable, or rather which dissolve like the expanses of grass just as one thinks one is getting near them.

Such are the plains of the Rupshu into which to-day's march has brought us. I chose this much longer and much more difficult route for my return journey not only because a great part of it was new to me. In the Rupshu also there was something I did not yet know and that I wished to know, and that was the human life which goes on there during the summer months. I had been there in spring, when the country up here had not yet abandoned its winter garb: there was not much snow on the ground, at least not everywhere, but there were violent storms accompanied by whirlwinds; these I experienced particularly on the day on which I eventually reached the great sheet of ice of the Morari-tso. The conditions, then, were those of winter, and the Rupshu plains were desolate and empty of life. But in summer they are populated with Changpa shepherds, and it was they whom I wished to come upon in the midst of their pastoral life.

My plan, in fact, was to go and pitch my tents close to an encampment of Changpa, the encampment of Rukchen. But although my men, after a march of some hours during the afternoon, kept on telling me that the encampment was quite close, it never appeared. And when they pointed out to me that it lay in a short lateral valley, also wide and flat, I ceased to have any faith either in them or in what they were pointing at, waving their arms and hands. All I could see was some large clumps of bushes and light puffs of a mist which was coming up in the first cold of the evening. But this also was a mistake, and what I saw was the shepherds' tents with smoke coming from them.

We are, in fact, at Rukchen, in the little lateral valley, and near us, scattered over the flat valley-bottom and up the first smooth slopes, are from thirty to forty Changpa tents—a complete encampment. I am very glad that I faced the monotony and the wind of the Rupshu and the uncertainty of the passes, for I am certainly learning something here.

The Changpa are typical inhabitants of the Tibetan plateaux: they are also typical Mongols, except when they have undergone some infusion of Ladakhi blood; they are, in fact, typical shepherds. Theirs is a pastoral life which goes perpetually backwards and forwards between summer and winter pastures. But whereas in the winter the nomad Changpa collect in the wide valley of the Indus not far off and in the district round Lake Pankong and remain there stationary, in the summer they disperse among the nearest lateral valleys, and especially over the Rupshu plateau, and move about to different localities according to their requirements and opportunities of finding pasture.

I knew them well, the Changpa: they had once given me hospitality, when I was travelling very light, without taking even a 'Whymper' tent with me. If anyone thinks that he can become a traveller, still more an explorer, without being prepared to give up ordinary habits and everything that he thinks to be absolutely necessary to life, he must either stay at home or learn to do so. After my first winter excursion last time I was out here, I had already learned that native houses were preferable to tents, and I gave up my tent, thus becoming also more mobile. I did actually sleep in the open air, in my sleeping-bag, and in the middle of winter, at a height of 16,400 feet here on the Rupshu; and I should have slept perfectly if my head had not been heavy with the perfume (not exactly of benzoin!) which came from a fire of the only fuel I could come by—yak-dung, wet with snow. Aspiring travellers, please note! And so, when I later came upon an encampment of Changpa and invaded one of their tents—in the same way in which I was accustomed to invade houses in the villages—the shepherd's tent seemed to me like a royal palace. It certainly had advantages over a 'Whymper' or a 'tropical tent': at least one could have a fire if one wanted it—always of sheep- or yak-dung, of course, but quite dry, and which burns well and gives a pleasant heat. One must only hope that it will not smoke!

The 'rebo', the typical tent of the nomad shepherds of Tibet, is made of a coarse cloth woven from yak-hair, black or brown, and sewn together in such a way that, when the tent is put up, it takes the shape of half of an egg cut lengthwise. It is therefore more or less elliptical, so that it has two long sides, connected by two shorter sides on a regular curve. Half-way along one of the longer sides the tent has a vertical opening, a kind of slit, the side-pieces of which are easily moved: this slit serves as entrance. There is a second slit in the roof of the tent, crosswise and corresponding with the entrance; little rods keep the sides of it apart, making a long, thin opening which serves to let out the smoke. Two vertical posts of moderate size, in the width of the tent and at the two ends of this smoke-opening, serve to hold up the roof. These in themselves would be an insufficient support; so, in order that the *rebo* may take its proper shape and keep it as long as it stays up, ropes are attached at a certain height to the coarse cloth of which it is made, and are held firm on the ground all round, with their ends free, by means of big stones; to keep them taut each one is passed over a vertical pole planted outside the tent and forked at the top. These external poles are often adorned with a coal-black yak's tail, or a little festoon of banners printed with prayers runs from one to another, for it must not be forgotten that we are still among Tibetans.

Apart from its characteristic shape the *rebo* also has a characteristic internal structure. Entering through the vertical slit that forms the door, one is immediately aware of a special internal arrangement, which is always the same and whose character is fixed and unchangeable, its symmetry centring about the narrow part of the tent immediately corresponding with the entrance. First there is the vertical pole which supports the roof of the tent; then a little square enclosure formed by three slabs of stone placed upright and open on the fourth side towards the middle of the *rebo*: this serves as deposit for the excrement of sheep and goats, which is the fuel generally used. Then, right in the centre, is the hearth—three large stones arranged so as to form a triangle. Then there is a second little enclosure for animals' excrement; then the second supporting pole. Finally, against the side of the tent opposite the entrance, there is a raised place made of earth and stones which is the little family altar: on it there are one or two statues of Buddha or of divinities or venerated lamas, one or two *kau*, and one or two brass cups to hold wicks or offerings of grain or rice, water or tea. Right round the inside of the *rebo* runs another smaller raised step of earth and stones; this is used for putting sacks of provisions on, tools, garments, stuffs, wool, and also, carefully shut up in a box, the little family treasure; it corresponds to the *bsot* or store-room in the houses of the Ladakhis. And one or two pieces of cloth, or even carpets, spread on the ground, show the place where the members of the family sleep peacefully after the day's work.

This work of theirs starts with the dawn and ends with sunset, and is distributed among them all with an organization which seems almost perfect.

Now it must be explained that each encampment constitutes an aggregate of human beings comparable to a village, or rather, to more than a village. The head of the Rukchen encampment is not, in fact, a *lambardar* (which is something like a mayor), but is a *zaildar*, which in the region of Ladakh means the head of a group of villages. An encampment, therefore, represents a fairly important collection of human beings. It is a kind of tribe which moves about together, following fixed and traditional rules in its movements, in its use of pastures, and also in its everyday customs. I do not know whether groups of individuals of lesser and subordinate rank are to be distinguished within an encampment. I only know that each tent represents the unit of a family. And I know also that possessions do not belong to the tribe but to separate families, as is shown by the relative wealth of some of the tents and the poverty of others. Then there is also one tent at Rukchen smaller and decidedly poorer-looking than any other, with bits of it all in holes. It is inhabited by a small family, badly clothed and wretched in appearance. It is a family that apparently does nothing, and never works; they seem to have complete leisure in their poverty, doing nothing but enjoy the sunshine as much as possible, squatting by the entrance of the tent. Who in the world can they be? They are the *mon*, the musicians, just as in every village in Ladakh. They belong, in a way, to the tribe, they move about with it, but they have no herds and therefore no work. They live on the generosity of the others, for whom they play their trumpets and their little drums on every solemn occasion or when, apart from any special solemn occasion, they are seized with the desire to have a *tamasha*.

It is extraordinarily interesting to watch the life of an encampment of nomads. When we arrived at Rukchen, domestic life was still going on busily outside the tents. Women were spinning wool; others were dyeing it that beautiful dark wine-colour which the fashion of Leh has brought even up here on to the Rupshu; others again were weaving on primitive looms placed flat on the ground. The men seemed to be less numerous, and perhaps less busy too. I started at once to go round among the tents; often, near them, there were odd little walls, perfectly built, but not of stone; they were composed of small bags, crammed with I know not what merchandise—probably salt and tea—two of which form the load of one sheep or goat. For even sheep and goats are beasts of burden here. I am hoping to see them in working order on the road.

The *zaildar* of the encampment invited us into his *rebo*: a row of wicks were burning dimly in front of an exquisitely modelled Buddha, and on the family altar there were *kau* of surprising fineness. We had excellent Tibetan tea, but not of the kind that is boiled with butter and salt so as to be like bad soup; this, on the other hand, was boiled with milk and plenty of spices, and I did not find it at all unpleasant. We were given red raisins, sweet apricot-kernels, and extremely hard little cakes, all of which were kept in little bags, together with bags full of rupees, in the box which obviously holds all the family treasures. But it was a frank, happy, spontaneous hospitality which was typical both of Tibetans and of shepherds. And these people, after all, are Tibetan shepherds.

The family of the *zaildar* of Rukchen is evidently a rich one, as one immediately realized on seeing the woman of the family. Her clothes seemed only just to have been made, so new they looked, and the stuff was without holes or tears, and bright-coloured. The wide skirt and the sleeves and neck were trimmed with beautiful embroidered bands. And her ornaments were of an abundance, a variety and a richness such as might have made the most elegant ladies of Leh envious. And besides, her costume was almost entirely in the Leh fashion. These women of Rukchen have kept nothing of the old Changpa

287

costume except a *kau* of embossed silver, rectangular, but very narrow and very long, which they wear on the forehead as a sort of starting-point of all the ornaments which thickly cover the flaming *perak*. Otherwise there is no difference. Only among rags which had become useless did I see some of the stuff with narrow stripes of every colour which was formerly used for the women's petticoats. It is a pity they have given it up; it was so extremely picturesque! The men also now dress like the Ladakhis; but they always have a tendency to wear their great robe shorter, because it bulges out more above the girdle tied round the waist.

When I came out of my host's *rebo* the appearance of the encampment was beginning to change. The sun had set behind the smooth hills near by and, as always, the sky was rapidly growing dark. There were no more women spinning or dyeing wool or weaving on primitive looms, but all the *rebo* were sending out smoke through the long openings in their roofs: preparations for evening tea were going on.

Shortly afterwards something very surprising began to happen. The ground, down at the bottom of the large valley into which the valley of Rukchen opens, appeared to be covered with curious dots which till then had escaped my notice— though I can claim that I am always observant of everything. There were whitish dots which looked as if they might be large stones, alternating with black dots which looked like bushes. It was indeed odd that I had not noticed them before! I now fixed my eyes upon them.

Then I saw that these strange dots were obviously not attached to the ground, but were slowly moving. But in order to realize this I had to keep my eyes firmly fixed upon them. As they slowly moved, so they also slowly grew larger. Then, at a particular moment, they began to take shape. Of course they were not stones or bushes! They were the flocks belonging to Rukchen—thousands and thousands of sheep and goats, and a few larger black spots were the yak.

They continued to advance in this way, very very slowly: in fact they nibble at the grass as they go, until the moment that they arrive at the tents. There were a few men behind each flock, with long goads. They looked as if they were paying little attention as they came slowly on, stopping at almost every step. But appearances were deceptive: actually they follow the movements of each one of their beasts, especially of those that have a tendency to lag behind or to stray off at the sides from the main part of the flock. Then the men whistle sharply to make them close in again. In front, like a guide, a big dog goes slowly, often stopping to give the beasts time to nibble and turning its head this way and that as though to inspect them.

Finally the flocks arrive, one after the other, from every side and every direction, and they seem to fill the whole wide valley of Rukchen. For a brief moment life swarms round every tent. The dogs are tied up firmly and immediately lie down, but are ready to leap out, snarling and showing their teeth, directly they see anyone who does not look like a Changpa belonging to the tribe. The yak also are tied up, and in a very odd fashion: a big rope is tied to the iron ring which hangs from their great fleshy nostrils, its other end being passed round a small stone on the ground; and the great beasts, ignorant of their strength, remain motionless where the shepherd has put them. The sheep are at once driven into the circular enclosures of stone where they pass the night. But not so the goats: the goats belonging to each family are lined up close together, head to head in two long rows, and the women pass from one to another for the evening milking. Then they too are shut up in their own special stone-built enclosures. The latter are called 'le': can it be that the capital had its origins in a primitive shepherds' encampment?

Meanwhile night has descended. Everyone has disappeared inside the *rebo*, from which a thin thread of light still shows for a little. The light vanishes, and all sound ceases. The whole encampment sleeps. Only, at times, one of the dogs, made suspicious, perhaps, by some rustling in the grass and a shadow of some small wandering cloud, gives a short, sharp bark as though challenging some enemy or intruder. Another dog answers near by; then another, farther away; then all the dogs of all the *rebo* in Rukchen. For five minutes there are desperate snarls and barks and howls, echoed and infinitely multiplied amongst the hills. Then, as if by general consent, they all stop and lie down again, and the solemn silence of night again falls on the sleeping encampment—until the next rustling in the grass and the next shadow of a cloud wandering across the moonlit sky.

But in the morning, the moment the air is tinged with the pale pink that announces the dawn and makes visible the vague outlines of the nearest hills, the whole encampment awakes. Sheep and goats are driven out of their pens, dogs are let off their leashes, yak are freed from their imaginary bondage. Men come out of the *rebo* armed with their long, thin goads. The flocks go off with their safe advance-guard of dogs, their rearguard of whistling shepherds. They go off one after another, in every direction, dispersing here and there according to the pastures for which they are bound. They go very slowly, for both goats and sheep nibble at the grass from the very beginning. Then as they get farther away, they lose shape, until they merely look like odd little dots on the ground —white stones and dark bushes—and end by disappearing altogether.

Here, in the meantime, the women have begun their wool-spinning again, others their dyeing, others, again, their weaving on the wretched primitive looms. A silvery voice is heard calling from one *rebo* to another; here and there a mournful song accompanies some task which is being done inside the tent; there are cries of children, urchins wailing, and the *mon* execute flourishes on their trumpets and roll their drums as they practise their art.

And so on till the evening, when the flocks return and there is again a short, busy moment as the various tasks are performed —as they are performed day after day, everlastingly.

Such is the life of the Changpa nomads, both here at Rukchen and in their other encampments.

Rukchen, on the Rupshu Plateau, September 29th, 1930.

CHAPTER XXVII

THE RETURN TO INDIA

These last stages of our journey have been of formidable length. My readers partly know the reason, for it is the same reason for which I put forward my departure from Leh and gave up the short détour towards Morari-tso. This route, which in general is little, if at all, used by travellers, crosses the Himalaya, not—like the route towards Kashmir—at a part where it is a clearly defined mountain-range and comes down to a single, deep-sunk pass. Here, this vast fold in the Earth has not the character of a distinct chain, but spreads out into a tract of plateaux which are a prelude to the great Tibetan plateaux beyond, so immense that they seem endless; and it has to be crossed, not by a single, low pass, but by a number of saddles one after another, all of them very high. Even when the first snows come, on the Kashmir route only one effort—and that not a very great one—is needed to cross the chain, and there are villages quite close on both sides of the pass. But here, going towards Lahul, if the first snows are heavy, no effort is adequate and there is no possible help from inhabitants: caravans caught on the way have to be unloaded, sometimes they have to go back, and in any case the road is closed, and remains hopelessly closed, until late in the following spring. It is already closed, if not actually, at any rate officially: one fall of snow—and who knows where we should be! That is why I started earlier and why I have done long and exhausting marches; it is also why, until this morning—for it was only this morning that I crossed the third of the high passes—a certain amount of anxiety disturbed the peace of mind which I felt I had earned at the end of my journey.

Our marches were long. Perhaps a march of eight or nine hours a day, even though we were urging on our mounts as much as possible, may not seem an effort to be considered really excessive. But one must take into account all the time the

291

conditions of my present caravan. They are not Ladakhis, to begin with, but Punjabis, who are slow and indolent in all their movements, and are talkative and quarrelsome. In the morning, by the time they have loaded up all the mules, it is past 9 o'clock, however much I may urge them on. And the days are short now, so that the caravan always arrives at the end of the day's march in the dark, sometimes well after nightfall. Waiting in the darkness and the cold of these first autumn evenings, often in bad weather and at a great altitude, was not particularly pleasant or attractive. And when the caravan did arrive, all these Punjabi drivers do is to unload the mules in an untidy fashion and then go off on their own account; it was left to us to go in search of the loads required for pitching the camp, preparing the dinner and putting up the tents, assisted only by three Ladakhi servants, and in the feeble light of a few little lanterns. This is why these five stages—or rather six, if one includes the march up the Upshi Valley—have seemed to me so long and exhausting. Also, they have been all the time at a great altitude and have taken us over three very high passes.

On the 30th, the last day of September, I was anxious to see the departure of the flocks from the encampment of Rukchen and the beginning of the daily life of my new friends, the Changpa. I sent the caravan on, being sure that I would come up with it and even pass it on the road, and amused myself for some time, so great was the interest aroused in me by this primitive, simple, monotonous life among the nomad shepherds of the Tibetan plateaux. After this we should be going through an uninhabited zone for some days, so it was better to take advantage of this occasion.

That day I crossed the most westerly extremity of the Rupshu, an immense, perfectly flat, level depression between smooth, rounded heights of moderate size. The weather was fine, but there was a very strong wind, which lashed us full in the face all day long. We did not succeed in finding shelter even for our midday meal. Our only distraction on this dull, monotonous march, going as fast as possible but struggling all the time against squalls which blew with ever-increasing violence, was the herds of wild asses, or *kyang*, which would be quietly feeding and then, as we drew near, would rush off at a gallop in a crowd, until they had reached a safe distance from the danger which had scared them; then they would slacken their speed, still prancing about, and would finally stop again and start feeding in safety. It was already dark that evening when we pitched our camp at the confluence of two valleys (as is indicated by the name of the locality, Sumghiel), a deep depression at the extreme edge of the plateau, where the latter begins to be broken up by the tributaries of the Zanskar. It was a miserable camp, huddled between a precipitous cliff above the river and another which rose behind our tents to the flat summit of a short terrace.

The following day our march was even longer and more exhausting. The weather would have seemed fairly fine if we had not still had in front of us two more high passes to cross, but actually little clouds, white as cotton-wool, were appearing from behind the top of the ridges towards which we were going, and they might be the forerunners of a period of bad weather. All the morning we were passing through extremely picturesque country, along a valley that cut through mountains of dolomite. At first it was extremely narrow and looked as if it were blocked by a huge chaos of rocks which had hurtled down from the precipitous walls. The track went up through the middle of them, laboriously and with infinite windings; the mules panted and stopped at every other step, and the drivers shouted and swore to make them go on. After we had got over the 'mauvais pas' the valley became almost regular, but still so narrow that there was not room for the path along the bottom and it had to go over the rocks and loose stones of the slope. Above, on both sides, were bold mountains and precipices worthy of the Dolomites. Farther on, the head of the valley, as though in contrast to these, lies in a narrow belt of schists, which explains the gentle, wide smoothness of the pass at its end, the Lacha-lung-la, at a height of 16,730 feet.

Two of the high passes had now been crossed, but the road was none the easier for that. Coming down from the pass into the bottom of a valley, we crossed it and went up the opposite side in order to avoid the narrow and indescribably wild gorge which forms a part of it. We went up and down the side, at a height of over 16,400 feet almost all the time, and on the edge of apparently bottomless abysses. It was well after nightfall when we again descended to the bank of the Sarap—

one of the main branches which form the source of the Zanskar
—and pitched our camp in a hasty and disorderly fashion owing
to the darkness and our own weariness. It was only later on
that the moon lit up fantastically the wild and gloomy grandeur
of the surrounding landscape.

However, we were not alone that day on our long march.
We overtook and were overtaken by endless flocks migrating
on their long return journey towards the more southerly valleys.
This also was something that I had always wished to see
happening. It is not only for the sake of pasture—though this
would be a sufficient reason—that sheep and goats, and especially sheep, migrate between the plateaux of the Chang-tang and
the valleys of Lahul. Each sheep carries its 26 pounds of merchandise, divided into two equal loads, on either side of its
woolly back; one cord serving as breeching, another as martin-
gale, so that the loads shall not fall when they go up or down.
They carry rice and sugar and also cheap cotton goods when
they go up from Lahul towards the Chang-tang, and bring back
salt and wool and *pashmina* when they come down again from
the Chang-tang to Lahul. On the way, and then on the
plateaux, they feed almost for nothing, while the shepherds also
make a profit as caravaneers and as merchants. And it is no
mean profit, when one thinks that a flock of a thousand sheep
can transport more than 10 tons. They obey a mere whistle
from the shepherds—slowly, because they feed as they go,
whenever the condition of the ground and the meagre vegetation
permits—but they go on from morning till evening even on the
long, suffocating summer days, and traverse in a day distances
so great that to us, though we are on horseback and have all
the comforts allowed by a hard caravan life, they seem really
tiring. They go slowly, poor beasts, but apparently without
fatigue; but if it happens that the shepherds urge them to
quicken their pace and go aside to give place to a caravan meeting or passing them, then one can see, from the effort they make,
how really tired they are: they limp with their fore-legs, dragging
their hind legs, and their whole body sags as though weighed
down under a load too heavy for them.

Yesterday also we passed several of these flocks migrating
towards the valleys of Lahul. It looked as if they too, like us,
were trying to hasten their slow progress. Yesterday was a

stormy day, certainly the worst of our whole journey, apart from the days when we were crossing the Italia Pass. It was an easy, but long, march, along the bottom of the valley the whole time, over alluvion and among moraines. The scanty cotton-wool clouds of the day before had thickened, and merged into a heavy sky in front of us, uniformly grey with storm-clouds. There were violent squalls of icy wind, also showers of snow, which pricked one's face like so many pin-points. Never in my life have I suffered so much from cold as yesterday during the late afternoon, while we were waiting for the caravan to catch us up. It was difficult to find a slightly sheltered place for the camp. We came to the end of our day's journey after nightfall; the tents were put up in the dark and the loads were scattered in complete disorder all round. I spent an almost sleepless night, owing to the mules searching about and fighting amongst themselves for a little grass.

To-day at last we came to the last pass, the Bara Lacha-la. It seemed almost humiliating—only 16,080 feet—to us who were now accustomed to the 16,400 level! And how cold it still was this morning! The point where we encamped yesterday evening was just at the lower edge of an immense moraine-field which fills the entire head of the valley. It would be hard to find finer moraines than these. They form a whole series of gigantic curving banks, with the hollow side of the curve towards the top of the valley. They are all connected like a great steep staircase, with a flat space on top of each step. Often, instead of a plain flat space, there is a little lake, or a flat stretch of clay, the traces of an ancient-lake. It is only the last and highest of these banks of moraine that encloses a larger lake: this is the Yunam-tso, and near its shores it is already covered with a sheet of ice. And how cold it is this morning, even though the sun is out!

After it had followed along the shore of the Yunam-tso the road up to the pass is short and easy. This, at last, is the pass which starts us on our way down over the southern slopes of the Himalaya. After crossing so many plateaux, so many chains and buttresses, we are at last on the watershed of the great mountain-range. It is also a climatic boundary. Just as on the other side there was a clear sky and intense cold, im- mediately on this side there is a completely overcast sky and a milder temperature. At the beginning of the descent it was still snowing a little, but no more after that. And our hearts are light, for the last threatening pass has been crossed.

We came quickly down the valley by a fine caravan-road which goes in wide loops; here and there, however, it had been swept away by the overwhelming force of some great lateral torrent. At nightfall we arrived here at Patseo, where there are again the first signs of human occupation—a few temporary huts built by shepherds and also a bungalow. But the road, as I have said, is already officially closed, and so the bungalow-keeper has gone down to the plains. However, the *serai* is open and quite new, as though it had been made specially for us to stay in.

Patseo, October 3rd, 1930.

Patseo was an important stage on our journey: not only did it mark the end of all possible difficulties, and our final descent to below the 13,120 feet level, but also the beginning of human life. Not only was there the little bungalow with its brand-new *serai*, the little shepherds' huts, several shelters and temporary cabins roughly built in stone by caravaneers (for it is here, in the summer, that the trade-caravans exchange their merchandise: the Changpa go no farther down, and the Lahulis no farther up), but there were also the first beginnings of trees, a few sickly birches clinging desperately to the rocks of the mountain-side. We had already seen fairly plentiful grass the day before, not much below the Bara Lacha-la; it was grass of a curious orange colour, which, when we had come some way down the valley, became red, then darker and darker and more of a wine-red. These were the colours of autumn. The scanty foliage of the birches was also of a bright yellow, which varied as the wind moved or turned the leaves.

We went rapidly down the valley of the Bhaga, one of the "five rivers" which give the name of "Punjab" to the great flat region below. Our progress was quick, because the road— still the caravan-road—is very skilfully cut out of the valley-side as it descends. Now gradually the birches clinging to the rocks were growing more frequent, but up above, the slopes were a curious wine-red from the autumn colour of the grass. Then there began to be other trees, reduced in size so that they looked like bushes, and extremely dark, in contrast with the yellow of the birch-foliage: these were junipers. And gradually, as we went farther down, the junipers became more like proper trees, also more numerous, and took more regular shapes, either more tapering or more spreading, but in such a way as to remind us at times of firs, cypresses, or even thuias. Farther down they were very numerous and thick and grouped with a particular kind of irregularity that gave the whole landscape a special character, making it look like a great, picturesque natural park.

Then came the first cultivated fields and peasants' houses, just after the caravan-road reaches the bottom of a valley near a point where several streams join. It was strange, but the first houses are typically Ladakhi, and their inhabitants are Ladakhis—men in long white robes and blue girdles and caps with woolly turned-up edges, and women in dark wine-coloured dresses and great black fans behind their ears and flame-red *perak* on their heads—a little island of Ladakhis on this side of the Himalaya. I had my last greeting from Ladakh in the 'ju' and the smiles of these Ladakhi colonists in a country that is not their own.

From the moment when I reached the first houses and fields the journey seemed to be finished in a flash, even though the individual stages were no longer than before. For each stage brought us farther down to where fields and houses became even more frequent, and, like the whole landscape, took on an appearance more and more different from the country we had known in Western Tibet. An obvious Tibetan influence could be seen at first in the upper Bhaga Valley, but a change, after that first settlement of Ladakhis, became gradually visible. The houses gradually tended to lose their Tibetan architectural characteristics and assume others, of, I suppose, Indian influence. However, the inhabitants, the Ladakhis, were still Buddhist, though their Buddhism is much less sincere and much more influenced by the Hinduism of the valleys nearer the plain. It is true that we met one or two lamas in flame-red robes on the road and also saw one or two rough *mani* and one or two miserable, half-ruined *chorten*. But there were no *gompa*, no temples, no chapels, no *lato* in sight, and man had contributed no signs of festivity and grace and gaiety to the natural landscape. But

297

the people were gay, and the women wore a characteristic costume, especially as regards the few but strange ornaments which they wear on their heads. The hair is parted into a number of small, tight plaits hanging down the back and joined only at the ends, low down, in a little tuft of black wool; but where they are joined, they are covered with a great square plaque cut from the outside covering of a marine shell—which, when whole, must be perfectly gigantic—and adorned with carving in very simple ornamental designs. But this is evidently an older custom; the majority of the women actually wear, instead of this white, translucent plaque, another of exactly the same shape and size and with the same little ornamental carvings, but made of silver, with a big turquoise in relief in the middle of it. And these women of the upper Bhaga Valley wear on top of their heads a curious sort of little bowl of worked silver adorned with stones, and on both sides, just behind their ears, two enormous, really enormous, pieces of yellow amber; one wonders how they keep in place and why they do not become very wearisome to the wearer.

We went on down the Bhaga, stopping in well-built and well-furnished bungalows. The caravan-road goes up high again over the side of the valley, the bottom of which again goes through rugged gorges and rocky defiles. We have again passed numerous migrant flocks of sheep laden with their neat little bags stuffed tight with *pashmina*, which weighs heavy and is expensive. Towards evening they stop, and the men of these strange caravans use the little bags to make long, low walls which surround a regularly formed enclosure in which they light their fires and pass the night in shelter from the wind. They are a very curious sight, these encampments of flocks coming down from the Chang-tang.

Cultivated areas become more frequent and also more varied the farther one goes down the Bhaga. Houses are also more numerous, and little villages more frequent—generally placed where there is only a very small flat space on the mountain-slope. From far off they would look like Alpine villages were it not for the whiteness of the houses.

So we went on till we came to the confluence of the Bhaga with the Chandra, up which we had to go for two good days' march—in fact until we came again to the upper limit of the villages, then of the fields and then even of the junipers. Moreover, it is a valley which is much more rugged, much barer, and much less cultivated and inhabited than that of the Bhaga. The bungalows also looked rather deserted, though they are on the same road that leads from the Bara Lacha Pass into India—India which is now quite near.

We crossed the river and mounted steeply up, twisting backwards and forwards, over the left side of the valley, till we came right to the summit and over the summit—yet another pass, our last, the pass that will finally take us away from the interior valleys of the Himalaya on to its southern slope. This was the Rohtang-la. But it was quite a tame pass—flat, wide, and only 12,795 feet high—very inferior!

Beyond, there was a rapid descent through continuous pasture-land of Alpine character, interrupted only by crags of rock. This pasture was luxuriant, thick and green, very like that of the Alps, and even if one did not know it one could see that we were on the southern slope of the great range. Then, the moment we reached the foot of this long, rapid descent, and, with it, the bottom of the valley (this is the valley of the Beas, another of the "five rivers" which give the Punjab its name), we found ourselves right in the Himalayan forest.

Our last stages lay beneath shady, wonderfully thick and majestic vaults of fir-trees, cedars, pines, gigantic holly-trees, chestnuts, walnuts, and the hundreds and hundreds of other kinds of trees which go to make up this incomparable forest. The thick shade, the luxuriant undergrowth of ferns, and the continual murmur of springs and brooks, little torrents and waterfalls, give an indescribably pleasant feeling of freshness, though the sun, whenever we came to cross a clearing, seemed intolerably hot and scorching. And naturally so, for we have come down from the heights to which we had grown accustomed, to little over 3,300 feet.

But it is not only that! The worst of it is that here, at Sultanpur, there is a motor-road coming up from below, and one hears the continual throbbing of an engine. And there is nothing, absolutely nothing Tibetan, or even remotely resembling Tibet, nothing but Indians dressed in every sort of way and in every colour, faces of every type or of no particular type, a superabundance of feminine ornaments of every variety, but nothing picturesque, as in Ladakh.

Ladakh, Ladakh . . . Ladakh comes back to my mind all the time, and I compare everything with it. But it always seems to me incomparable.

I have dismissed the caravan-crew of little, meagre, chattering, quarrelsome Punjabis. All the baggage is heaped up on the grass in front of the bungalow and looks pathetic in its disorder; but it is much sadder to think that it will no more be carried by a coolie or a mule, a yak or a horse. Three large lorries are already ordered, to take it to-morrow over its last stage through the Himalayan valleys.

And we go too, with the baggage, towards the plains. It is sad, very sad, to have to put the word "finis" to an enterprise so long desired, a journey so very wonderful, perhaps the last of one's life. The last of my life? I do not like to think this. Not the last, yet!

Sultanpur, October 10th, 1930.

INDEX OF PERSONS

GENERAL INDEX

74°   75°   76°

36°

35°

34°

33°

GILGIT AGENCY

Hunza
Nagar
Gilgit

INDUS R.

G R E A T

M. Nanga Parbat

Astor

K A S H M I R

Rondu

Skardu

Burgi-la

DEOSEI
PLATEAU

Gurais

Kishen Ganga R.

Sonamarg

Dras R.

Kolahoi

Zoji-la

Srinagar

Dras
Suru R.

P I R   P A N J A L   R A N G E

Chenab R.

Kishtwar

Hispar Glacier

Hispar Pass

Biafo Glacier

Muz-Tagh Pass

K2

Baltoro Glacier

Ascole Braldo R.

Shigar

Tolti

Khapalu

Kaimang

Kargil

Mulbe-
Gompa Fotu-la

Suru

L A D A

PADAR

Punjab Sta

Scale

Miles 20   10   0   20   40   60   80   100

74°   75°   76°

77°   78°   79°   80°

1913-14
1930

KUNLUN
MOUNTAINS

Suget

Karakash R.

Suget Pass

36°

Yarkand R.

Chaksgam Valley

Teram Kangri

Karakoram Pass

AKSAI-CHIN

Siachen Glacier

Base Camp

Rimo Glacier

Haro R.

Nubra R.

Saser-la

Murgo

Depsang Plains

35°

Chimo

LINGZI TANG

Panamik

Shyok R.

Tegur

Deskit

Khardung

Chang Chemmo R.

Khalatse

Khardung-la

Lamayuru

Nimu

Leh

Diggher-la

Basgo

Piang

Shyok

Tankse

34°

Zanskar R.

KH

Chang-la

Chimre

Pangong Lake

Indus R.

Ghia

Shushul

Stakalung-la

Tsaka Pass

Padum

Rokchen

Gnima

Thangra

Puga

INDUS R.

Lachalung-la

33°

Morari-tso

Bara Lacha-la

GES

Parang-la

Chandra R.

Rohtang-la

Spiti R.

KULU

77°   78°   79°   80°

For Product Safety Concerns and Information please contact our EU
representative GPSR@taylorandfrancis.com
Taylor & Francis Verlag GmbH, Kaufingerstraße 24, 80331 München, Germany

www.ingramcontent.com/pod-product-compliance
Lightning Source LLC
Chambersburg PA
CBHW050641270326
41926CB00035B/2180